Checklist for Change

Checklist for Change

Making American Higher Education a Sustainable Enterprise

ROBERT ZEMSKY

RUTGERS UNIVERSITY PRESS
New Brunswick, New Jersey, and London

Library of Congress Cataloging-in-Publication Data

Zemsky, Robert, 1940– author.
  Checklist for change : making American higher education a sustainable enterprise / Robert Zemsky.
      pages cm
  Includes bibliographical references and index.
  ISBN 978-0-8135-6134-9 (hardcover : alk. paper) — ISBN 978-0-8135-6135-6 (e-book)
  1. Education, Higher—United States.   2. Educational change—United States.   I. Title.
  LA227.4.Z44   2013
  378.73—dc23

                                                      2012038526

A British Cataloging-in-Publication record for this book is available from the British Library.

Visit our website: http://rutgerspress.rutgers.edu

Manufactured in the United States of America

For the Tie-Dye Gang—Ann, Peter, Clara,
Gabrielle, Oscar, Stella, Tobi, Michael,
Noah, Willa, Jeffrey, Courtney, Eli, Jo

Contents

Acknowledgments

I am almost embarrassed at just how extensive a list of acknowledgments I owe for a volume that was expected to be a personal summing-up—almost, but not quite. For me at least, one reward of writing is learning how to ask for and accept help. Other people's opinions do matter, and, when they contribute their ideas and concerns freely and frankly, the resulting product is inevitably better.

As so often in the past, I have depended on the insights and generosity of Greg Wegner of the Great Lakes Colleges Association. His several readings of *Checklist for Change* played an important role in shaping my narrative as well as making certain—or at least as certain as I would allow him—that I kept my penchant for wordplay reasonably in check. Rick Morgan had the unenviable task of being the first reader of nearly every snippet of prose that came to make up this volume. Even before Greg turned his hand to making sense of what I had written, Rick filled in the missing words, corrected the malapropisms, and inverted the sentences that made no sense as I had written them. Ann Duffield again played the role of tough taskmaster, challenging me to be bold and, when I went too far, reminding me that I wanted real people with well-developed sensibilities to take seriously what I had to say. With a cool sense of the possible, Pam Erney managed the four case studies that are at the heart of this volume. Jody DeMatteo performed that final edit with vigor as well as grace. As twice before, Lisa Jerry was responsible for the final copy-edit for Rutgers University Press—a task she performed with an academic sensitivity that helped me see when and where I was wide of the mark.

My Penn colleagues Laura Perna and Joni Finney scrubbed the chapters focusing on public policy, student financial aid, and faculty responsiveness. Sandy Baum, from whose detailed reporting on federal student aid I borrowed shamelessly, scrubbed the chapter on student financial aid as well, though she would no doubt point out that on some issues we have continued to disagree. Mark Huddleston, Lisa MacFarlane, and Mark Rubenstein reviewed and corrected my description of conflicts at the University of New Hampshire in which they collectively played important roles. Sharon Herzberger and Jim Dunkelman, performing the same task for my analysis of the ongoing transformation of Whittier College, allowed me to talk as bluntly about Whittier's challenges as well as its hoped-for successes. At the University of Minnesota Rochester, Stephen Lehmkuhle and Claudia Neuhauser reviewed the UMR chapter for accuracy, but not opinion, and trusted me not to make their colleagues on the U of M's Minneapolis-St. Paul campus overly nervous about what was transpiring just to their south in Rochester. Along with her Provost Lane Earns, Lori Carrell, who was the shepherdess in my telling the tale of curricular reform at the University of Wisconsin Oshkosh, allowed me to watch and transcribe their efforts even when they were not at all certain those efforts would prove successful. Then, once success was in hand, professors Carrell and Earns made certain I told the Oshkosh story correctly. Susan Shaman was responsible for the analysis of the Oshkosh data and for enriching my understanding of what all those numbers meant. She was aided early in the analysis by Trish Burch of the Stillwater Group. Bill Massy leant me early drafts of his papers on disruptive change and then engaged me in a spirited argument about what was about to happen next. The chapters on the curriculum and curricular change were made possible through the generous support of the Spencer and Teagle foundations and their respective presidents Michael McPherson and Richard Morrill.

Bill Tyson, of Morrison and Tyson Communications, has served as my link to the media for more than a decade. Each time I contemplate a new project, he reminds me that I write, not for myself, but for that often ill-defined and frequently uncaring audience "out there." If he has succeeded in focusing my aim once again, then this volume will find an audience that comes to both care and take my ruminations seriously. Marlie Wasserman of the Rutgers University Press has blessed as well as promoted this effort, though with her ever-present healthy dose of skepticism. Finally, Doug Lederman of *Inside Higher Ed* provided the spur for me to write *Checklist for Change*. Thanks, Doug.

Checklist for Change

1 | Trapped in an Ecclesiastes Moment

In the late 1980s I briefly shared the stage with Robert Reich—not yet a member of a president's cabinet but already a major commentator on securing America's economic future. In those days the big accounting firms regularly brought cadres of university officers to Florida or some other sunny location to network with each other and their partners who were responsible for the firm's higher education practice. Golf, of course, was also on the agenda, along with a smattering of talking heads who were expected to lend an air of intellectual respectability to what otherwise amounted to a perk for being among the handful of university and college officers who decided which firms got the contracts to conduct their institution's financial audits.

That Saturday morning Reich and I were expected to supply the necessary veneer of respectability. I had never met him before so did not know, as he noted when introducing himself, that he was "height challenged." It was something we all quickly forgot as Reich launched into a mesmerizing tale of a Monday morning in October 1987 when he had appeared on the *Today Show.* "I was asked," he said, "whether the stock market was due for a major correction. I clapped my hands and said 'Of course—it could happen any time now; indeed I wouldn't be surprised if it dropped 500 points today' [500 points being the equivalent of 2,800 points or 23 percent in terms of today's stock market]! And that," he continued with a second thunderous clap of his hands, "is precisely what happened—a more than 500-point drop in a single day. Well, for the next six months my phone didn't stop ringing—everybody wanted to know what was going to happen next, and they were more than happy to pay me to make my next big prediction under their auspices. But do you want to know the question nobody asked me?" The ballroom in which we had congregated was beyond silent as we all leaned forward to get the word. "No one ever asked me if I had made such a prediction before. And had they asked I would have had to tell them. 'Yes, as a matter of fact, I had been predicting every Monday morning for the last three years that the market was due for a 500-point correction.'"

What followed was near pandemonium—a startling mixture of guffaws, delighted shouts, and thunderous applause. Neither I remember nor, I suspect, anyone else remembers what I said that Saturday morning when I followed Reich at the podium. But I vividly recall the lesson Reich taught us that morning: in this world, interesting predictions come in all sorts of sizes and flavors; the most interesting are those that try to track how institutions and industries, often buffeted by conflicting forces, change and do not change. At the heart of Reich's parable is what everyone in Las Vegas knows as the "money bet": yes, you can imagine big changes and hence big winnings, but the safest course is to continually bet with the house, which means essentially betting there will be no change at all. The alternative is to bet the house will lose, with the full understanding that you could go three years or longer before being proved right. If you can afford the losses such a strategy promises, then the gains in increased notoriety, not to mention booking fees, can more than offset the intermediate loss of credibility.

For three decades now, higher education's truth tellers and prognosticators, including me, have been predicting that American higher education is about to change because it has to change. Every Monday morning or so, it seems, we lay out all the pressures—rising costs, unequal access, confusing curricula—that, like the signs of an impending earthquake and accompanying tsunami, are but announcements that all the wrongs of American higher education are about to be swept away.

For all these decades, however, the money bet has remained the same: higher education will change little if at all. Prices and, more important, costs will continue to increase faster than inflation. The participation and attainment gaps separating the experiences of majority and minority citizens will not be closed; rather, they will continue to resemble parallel railroad tracks across the graphs charting the percentage of each group that enters college and emerges with a baccalaureate degree. Curricular discussions and experiments may abound, but what actually happens in the classroom and lab will stay largely the same. The sage will remain on the stage.

To understand just how completely the money bet has prescribed higher education's future, it helps to go back to the 1980s when, just as now, the forces of change appeared on the verge of combining to produce a radically different higher education landscape. Mostly these predictions of necessary, but not necessarily imminent, change were put forth in various thoughtful commentaries, often signed by some of higher education's most respected leaders and commentators.

A Nation at Risk

First came *A Nation at Risk,* still the most referenced and often quoted of the reports, white papers, and commentaries the 1980s produced. Best remembered about *A Nation at Risk* is its stinging indictment of an educational system that was being engulfed by a "rising tide of mediocrity":

> We report to the American people that while we can take justifiable pride in what our schools and colleges have historically accomplished and contributed to the United States and the well-being of its people, the educational foundations of our society are presently being eroded by a rising tide of mediocrity that threatens our very future as a Nation and a people. What was unimaginable a generation ago has begun to occur—others are matching and surpassing our educational attainments.
>
> If an unfriendly foreign power had attempted to impose on America the mediocre educational performance that exists today, we might well have viewed it as an act of war. As it stands, we have allowed this to happen to ourselves. We have even squandered the gains in student achievement made in the wake of the Sputnik challenge. Moreover, we have dismantled essential support systems that helped make those gains possible. We have, in effect, been committing an act of unthinking, unilateral educational disarmament. (NCEE 1983, 9)

Equally memorable was the ease with which the leadership of American higher education made *A Nation at Risk* a report about "them"—the dreaded K–12 system in general and American secondary schools in particular—and decidedly not about "us"—the nation's colleges and universities. Again most commentators and public policy wonks remember how the report sparked a major effort to reform public elementary and secondary education in the United States, a reform effort that culminated with George W. Bush's No Child Left Behind Act of 2001.

The irony is that the National Commission on Excellence in Education that authored *A Nation at Risk* included among its members a remarkably strong higher education contingent: David Gardner, then the president of the University of Utah and already president-elect of the University of California, who chaired the commission; Norman C. Francis, president of Xavier University of Louisiana; A. Bartlett Giamatti, president of Yale University; Shirley Gordon, president of Highline Community College; along with Gerald Holton, Mallinckrodt Professor of Physics and Professor of the History of Science, Harvard University, and Glenn T. Seaborg, University Professor of Chemistry and Nobel Laureate, University of California.

They, at least, were clear that the "rising tide of mediocrity" pertained as much to higher education as it did to primary and secondary education. The commission's charter included six specific charges to which the commission gave particular attention:

- assessing the quality of teaching and learning in our Nation's public and private schools, colleges, and universities;
- comparing American schools and colleges with those of other advanced nations;
- studying the relationship between college admissions requirements and student achievement in high school;
- identifying educational programs that result in notable student success in college;
- assessing the degree to which major social and educational changes in the last quarter-century have affected student achievement; and
- defining problems that must be faced and overcome if we are successfully to pursue the course of excellence in education. (NCEE 1983, 7)

Except for the absence of a concern with rising costs, the commission's charge has a remarkably contemporary ring. Of first importance is the quality of teaching and learning, followed by a concern with American competitiveness. For the first time, the alignment between what happens in high school and then in college is singled out for special attention as a means of improving "student success in college." This recapitulation of the commission's charges is also notable for making clear that the subject at hand is "our Nation's public and private schools, colleges, and universities"—a linking that was repeated frequently in the text.

Two other passages are worthy of note. The first is the commission's lamentation. In summarizing what it had learned from a parade of witnesses, *A Nation at Risk*, first paid homage to that sense of hope often found among those who teach and learn and then observed: "We could also hear the intensity of their frustration, a growing impatience with shoddiness in many walks of American life, and the complaint that this shoddiness is too often reflected in our schools and colleges. Their frustration threatens to overwhelm their hope" (NCEE 1983, 13).

Ultimately, *A Nation at Risk* specified what it saw as the requirements for a Learning Society in which all members of society are engaged in the process of continuous learning and self-improvement. The problem was that, as a nation, the United States was moving away from the ideals embedded in the concept of a Learning Society:

> For too many people education means doing the minimum work necessary for the moment, then coasting through life on what may have been learned in its first quarter. But this should not surprise us because we tend to express our educational standards and expectations largely in terms of "minimum requirements." And where there should be a coherent continuum of learning, we have none, but instead an often incoherent, outdated patchwork quilt. . . . The ideal of academic excellence as the primary goal of schooling seems to be fading across the board in American education. (NCEE 1983, 15)

Integrity in the College Curriculum

One of the commission's principal complaints concerned what it called the "curricular smorgasbord" and an overemphasis on "student-choice" that yielded "a cafeteria-style curriculum in which the appetizers and desserts can easily be mistaken for the main courses" (NCEE 1983, 18, 21). Two years after the publication of *A Nation at Risk*, the Association of American Colleges (then AAC, now AAC&U) issued a special report with the misleading title *Integrity in the College Curriculum*—misleading in the sense that the report made embarrassingly clear there was little if any integrity in the college curriculum. Part of a larger AAC project on Redefining the Meaning and Purposes of Baccalaureate Degrees, *Integrity* was produced by a Select Committee largely drawn from the ranks of higher education and those institutions committed to the liberal arts and what would later be classified as liberal learning. Among the notables who worked on the project were Arthur Levine, David Breneman, Robert McCabe, Gresham Riley, Martha Church, and Williams College's Fred Rudolph, who is generally credited with drafting the report.

That text began quietly enough by noting that when the Select Committee began its work in 1982, it thought it might be a "voice crying in the wilderness." By the time *Integrity in the College Curriculum* was issued in 1985, two years after the publication of *A Nation at Risk*, the committee understood it "had joined a chorus." There was nothing either quiet or choruslike about what followed. The report was a scorching indictment of higher education. The chapter addressing the issue of the status of the baccalaureate degree was pointedly titled "The Decline and Devaluation of the Undergraduate Degree." Nothing escaped the Select Committee's barbs:

> The business community complains of difficulty in recruiting literate college graduates. Remedial programs, designed to compensate for lack of skill in using the English language, abound in the colleges and corporate world. Writing as an undergraduate experience, as an exploration of both communication and style, is widely neglected. College grades have gone up, even as Scholastic Aptitude Tests and American College Testing scores have gone down and the pressures on teachers to ease their students' paths to graduate schools have increased. (AAC 1985, 1)

The committee saved its harshest criticism for the college curriculum itself:

> As for what passes as a college curriculum, almost anything goes. We have reached the point at which we are more confident about the length of a college education than its contents and purpose. The undergraduate major . . . in most colleges is little more than a gathering of courses taken in one department, lacking structure and depth, as is often the case in the humanities and social sciences, or emphasizing content to the neglect of the essential style of inquiry on which the content is based, as is too frequently true

in the natural and physical sciences. The absence of a rationale for the major becomes transparent in college catalogs where the essential message embedded in the fancy prose is: pick eight of the following. And "the following" might literally be over a hundred courses, all served up as equals. (AAC 1985, 2)

What caused this state of affairs? "The curriculum has given way to a marketplace philosophy: it is a supermarket where students are shoppers and professors are merchants of learning. Fads and fashions, the demands of popularity and success, enter where wisdom and experience should prevail. Does it make sense for a college to offer a thousand courses to a student who will only take 36?" (AAC 1985, 2). No one escapes blame in this calling out of higher education's curricular foibles. Boards of trustees or state office holders are responsible for both funding and superintending their public systems of higher education, but they have so surrendered themselves to a culture of "numbers and money that they and academic administrators neglect energetic scrutiny of their true mission." And certainly the faculty deserves criticism, given that "the development that overwhelmed the old curriculum and changed the entire nature of higher education was the transformation of the professors from teachers concerned with the characters and minds of their students to professionals, scholars with Ph.D. degrees with an allegiance to academic disciplines stronger than their commitment to teaching or to the life of the institutions where they are employed" (AAC 1985, 6). When *Integrity* was about to be published, the staff of AAC came to Penn's Institute for Research on Higher Education (IRHE) and asked if there was a way of validating the Select Committee's conclusions that the baccalaureate degree across American higher education lacked both structure and coherence. My IRHE colleague Susan Shaman and I agreed to undertake such an analysis as long as AAC would not only provide the funding (it eventually came from an unusual partnership between the National Science Foundation and the National Endowment for the Arts) but also help persuade a broad enough sample of institutions to let us analyze the complete transcripts of the previous year's graduating class. AAC more than met both conditions; they enlisted the active cooperation of thirty institutions, each of which allowed us to map how seniors graduating in the spring of 1986 with a baccalaureate degree in arts and sciences, business, and/or engineering had satisfied the institution's degree requirements.

Susan and I had always assumed, though we never asked, that AAC was worried about *Integrity*'s reception, given that its conclusions could too easily be dismissed as the anecdotal tales collected by members of the Select Committee along the way. Hard evidence was lacking—and that was what we were contracted to supply. Our statistical analysis not only confirmed *Integrity*'s critique, but also in several important ways the numbers yielded a more complete understanding of what had gone wrong. Published in 1989, *Structure and Coherence, Measuring the Undergraduate Curriculum* presented our principal finding:

> Those who would argue that the current critique of the undergraduate curriculum exaggerates the problem will derive little solace from our findings. To the extent that the institutions in our sample are representative of colleges and universities in general, we find the undergraduate curriculum in the liberal arts lacking sufficient breadth of study, particularly in the natural sciences and mathematics, and lacking substantial depth as measured by either structured or temporally focused coursework. (Zemsky 1989, 36)

Diversity, Competition, and Costs

Beyond the concern with teaching and learning often expressed as a loss of structure and coherence in the undergraduate curriculum, there was, throughout the 1980s, a growing sense that among the nation's most selective private colleges and universities the competition for top students, like the broom in the tale of the sorcerer's apprentice, had taken on a life of its own. Katharine Hanson, then the executive director of the Consortium on Financing Higher Education (COFHE)—higher education's most exclusive cartel of the thirty-one most expensive, most selective undergraduate institutions in the country—commissioned a small study group to look at what that competition was doing to her members and to the students they enrolled. We were an interesting group: columnist Ellen Goodman; psychologist Howard Gardner; Fred Hargadon, then dean of admissions at Princeton (formerly dean at Swarthmore and then Stanford); and Larry Litten, then COFHE's principal researcher. I chaired the study group's meetings and with my colleague Gregory Wegner wrote the white paper that summarized the group's deliberations.

The discussion paper that Greg and I distilled from the study group's deliberations had a deceptively academic title—*Diversity,*

Competition, and Costs: A Candid Look at Selective Admissions.
Among the limited number of people who actually read the paper, it
was known simply as "Tobi's Lament," having begun with a summary
of my daughter's tale of applying to and choosing among four COFHE
liberal arts colleges. The story begins with my mistakenly asking Tobi,
now that it was over, would she mind sharing with me how she went
about making her final decision:

> With an innocence of the etymology of the phrase she used with
> such abandon, she turned to me and hissed, "Dad, you just don't
> understand. College choice sucks!" In the nearly hour-long solilo-
> quy that followed, Tobi detailed what 18 months of worry about
> choosing a college had done to her and her friends—how it had
> affected the terms of their friendship, their sense of priorities in
> the last year of high school, and finally, their confidence in their
> ability to make mature, responsible decisions. Despite each of
> their successes, neither Tobi nor her friends really felt they under-
> stood how or why they made their choices, or what they were
> expected to learn from such a process except, perhaps, that life
> was a crapshoot. (Zemsky and Wegner 1987, 1–2)

Tobi's lament neatly framed what, by the mid-1980s, was already
becoming a potent indictment of the admissions practices at the
nation's most prestigious and expensive undergraduate institutions.
How these institutions annually recruited and admitted their freshmen
classes was:

- overly competitive,
- detached from and disruptive of the youngster's schooling, and
- unacceptably stressful in terms of social and family relations.

Among the study group's members, Howard Gardner was the one
who had produced the most extended critique of the principles and
criteria then being used to discriminate among the growing number
of applicants applying to selective colleges and universities. Gardner
wanted to abandon the SAT, not because it was culturally or politically
biased, but because it "taps only two intelligences and does so in a
relatively narrow way."

> Instead, Gardner favored policies which provide more useful and
> *discriminating* information about colleges and which yield useful
> insights concerning the individual student. "We know that such

processes take time. Rather than compressing the whole experience into a few months in the senior year, I favor a gradual famil-
iarization with college during the high school years. At the same
time I favor the collection of indices, like projects and portfolios,
which record information about the student's personal and cognitive growth over significant periods of time." (quoted in Zemsky
and Wegner 1987, 4)

While Gardner's critique focused principally on educational goals,
most commentators, including most of the study group, were coming to
focus, as Tobi had, on the competitiveness of the process, which pitted
not only student against student but institution against institution.
What the study group added to this critique was the realization that the
process consumed dollars at about the same rate that it flattened egos.
As a COFHE initiative, the study group had full access to COFHE's otherwise secretive archives documenting the competitive power of its
thirty-one member institutions. In 1985, COFHE institutions received
applications from 88,889 individual high school seniors for just 24,000
admissions spots. Among all the successful applicants to one or more
reporting COFHE institutions, 67 percent matriculated at a COFHE
institution. Among the most selective universities the yield was even
higher, 72 percent.

As *Diversity, Competition, and Costs* made clear, these successes
came at a considerable price. Among COFHE universities admission
staffs averaged 29.5 full-time equivalent employees; at COFHE colleges
the average per institution was 15 full-time equivalent staff. More staff
translated into substantially higher average admission costs per matriculating student: for COFHE universities those costs equaled, on average, 9.7 percent of the tuition income realized from those students in
their first year of enrollment. For the colleges, the relative cost of
matriculating the class was equal to 13.7 percent of the tuition charged
to these students during their freshman year.

Finally, *Diversity, Competition, and Costs* documented how the
cost of admitting each new freshmen class had been increasing faster
than inflation as measured by the Higher Education Price Index. While
that index increased 73 percent between 1979 and 1986, admissions
costs increased 118 percent at COFHE universities for the same period,
and they increased 146 percent at COFHE colleges. And as the study
group's report noted, these "increases in admissions costs are not a
function of a relative shortage of applicants. The most selective and

attractive institutions among our membership have made the same investments in staff, travel, and marketing materials as those with less robust applicant pools" (Zemsky and Wegner 1987, 10).

The fundamental question *Diversity, Competition, and Costs* next asked was simple: Why? Why did the nation's most prestigious as well as most selective institutions need to substantially increase their efforts to market their institutions to prospective students and their families? The answer was simple enough: marketing, the COFHE institutions had decided, was essential to broadening the pool of students who considered top-tier private colleges and universities.

> The reason to expand admissions staffs, increase travel budgets, and purchase marketing materials was to enable the institution first to identify talented youngsters who could bring social, ethnic, and financial diversity to the applicant pool, and second to persuade substantial numbers of those students to enroll. The purpose of the new admissions investments was to increase the diversity of the class, whether through the use of Search, special mailings to targeted youngsters, or additional travel to high schools and college fairs. Perhaps ironically, many of us first engaged in professional marketing as part of our commitment to increase the social diversity of our institutions. (Zemsky and Wegner 1987, 11)

That was the contribution of the 1960s. The 1970s brought near financial panic—or, as *Diversity, Competition, and Costs* told the story, unimaginable financial shock: uncontrolled expense, unforeseen deficits, constant wrangles over budget, and a sense of economic decay. Bud Cheit perceived the imminent changes in the title of his 1971 study, *The New Depression in Higher Education.*

> Still, our institutions learned to cope. We invested heavily in financial planning and management. We reduced staff, deferred maintenance, and postponed new construction. We also came to appreciate the financial importance of tuition income. Our first instinct was to maintain price, while slowly expanding enrollment to ease the pressure of the budget. By becoming co-ed, all male colleges were able to expand enrollment, and hence tuition income. When, by the mid-1970s, most of our institutions could no longer expand enrollment without significantly increasing both physical plant and faculty capacity, we began to accelerate

our tuition increases while trying to hold constant our expenses, particularly for salaries. (quoted in Zemsky and Wegner 1987, 12)

Did the growing investment in admissions marketing achieve the twin goals of diversifying COFHE's freshman classes while simultaneously assuring each institution a consistently increasing supply of tuition income? Not exactly. *Diversity, Competition, and Costs* was impolitic enough to observe that the goal of increased tuition had more than been met, justifying in itself the costs of the added investment in admissions. Selectivity as measured by both admit and yield ratios had increased, while either maintaining or slightly increasing the size of the freshman class, all the while increasing tuition rates substantially faster than the underlying rate of inflation. To make its point that not everyone was happy with COFHE's successes, *Diversity, Competition, and Costs* first quoted a recent headline from the *Washington Monthly:* "Highbrow Robbery: The Colleges Call It Tuition, We Call It Plunder." More disarming as well as troubling was Terry Hartle's observation. Then serving as a principle education analyst for Senator Ted Kennedy and later to become the American Council on Education's senior vice president, Hartle presaged the argument that over the next thirty years would come to haunt American higher education:

> All sorts of reasons have been put forward to justify the sharp tuition increases of the early 1980s: the cost of quality, expensive equipment, institutional aid, faculty raises, the catching up for the 1970s (the last one is starting to sound pretty stale). Regardless of whether or not these are true, it seems clear that the basic laws of supply and demand are really what is at work in the selective institutions: There are more qualified applicants than places for them. As a result, there is little need to exercise restraint. Prices go up, the number of applicants stays stable (or goes up), so prices rise further. Not much mystery in that. (quoted in Zemsky and Wegner 1987, 13)

Equally disconcerting was the fact that, despite initial successes, the marketing campaigns had not substantially increased the diversity of COFHE campuses. Here *Diversity, Competition, and Costs* quoted one of Princeton's William Bowen's last major reports as president to the Princeton community: "Whereas there was a clear increase in the percentage of the class that came from low- and middle-income families between 1968 and 1980, that increase appears to have been erased in the most recent five years. . . . [W]e are now back to approximately the same income distribution that prevailed in the late 1960s, and no one can be sure whether this most recent trend will continue" (quoted in Zemsky and Wegner 1987, 14). All that was left was for *Diversity, Competition, and Costs* to deliver its coup de grâce:

> What is clearer today than it was a decade ago is that the marketing techniques we have developed to recruit our students are primarily successful among the middle and upper middle class—a fact that is not surprising since most of those techniques were first developed by service industries for selling reasonably expensive products to the same segment of the population. The people who respond most often to our techniques are high achievers from families that value education and that, for the most part, can afford its costs. While upwards of 40 percent of our undergraduates qualify for need-based aid, nearly 60 percent of our students come from families that can afford more than $16,500 per year per child in educational costs. There is little social or cultural diversity among American families capable of meeting such costs. It is also clear that high tuitions and fees create much of the need that justifies student aid. More than half of the aided students at our institutions come from families that can pay substantial sums for the education of their children. (Zemsky and Wegner 1987, 16)

Seeing Straight Through a Muddle

Then in 1987 the Pew Charitable Trusts, a foundation at the time relatively new to the task of helping to define the nation's agenda, launched a major initiative with an awkward title: The Higher Education Research Program Sponsored by the Pew Charitable Trusts. Most, however, would come to know the effort as the Pew Roundtable in recognition that its principal activity was the convening of twenty-plus higher education leaders and experts in quarterly roundtable discussions of the future of American higher education. I served as the roundtable's convener and, again along with Greg Wegner, as its principal amanuensis.

I was once asked what qualified one to be a member of the roundtable—and without thinking responded, well, you have to be a pooh-bah in waiting. And so they were, and most in the intervening thirty years have in fact become pooh-bahs in full standing: Arthur Levine, now president of the Woodrow Wilson Foundation; Virginia

Smith, the former president of Vassar and Clark Kerr's California side-kick; Bruce Johnstone, at the time chancellor of the State University of New York (SUNY); Arturo Madrid, then president of the Tomas Rivera Center and currently the Murchison Distinguished Professor of Humanities at Trinity University; Mary Patterson McPherson, then president of Bryn Mawr College and now executive officer of the American Philosophical Society; William Massy, professor emeritus of business administration and education as well as vice president for finance at Stanford University; and Patrick Callan, then vice president of the Education Commission of the States and currently president of the National Center on Public Policy and Higher Education, which is responsible for higher education's biennial national report card *Measuring Up.*

The roundtable spent its first year defining for itself a higher education reform agenda—an agenda it made public in the fall of 1988 in an essay entitled "Seeing Straight Through a Muddle," published as the inaugural issue of *Policy Perspectives.* In casting its agenda the roundtable sought to sum up the efforts of reform that had preceded it—*A Nation at Risk* and its warning of a "rising tide of mediocrity," *Integrity in the College Curriculum*'s charge that American colleges and universities no longer had "a firm grasp of their goals and missions," and the 1986 charge by the nation's governors that "today's [college] graduates are not as well educated as students in the past." What puzzled the roundtable then and subsequently was how loud, even shrill, the calls for reform had already become. Noting that "American colleges and universities are openly troubled by a sense of diminished opportunities and lessened capacities," "Seeing Straight Through a Muddle" went on to caution: "The agenda for reform has come to resemble the campus kiosk—plastered with redundant bills layers thick. No group or faction today hesitates to shout its opinions on what higher education should be or do. Restore Plato to the heavens! Increase productivity! Cut costs! Make professors teach! Measure value added! Reward excellence!" (PHERP 1988, 1). It is important to remember that all this was written more than thirty years ago, but in its language and thrust, "Seeing Straight Through a Muddle" could have been written yesterday.

Thirty years ago, the roundtable's strategy for productive reform was to impose self-discipline on the academy's would-be change agents. In heeding its own advice, the roundtable defined just three "principal issues": costs, teaching and learning, and what it called "sorting," which "Seeing Straight Through a Muddle" defined as "the increasing proclivity of colleges and universities to 'sort out' and 'sort down' the economically disadvantaged." Controlling costs meant both understanding and coming to accept why "the American press had declared unequivocally and unambiguously that colleges and universities are too expensive. While the American public and their elected representatives . . . are more than a little puzzled by the unexplained rise in the price of a college education, and by the seemingly insatiable appetite by colleges and universities for new funds." A renewed as well as tough-minded focus on teaching and learning ought to result in a practical framework built around just three principles: First, good teaching requires an "awareness of learning," per se. Second, "assessment is a useful tool only when it measures student learning." Third, while "rhetoric is important, it is institutional practice that must change." To address a set of sorting functions that were producing an increasingly stratified higher education, it was necessary to begin by admitting that the reform efforts of the last twenty years have "produced only failed programs and broken promises. We tell ourselves we have tried, but the problem has proven to be too big, too intractable, too far beyond the traditional calling and expertise of the academic enterprise" (PHERP 1988, 2–5).

An Ecclesiastes Moment

I have begun with these four calls for change from the 1980s to demonstrate that those of us in higher education really are living in an Ecclesiastes moment—change may be all around us, but for the nation's colleges and universities there really is precious little that is new under the sun. For thirty years, the very thing that each wave of reformers has declared needed to be changed has remained all but impervious to change. Even the language of reform has remained constant; the four essays summarized here really are indistinguishable from today's calls for change.

This much is also clear: the 1980s failed as a precursor of change despite, or perhaps because of, the elegance and rhetorical punch of the critiques that decade produced. For me personally, this sense of missed opportunity provided both context and motivation for reconsidering how purposeful change might yet come to American higher education.

I began by trying to be more specific about the three lessons I eventually drew from higher education's continued inability to control costs, provide broad access, and place teaching and learning at the center of the enterprise.

Lesson 1

The notion that American higher education changes slowly but purposefully is wrong. The nation's colleges and universities are not slowly evolving. They are, in fact, pretty much stuck where they were in the 1980s—largely unable to control their costs, locked in a competition for students that Michael McPherson, then professor of economics at Williams College and now president of the Spencer Foundation, rightfully identified as an "admissions arms race." The nation's colleges and universities are increasingly more stratified socially and economically, while being less able to tell themselves, their students, or their benefactors what their students are learning or whether that knowledge is likely to prove useful. A corollary to this first lesson is that American higher education will not change—or be changed—one institution at a time. The pressures to preserve the status quo are simply too great for an institution to break out of the pack and then have its success become a model for its competitors.

Lesson 2

Change will not be stimulated either by reports or analyses—no matter how elegant or prescient or tough minded. My library is filled with such efforts—alas more than one in whole or in part written by me. The failure of the Spellings Commission, the most recent attempt to summon both the nation's and higher education's conscience in support of an agenda for purposeful change, should remind all would-be reformers that it is not what you say or even how well you say it; when it comes to changing higher education, those who matter most are not listening.

Lesson 3

Required is one or more dislodging event(s) of sufficient magnitude so that the gridlock that now holds higher education hostage is broken. In *Making Reform Work* I defined a dislodging event as one generating sufficient force that the academy writ large begins to consider changes that no one institution on its own will likely pursue. In this original formulation, I had imagined that institutions would, of their own volition, choose to change themselves rather than face the prospect of being changed by someone or something else. Today I am not so optimistic, having among other things come to better understand the dominating role federal student aid funds play in setting the context in which individuals as well as individual institutions make decisions and prioritize their educational investments. My unhappy conclusion is that reform will not come to higher education until and unless the federal government becomes an active sponsor of change; in other words, the dislodging events that come to matter most will be those the federal government helps puts in play.

Defining the Task at Hand

I am aware that I have now written myself into something of a corner. If, as I have just argued, no report or analysis will in itself spark the kind of change I have in mind, why bother to write yet another book that won't matter? There are several explanations for my stubborn insistence on continuing to write about how American higher education needs to and can in actuality change. The first derives from a conversation with *Inside Higher Ed*'s Doug Lederman, who wanted to write a profile of me that coincided with the publication of *Making Reform Work*. Having read the book, Lederman told me it sounded like a "summing up" of a long career as one of higher education's more persistent critics. I was somewhat taken aback by his suggestion, not so much with the idea that I was a persistent critic, but rather with the notion that I was offering an end-of-career summing up. Having assured him that I would be heard from again, I hung up, and spent much of the next year with Lederman's observation echoing in my mind.

Checklist for Change is the product of those ruminations. It is in fact a summing up, as well as a checklist, of what would have to happen if American higher education were to change. An argument in three parts follows. The first (chapters 2 through 6) details the traps—as in the bunkers that dot competitive golf courses—that over the last thirty years have sucked the air out of every credible reform movement seeking to change American higher education. Next comes a set of vignettes (chapters 7 through 9) that examines current reform efforts that might serve as harbingers of the kinds of change needed. The last section (chapters 10 through 12) provides, in as much detail as I can muster, a description of the twenty principal changes that must occur as an integral part of that change process: a fundamental recasting of federal financial aid; new mechanisms for better channeling of the competition among both colleges and universities for students; an equally fundamental recasting of the undergraduate curriculum; and a stronger, more collective faculty voice defining not why, but rather how, the enterprise must change.

A second explanation for writing *Checklist for Change* is my somewhat belated realization that the number of people on whom real change within higher education actually depends is substantially less than a thousand: senior federal officials, including the president and the secretary of education and their staffs and principal advisors; the chairs of key Senate and House committees and their staffs; the leaders of the Washington-based higher education associations; the leaders of the few philanthropic foundations still interested in reforming higher education; maybe a dozen journalists associated with major media outlets; the heads of the nation's state systems of public higher education; the governors of those states along with their key budget and policy officers and the leaders of their state legislatures; the leaders of the disciplinary associations to which most faculty belong; the leaders of the principal faculty unions across the country; maybe three dozen well known and outspoken college and university presidents; the heads of the nation's six regional accrediting agencies along with the leaders of the best-known professional accrediting agencies; and finally, the twenty or so higher education policy wonks who have made a career of both predicting and promoting change. *Checklist for Change* is addressed first to the thousand or so education and political leaders on whom changing American higher education ultimately depends. It is their checklist, were they to be organized well enough to put its precepts into practice.

And then I offer the third explanation for the writing of this volume—the possibility that now is the moment to bet against the house. Having predicted every Monday for the last thirty years that higher education was about to change and then been proved wrong, it is just possible that the reordering of the nation's economy along with an up-ending of local and national politics will produce the necessary dislodging events. In that case I hope *Checklist for Change*, like a Robert Reich prediction of a single-day sell-off in the stock market, will prove unexpectedly prescient.

2

A Faculty Encamped Just North of Armageddon

This volume is predicated upon a simple axiom and its inconvenient corollary. The axiom holds that changing American higher education ought to be the business of the faculty. Although often used as a shield against those who want faculty to teach more, the truth is that: learning and research are joint products in which, necessarily, the former proceeds from the latter. Faculty teach what their research and disciplines have taught them. Faculty are content experts as well as pedagogues who teach by both example and precept.

To be sure, some instructional models sever learning and research when a cadre of instructors, responsible for neither course design nor creation of course content, deliver the specified curriculum to their students. Many of the biggest and most successful for-profit higher education institutions have invested in this model by staking their future on creation of standardized courses centrally designed and monitored. Most e-learning programs similarly separate responsibility for delivering instruction from the design of course content. Even these efforts, however, essentially harvest the work of faculty at traditional institutions who see their research as the foundation on which the curriculum is built.

If, as I am about to argue, changing American higher education requires a rethinking of how the nation's colleges and universities organize, and ultimately deliver, more efficient curricula, then changing American higher education is a faculty responsibility. Faculty own the curriculum just as certainly as each faculty member owns his or her courses and research. Faculty are, and are likely to remain, the essential workforce; in traditional institutions that focus on scholarship as well as teaching, there will likely be neither change nor reform without them.

And yet, most faculty members do not believe that change is either necessary or inevitable. They are not yet committed to changing what they believe they do best—and that is the inconvenient corollary to my axiom on the necessary role faculty must play if change is to prove purposeful. Faculty are not oblivious to the changes that swirl about them. They know too many lawyers and physicians whose professional lives have been uprooted by the new electronic technologies and new forms of financial management; the faculty do understand the power of the currents reshaping what were once considered independent professions, akin to professorial appointments. They have seen public appropriations for higher education dwindle and in some cases slashed, and they have heard the political voices warning that the worst cuts are yet to come. Though faculty have increasingly come to see themselves as victims, most are not so much angry as they are doubtful—uncertain that the changes now being championed by that growing army of policy wonks and political operatives will do anything but lessen the academy's value and independence. To their critics, faculty have responded as standpatters have always responded, by claiming that what is not demonstrably "broke" doesn't need fixing. Where, they ask, is the proof that change is necessary? And above all, they ask, why now—why not when the economy is once again healthy, when the disruptions of the present moment have faded (as surely they must), and when there can be more certainty about the true value and sustainability of the fixes being so readily bandied about?

Such faculty are encamped just north of Armageddon. They can look over the ridge and see the destruction that would await them, were they to be so foolish as to charge headlong in pursuit of change. Among the faculty there are those who believe something must be done to recapture the initiative and thereby ensure that the academy is not flattened. But most faculty simply worry about that which they cannot control, all the while saying with increased conviction, "I think I'll sit this one out."

It is also the case that most faculty have long since become impervious to rant as well as to challenge. To be sure, faculty do not like to be disparaged. When attacked, they are more than capable of giving as good as they get. But language—no matter how elegant or bombastic—will not change the faculty: not the siren call of *A Nation at Risk;* not the insider's indictments that *Integrity in the College Curriculum* so urgently pressed; not *A Test of Leadership*, the formal title of the Spellings Commission final report; not any of the myriad reports, studies, position papers, or simple pleas for change that have sought to command higher education's attention over the last forty years.

If purposeful change must necessarily engage the faculty, and if in great overwhelming numbers faculty would like to "sit this one out," then means other than rhetorical persuasion must be found to engage them. What is required, as I have previously argued, is a strategy that makes change possible. And the search for that strategy necessarily begins, not with an idealized vision of an alternative future, but rather with a different understanding of how, as faculty, we came to be the way we are.

The Professionalization of a Calling

In the last decades of the twentieth century, American higher education continued its expansive ways. Between 1970 and 2010, the number of degree-granting institutions of higher education more than doubled, total undergraduate enrollments increased from slightly more than 8.5 million to slightly less than 20.5 million. The size of the American professoriate grew even faster, nearly tripling between 1970 and 2009, while the number of Americans reporting having earned a doctorate degree quadrupled, as did the proportion of twenty-five- to twenty-nine-year-olds having earned a baccalaureate degree (NCES 2010).

Faculty salaries also increased relative to other professions. In 1970, the average full professor's salary was 71 percent of an attorney's and 92 percent of an engineer's salary. Four decades later, full professors, on average, were earning just 8 percent less than lawyers and were 18 percent better paid than engineers. The gap between full professor and physician salaries remained relatively constant over these decades, with full professors earning just over half of what the average physician earned (NCES 2010; BLS 1970, 2010).

What increased as well was the mobility of the American professoriate. Faculty everywhere began to talk as much about their careers as about the institutions in which they currently held an academic appointment. Faculty developed parallel loyalties, not just to their disciplines, but also to both the disciplinary specialties that had captured their attention and the specialized disciplinary societies to which they now belonged. Research and publication became ever more important, ultimately serving as the hallmarks of a scholarly occupation that was nonetheless a profession in the same sense that distinguished medicine, law, and engineering. The tweedy, slightly distracted, and almost always rumpled image of an absent-minded professor became something of an anachronism—replaced, in fiction at least, by Morris Zapp of David Lodge's *Changing Places*.

Perhaps paradoxically, the recasting of the American professoriate was accompanied by the rapid deconstruction of the American collegiate curriculum. While a generation of students, intoxicated by a whiff of revolution, proclaimed their right to "do our own thing," their faculty mentors knew best how to put the slogan into practice. Graduation requirements were relaxed. On most campuses senior theses and comprehensive exams became things of the past, and everywhere the specialty courses the faculty really wanted to teach became the curricular norm.

It was this drift that *Integrity in the College Curriculum* described and decried so precisely. Best remembered about *Integrity* is its description of an undergraduate education that had become mush—no structure, no depth, no coherence. In a less-quoted second chapter, the authors laid a substantial part of the blame for this state of affairs at the feet of the faculty. What had gone wrong, in a word, was the professionalization of the professoriate:

> Central to the troubles and to the solution are the professors, for the development that overwhelmed the old curriculum and changed the entire nature of higher education was the transformation of the professors from teachers concerned with the characters and minds of their students to professionals, scholars with Ph.D. degrees with an allegiance to academic-disciplines stronger than their commitment to teaching or to the life of the institutions where they are employed. (AAC 1985, 6)

What was required, *Integrity* proclaimed in 1985, was a revival of that sense of "responsibility of the faculty *as a whole* for the curriculum *as a whole*" (AAC 1985, 9).

To drive home that point, the authors used language that must certainly have startled their AAC sponsors: "What can be done to encourage American college professors to revive their corporate responsibility to the curriculum? How can they be inspired to reinvigorate the curriculum, making it an expression not of their special disciplinary interests but of their considered judgment of what a baccalaureate education ought to be?" (AAC 1985, 11).

In the early 1990s Harvard's Henry Rosovsky, in equally pointed language, called out his own faculty for their diminished sense of collective responsibility. In the spring of 1991, he was finishing his second tour of duty as dean of Harvard's Faculty of Arts and Sciences. In what amounted to his second farewell address to his colleagues, Rosovsky reminded his listeners of their obligations to be true citizens of the university. Those comments are important in part because of the directness with which he made his case and in part because Harvard itself looms large in nearly every academic's understanding of what constitutes excellence in higher education.

Rosovsky began by reminding his colleagues just how long he had been at Harvard, first as a graduate student in economics from 1949 to 1956, then returning from Berkeley to Cambridge as a tenured professor of economics in 1965. He began here for two reasons: first, to establish just how long and how well he knew his colleagues—their traditions, habits, and shortcomings; and second, to remind his colleagues how their lives as professors had changed over this span of time. In particular, what concerned him was a continually diminishing teaching load:

> Taking either date [1956 or 1965] as a starting point, I suspect that teaching loads have declined significantly. Indeed, it has become extremely difficult to say what constitutes standard teaching loads. Does everyone get full credit for shared courses? Do professors teach what they choose or does the department insist that certain basic courses be covered? Why do many humanists teach more than social and natural scientists? Last year I asked a number of large departments to describe their standard loads. One chairman replied that it was not possible for him to answer the question. All will agree that when they were students, teaching obligations were heavier.

Not only were his Harvard colleagues teaching less, they were also much more likely to be absent from Cambridge, even during term-time.

> We have every right to assume that a Harvard professor's primary obligation is to the institution—essentially students and colleagues—and that all else is secondary. I do not mean unimportant or unworthy, but I do mean secondary. The institution in which

we have a full-time job has the greatest claim on our effort. That implies a prolonged and regular physical presence in Cambridge, Massachusetts during term-time. (Rosovsky 1991, 1b)

Rosovsky's description of the activities that kept so many Harvard professors away from Cambridge is, in fact, a description of the life of the modern academic professional:

> There is a very close relationship between absences from Cambridge and the spread of outside activities. It is difficult to discuss because we have so little hard information, but I do have the clear impression that, for a significant minority of our faculty, the sum of their efforts outside Harvard is greater than their efforts inside Harvard. We are dealing here with a mixture of activities: business ventures, professional activities, lectures, consulting (worldwide) for governments, etc.

And that brought Rosovsky to the crux of his argument—a diminished "social contract" or body of rules linking professors to one another and to the institution they served:

> FAS has become a society largely without rules, or to put it slightly differently, the tenured members of the faculty—frequently as individuals—make their own rules. Of course, there are a great many rules in any bureaucratic organization, but these largely concern less essential matters. When it concerns our more important obligations—faculty citizenship—neither rule nor custom is any longer compelling. (Rosovsky 1991, 2b)

At about the same time as Rosovsky was ruminating over the changing context in which faculty at Harvard self-defined their tasks and responsibilities, the Pew Higher Education Roundtable was taking up the same subject as part of a larger exploration of why colleges and universities had become ever more expensive institutions to operate. In an issue of *Policy Perspectives* largely shaped by Bill Massy and me, the Roundtable put forth two explanations. The first was an "administrative lattice" that, much like a mathematical lattice, grew "to incorporate ever more elaborate and intricate linkages within itself."

Operating simultaneously was an "academic ratchet," which over the course of time had "drawn the norm of faculty activity away from institutionally defined goals and toward the more specialized concerns of faculty research, publication, professional service, and personal pursuits." Here, the *Policy Perspectives* essay, stepping beyond Rosovsky's more temperate description of a faculty in which professors individually defined the rules they would obey, argued that professors, in largely unanticipated ways, had become "independent contractors" with lifetime contracts. "The irony," *Policy Perspectives* concluded, having described the interactions of the lattice and the ratchet, "is that while administrative units have become more like academic departments—more committed to group processes and collective decision making—more and more faculty have become independent contractors largely unfettered by the constraints of institutional needs and community practices" (PHERP 1990, 6).

Nothing changed very much in the ensuing twenty years, except perhaps to make more pronounced the trends defining faculty members as independent contractors. Everywhere a common language abounds through which faculty declare the courses they teach to be "my courses," their students to be "my students," and the external funds they receive to be "my money." There is noticeably less collaboration, less collective design, less collective responsibility. In the 1990s Bill Massy and I conducted a study that involved interviewing department chairs at a wide range of institutions. Those interviews began with a simple question: "How are teaching schedules developed— through departmental meetings or by one-on-one meetings with the individual faculty members?" We were startled to learn that more than 60 percent of the chairs used individual negotiations with each member of the department. Even more startling was the vociferousness of these chairs in claiming that they wouldn't think of having the schedule arrived at by any collective process.

One consequence of this Balkanizing of the decision process is that professional norms become more important than institutional customs or traditions. In a related study we asked more than four hundred faculty at a wide variety of baccalaureate institutions to calibrate the amount of time they devoted to three instructional activities: course delivery, student assessment, and meeting with students outside of class. In particular we wanted to know whether faculty at private, selective, name-brand research universities taught their undergraduate courses differently than did faculty at private liberal arts colleges or public universities. Again, we were surprised by what we found:

> The answer is, by and large, "No." True, the faculty from private research universities were likely to devote less time to assessing

the performance of their students and more time to interacting with them outside of class. But those differences in themselves accounted for relatively little of the variance in how faculty allotted time to the key activities associated with teaching an undergraduate course. Rather, the general pattern that emerges from the data is one detailing the similarities of the undergraduate teaching function—a homogeneity that stretches across all institutional types. (Landscape 1999, 55)

This use of national and disciplinary norms rather than institutional traditions and customs is also characteristic of the world of sponsored research, though in different ways and for different reasons. In this domain disciplinary conformity is most pronounced. The reliance on peer review makes almost certain that institutionally specific criteria and values will not play a role in determining which proposals receive federal funding. It is also the case that, unlike teaching, sponsored research in general and big science projects in particular are collective endeavors—big teams, lots of space and equipment, critically important technical and administrative support systems. But they are corporate rather than collegial in structure and operation. The principal investigator (PI) at the top of the hierarchy calls the shots. The PI's reputation matters, and in order to secure a continued stream of funding the team seeks to protect the PI. The academically qualified research staff members, including both tenure-track and adjunct members of the faculty, follow in importance. The bulk of the technical work is performed by relatively large numbers of postdoctoral fellows (aka post-docs) and graduate students. As Goldman and Massy pointed out a decade ago, the key to understanding why American research universities enroll and train so many graduate students, who then become post-docs, despite little promise of a full academic appointment at the end of their apprenticeships, is the measurement of success: the size of these corporate-like research groups correlates principally with the research productivity of the group as measured in terms of papers published (Goldman and Massy 2001). The bigger and presumably the more tightly organized the research group, the greater the number of publications and the greater the probability of continued funding. In this calculus, however, institutional needs or values play at most tangential roles.

This withering of the institutional role in faculty cultures is also echoed in the declining role the formal apparatus of faculty governance plays in the lives of most faculty. When I first came to the University of Pennsylvania in the mid-1960s, the semi-annual meetings of the Faculty Senate, to which all tenured and tenure-track professors belonged, regularly drew upward of 350 voting members; a good crisis could draw 500 or more members of the Senate. By the mid-1980s, the Senate had trouble attracting a quorum so the minimum number of those present needed to constitute a quorum was reduced. By the mid-1990s, the Senate gave up having regular meetings and chose instead to rely on an executive committee to speak for the faculty as a whole. Today, the members of the executive committee are, for the most part, among the more obscure members of the faculty, and the collective faculty voice is all but muted. Within the individual schools that comprise the university, faculty still meet, but there too attendance is a problem, as is the lack of issues on which the faculty as a whole is expected to render collective judgment. It really is a persistent case of out of sight, out of mind.

What is true at Penn is increasingly true at colleges and universities across the country—small liberal arts colleges being the only notable exception. The mantra of "shared governance" is more familiar to scholars of higher education and the denizens of faculty executive committees or their equivalents than to faculty members who spend most of their time teaching, meeting with students, and engaging in the variety of outside activities Rosovsky believed had trumped too many of his colleagues' commitment to a professor's traditional calling. One fundamental problem with thinking about a faculty-led movement for changing higher education is the sheer absence of collective faculty organizations to lead such an effort.

The flip side of that observation is an even more troublesome tendency to make academic freedom an absolute right, with individual faculty members defining for themselves how an institution's rules do and do not apply. I have a senior colleague, for example, who, when told by one of our program directors that her students were questioning her teaching, responded that such a query on the part of an administrator was a violation of her academic freedom, as were all administrative attempts to either monitor or regulate her classroom performance. In the same breath she reminded the program director that she had no interest in participating in any kind of "group-grope" that was intended to make the program's instructional offerings less disjointed. What and how she taught was her business and her business alone. By invoking faculty autonomy and academic freedom, she evoked the ultimate defense against any reform effort that asked her to change anything.

The Rest of the Story

In one regard, however, faculty, mostly at public institutions, have embraced collective behavior as a means of protecting faculty autonomy as well as faculty compensation. To a surprising extent, the unionization of higher education faculty has been a story mostly untold. As late as 1998, Gary Rhoades, a leading analyst of the nature and structure of professional work across higher education, could ask:

> Why focus on faculty members who are unionized? More to the point, as I have often been asked by university colleagues: *Are there any faculty who are unionized?* To paraphrase Shakespeare, me thinks they doth project too much. With few exceptions . . . research university faculty (who do most of the writing about higher education) are not unionized. Such faculty assume that their condition is universal. It is not. (Rhoades 1998, 9)

The unionization of American professors is actually a story of explosive as well as unexpected growth. Faculty unions in small numbers with limited memberships date back to the years just after World War I. The 1930s were a period of modest growth and then contraction, as were the years immediately following World War II. Then in the 1970s faculty unions took off, becoming an integral element of an emerging system of what Rhoades called "managed professionals." By 1994 Rhoades could report that just under a quarter-million faculty on more than a thousand American campuses were represented by collective bargaining agents. By his calculation, roughly 44 percent of all full-time faculty and 29 percent of all campuses nationwide were covered by collective bargaining agreements. As extraordinary as they were, those numbers were more than a little misleading, given that 95 percent of unionized faculty were in public institutions, both two- and four-year colleges and universities. All in all, unionized faculty in private institutions just exceeded ten thousand. If one also excludes faculty at public research universities, then, by Rhoades's calculus, 89 percent of the faculty at comprehensive and two-year public institutions were unionized, allowing him to observe, "As a workforce, a higher percentage of faculty are unionized than of workers in the private sector of the economy (12 percent) or the general workforce (16 percent)" (Rhoades 1998, 10).

What the faculty in these institutions sought, almost universally, was protection. As Rhoades makes clear, the unifying tactic in the contracts that came to govern faculty-administrative relations in a unionized context was the commitment to standardized rules governing both compensation and work—across-the-board raises, standard teaching loads by field if not by institution, and the same rules for everybody covered by the collective governing agreement. Rhoades noted:

> Unions promote the collective interests of faculty as professionals. The most basic salary structure is across-the-board percentage raises. In a profession that is built on the ideology of individual meritocracy, that might seem anomalous, even anathema. However, in a profession that in practice has not realized a real increase in salaries from wage levels two decades ago, that is arguably a useful strategy to promote faculty's collective interests. (Rhoades 1998, 259)

And there is the nubbin of the issue: faculty as victims. Almost uniformly, unionization has proceeded in American higher education where faculty have felt not just threatened, but genuinely abused by either their public comprehensive institutions without the cachet of a research mission or their community colleges without much if any cachet at all. The faculty at these institutions have seen their salaries fall further behind those of other, similarly educated professionals. They have also sensed, most of the time correctly, that the public agencies that provide their funding want somehow to speed up their lives by having them teach more students, in more varied locales, in new and differing subjects, all without any commensurate increase in the resources at their disposal. To this litany increased accountability standards of dubious value, furloughs, and salary give-backs have been imposed—all to cover deficits in public funding occasioned by a business cycle beyond their control and a political mantra chanting that all taxes are bad and therefore any tax increase, no matter how necessary to preserve the quality of public services, is an anathema.

When organized as well as threatened, unionized faculty have fought back. Their principal weapons, however, bear little resemblance to those of industrial concerns. Rhoades is right when he stresses that strikes have been few and far between. Strikes seldom happen, have not proved successful as a negotiating tool, and run counter to the professionalism of many faculty. Where strikes have ended in a stalemate, they have engendered bad feelings that have festered. In the decade immediately preceding Rhoades's *Managed Professionals* (1998), the University of Bridgeport and Wayne State University had three separate strikes and Temple University two. In the latter case the university required more than a decade to redevelop the momentum responsible for its growth in the 1970s and 1980s.

The Durham Two-Step

In general, however, union tactics are less angry, though in some ways even more destructive of the faculty's ability to recast how and why they do what they do. In this regard, the history of labor relations at the University of New Hampshire provides an important cautionary tale. UNH sits in a classic college town, dominated by a university filled with campus buildings surrounded by lawns and walkways, a storied Greek row, and a coffee house aptly named "Breaking New Grounds" that is filled with wood tables and benches along with engaged students, though one is never sure exactly who is and who is not a UNH student.

Across New England, UNH is one of a handful of public universities that compete head to head with the region's private colleges and universities. Most of its students are still from New Hampshire, though out-of-state students now provide more than half of the tuition income UNH receives. Known for a strong, productive faculty, over the years UNH has honed a half-dozen niche programs into a national reputation for excellence and innovation—a reputation some faculty worry the university doesn't truly deserve. As both a sea-grant and a land-grant institution, UNH was one of the first campuses to make a meaningful commitment to sustainability as both a field of study and a mode of operation. Thanks to a steady flow of earmarks following the Republican capture of the U.S. Senate in the 1990s, the UNH Institute for the Study of Earth, Oceans, and Space (EOS) has helped set the standard for multidisciplinary scientific research focusing on the integrated behavior of the Earth and its surrounding universe.

Despite its setting and accomplishments, every three years or so the university is convulsed by a continuing labor conflict that dates back to the 1990s and an American Association of University Professors (AAUP) chapter founded in the 1920s. While most of the other public colleges and universities adopted collective bargaining to resolve questions of faculty salaries and benefits in the 1980s (and a few even earlier), faculty at UNH waited until the 1990s to choose the AAUP chapter as its collective bargaining agent. By then UNH faculty salaries had fallen significantly behind those of New England's other public flagships. The story of the coming of collective bargaining is somewhat cloaked in mystery, which befits a well-told tale. Some Durham denizens will tell you the final straw was an arbitrary increase in parking fees for faculty; others say it was an equally arbitrary decision by the board of trustees to solve a budget crisis by increasing the mandatory contributions from faculty and staff to cover the costs of their health and retirement benefits. Both stories are apparently true, though the larger point of each is simply that the faculty had tired of being treated as an afterthought by the trustees.

The coming of unionization was accompanied by one further development that would loom large in the years ahead. Through the 1980s the vehicle for shared governance at UNH had been an Academic Senate in which faculty were the dominant but not the sole constituency represented. After unionization, a new Faculty Senate was created in which only tenure-track faculty were represented. One characteristic of the AAUP chapter as a union organization has been its refusal to expand its reach by including the better than 200 research faculty at the institution or any of the 200-plus lecturers and other adjuncts. The exclusive focus on the university's full-time, tenure-track faculty—and that constituency alone—has led to a remarkably close relationship between the AAUP chapter and the Faculty Senate, in which the individual professors often serve as both senators and members of the AAUP chapter's executive committee and in which the Senate becomes an active player in the union's bargaining tactics.

The union has made increased compensation and the protection of benefits its principal, perhaps even its sole, bargaining objective; and in that realm the union's tough, at times abrasive, tactics have worked to a fare-thee-well. Having set achieving and maintaining parity with the other public flagships across the Northeast—now known in the language of the bargaining process as "comparator schools"—as its goal, the union recently found itself in the awkward position of arguing that UNH's achievement of that goal was the result of an anomaly rather than a testament to its own hard bargaining in the past. The *Fact Finder's Report* issued in the spring of 2011, however, clarified this point:

> There is no dispute that in FY10, the average faculty salary at UNH was 1.7% higher than at the eight comparator schools. Although the Association characterizes this as an anomaly caused

by the small number of retirements that year, there is simply no
way to predict with any degree of certainty whether or when there
will be a significant increase in faculty retirements or retirement
incentive plans offered in the next few years that would impact
average salary of UNH faculty in relation to their peers at comparator schools. (Cochran 2009, 26)

There has always been a second, more ideological dimension to
the union's position—a nearly absolute belief that contrasting with faculty virtue was the meanness of spirit of a management culture that
devalued learning in general and liberal learning in particular. Faculty
represented labor, in a near-1930s meaning of that term; the trustees
and university administration represented management and were,
along with their patrons in corporate America, responsible for the economic and political dislocations that had put public appropriations for
universities like UNH at serious risk.

This more ideological side to the union's bargaining positions is
often reflected in the role assigned to the Faculty Senate in the bargaining process. The tactics themselves derive from a curious understanding of how industrial unions disrupt production by employing what is
known as "work to rule"—that is, an industrial job action in which production workers do only the bare minimum of tasks the current union
contract requires of them. At UNH, the "principle of work to rule," as
the president of the union put it during the 2008 round of negotiations,
"is simple: unless explicitly ordered in writing, undertake no activity
other than teaching, research and work assignments internal to your
department."

The list of what a faculty member should not do under "work to
rule" is both long and specific: do no committee work except where
promotion and tenure is involved; do not participate in the Faculty
Senate; do not attend faculty meetings at any level—university, college, or department; do not participate in university outreach activities;
do not help the News Bureau; do not help with student recruitment;
attend "no ceremonial or social function arranged by the Administration."
Or, as the president of the union put it, "Our Administrators depend on
faculty volunteers to perform a host of tasks beyond teaching and
scholarly work. They expect faculty to continue no matter what.
Surprise them" (Barkey 2008).

In a university committed to the principal of shared governance,
"work to rule" means shutting down all decision-making processes

across the university—or, in labor terms, putting a spanner in the works. As such, "work to rule" puts direct pressure on any administration that has specific objectives it wants to achieve; at the same time, by making sure that nothing happens, "work to rule" makes certain that changes that might affect faculty lives are not considered at all.

Thus things stood in the spring of 2011; with bargaining again at an impasse, the union needed something that would make the faculty willing to impose "work to rule" in support of the union's bargaining position. Then in April, University President Mark Huddleston gave the union what it was sure it needed. Appearing before the New Hampshire State Senate, Huddleston asked that the draconian budget cuts already approved by the House of Representatives not be imposed on his university. Huddleston's plea was simple: give us time to put our strategic plan in place so that we can, through changed practices and a different business model, achieve the economies you have demanded of the university. It is worth quoting at length the key passage from Huddleston's remarks, which contain an elegant statement of the need for change, and the reaction they engendered, which provides an equally revealing glimpse into why, in organized faculties, change is so easy to disrupt and then thwart.

> When I unveiled UNH's new strategic plan just over a year ago, the first thing I said was that the business model for higher education—here in New Hampshire and across the nation—is broken. . . . Through our strategic plan, we have committed ourselves to fixing the business model—and to becoming, as a result, a model for the rest of America. This will mean changing almost everything we do: how we teach, what we teach, when and where we teach; how we organize ourselves internally and how we partner with others externally; who we think of as students and how they interact with one another and with members of the faculty; how we conduct research and what we do with the fruits of that research. This is hard work. Change always is, especially for institutions as steeped in tradition as American universities. Indeed, in many ways, the structure and fundamental operating assumptions of higher education haven't really changed a great deal in hundreds of years. Our academic calendars are still synched to the rhythms of a predominately agricultural society, where one semester ends just in time for spring planting and the next begins only when the fall harvest is in. We still too-frequently convey information in

fifty-minute lectures delivered by a "sage on the stage" to largely passive recipients in the audience three times a week for fifteen weeks a term—as if that schedule were Biblically decreed and as if that were the way that "digital natives" actually learn today. Worse, we remain wedded to a credentialing regimen of courses and majors and degrees that mainly reflect "seat time," rather than what students actually learn or need to learn. And perhaps worst of all, we still cling, occasional rhetoric aside, to a vision of higher education that is both a way-station and a world apart, where our primary mission is to take into our cloistered quadrangles a narrow band of eighteen to twenty-one year olds, educate and entertain them for four years, and then send them off, never to return, except for the occasional alumni weekend—as if we didn't live in a world where need for education and skill renewal weren't constant and society-wide, where students graduating this May will have multiple careers, including in fields that don't even yet exist, and where relationships between business and non-profits and government and other institutions are defined not by walls, but by bridges. Fortunately, we at UNH get this, and many long-overdue changes are already underway at our campuses in Durham, Manchester, Concord and beyond. (Huddleston 2011)

Huddleston spoke to the New Hampshire Senate committee on April 18. Within the next ten days, the union had conducted a vote in which a majority of those voting (64 percent) expressed no confidence in their president. What galled the union leadership were two passages in particular in the president's remarks—his assertion that higher education's business model was broken and the idea that too often a faculty member who lectured was nothing more than a sage on a stage. As one member of the union's executive committee observed in a letter to fellow faculty members that laid out the rationale for the vote:

Reading this testimony, I conclude that the president has contempt for and ignorance of the fundamental enterprise of teaching and learning that must be at the heart of the university. . . . I am deeply anguished, since the business model the president describes has no room for, or interest in, the life of the mind and imagination as I understand these. (quoted in Berrett 2011)

Huddleston's comments on higher education's business model reflected his admitted interest in Clayton Christensen's notion of how disruptive technologies succeed when they change both the mode of production and the underlying business model an organization uses to succeed in a competitive market. The idea that faculty ought to become "guides on the side rather than sages on the stage" was one of the reform slogans of the 1990s often attributed to Lee Shulman. As Huddleston noted in his remarks, both ideas had found more muted expression in the university's 2010 strategic plan, *Breaking Silos, Transforming Lives, Reimagining the University*, elements of which he had been bringing to the Faculty Senate during the previous year.

Following the union's vote of no confidence, the Faculty Senate asked Huddleston to appear and explain himself, which he did, and thereafter followed a senatorial debate on the merits of the president's point of view. The problem, several senators said, was that the president had talked about higher education in such a way as to cast doubt on the university's virtues—"UNH provides quality education now and will never be a business organization."

Two weeks later the Senate again debated the president's remarks as it considered a draft resolution that concluded: "We are concerned that President Huddleston's recent characterization of our pedagogical practices, curricular programs, degrees and students' capacities implied to the public that the faculty has failed in that responsibility. The remarks were ill-advised and the implication is false." Central to the Senate's argument that afternoon was the idea that "faculty have primary responsibility for pedagogical decisions." Accordingly, the Senate leadership sought a commitment from the president to appear regularly before it to engage in "copious deliberation." What the Senate approved, however, was a mild chiding of the president: "We are concerned that President Huddleston's recent characterization of the pedagogical practices, curricular programs, degrees and students' capacities in American higher education implied to the public that the UNH faculty has failed in that responsibility." And a remarkable peace offering followed:

> We recognize the importance of alternative learning environments. We commend members of the UNH administration and faculty who have taken the lead in their efforts to encourage new methods of instruction and affordable options in the education of our students. However, we also feel that teaching and learning through face-to-face interaction between professors and students remain central to a superior education at the University of New Hampshire.

The resolution "as amended was approved with nineteen ayes, eleven nays and four abstentions" (UNH Campus Journal 2011).

The divisions within the Senate reflected the fact that Huddleston was actually winning in the minds of many across campus. The student newspaper had already weighed in, first quoting Huddleston's remarks to the New Hampshire Senate and then observing:

> The union overreacted, blowing the quote out of proportion. Apparently, professors don't like being told they can improve. But they have no problem telling students the same. Many professors cited the quote as what prompted the vote. That's ludicrous. It's a trivial quote that the union hyper-analyzed and took the wrong way. (*The New Hampshire*, April 29, 2011)

One faculty member with a long history of being in but not quite of the union sent an e-mail to a number of his colleagues saying he was "not disturbed by the President's remarks" before putting Huddleston's case in the language of a faculty member who nonetheless still saw himself as a largely independent contractor.

> I believe that we will change. We have changed. The challenge is how do we define the core values and practices that make us distinctive while grafting new practices that will keep us viable in a changing world. Asking whether there is a better way to achieve our desired goals is a practice that each of us do regularly when we prepare our syllabi for an upcoming class. Am I reaching my students? Is there a better way to teach that concept, is there a better way to deliver my instruction, and am I current are all questions that we ask ourselves. (Confidential e-mail shared with the author).

More typical was the remark of a senior faculty member who told a colleague he thought Huddleston was right. However, when asked if he would make his views known publicly, he demurred, saying, "It wouldn't make a difference. People aren't listening. No one wants to change" (Confidential interview with the author).

This last comment most clearly defines the problem at hand. Most faculty at UNH do not want to be bothered. They are there to teach, to mentor their students, and to engage in the kind of scholarship that distinguishes them and their calling. Periodically, they will declare enough is enough and, in the case of UNH, mount campaigns to change the union and its leadership—campaigns that have consistently failed to muster the number of votes necessary to elect the alternate slate of candidates. The key question then becomes, at what point do these faculty conclude that collective action that promotes change as opposed to protecting the status quo is the better alternative?

A Circular Silence

In the specific case of the union and the Senate taking up Huddleston's testimony to the New Hampshire State Senate, little if any of the commentary mattered. Nor did the split vote within the Faculty Senate on the merits of Huddleston's remarks. Nor did the fact that the actual vote of no confidence was rushed through using the union rather than the Faculty Senate as the convening body. And finally, it did not matter that less than a third of the tenure-track faculty actually voted no confidence in the president. The union got what it sought—a shot across the administration's bow at a critical negotiating juncture. No one doubted that when the time came to impose "work to rule," the Senate would vote accordingly, and most of the faculty would comply. Preserving the status quo, along with protecting the economic security of the faculty, would prove once again to be what mattered most.

On campuses everywhere, those like UNH with successful unions, no less than those campuses without unions at which faculty are independent contractors in all but name, seldom acknowledged is the near-singular importance of protecting the independence of the faculty from the winds of change billowing all around them. Just as uncommented on is the fact that in their desire to be left alone to do their own thing, faculty bear as little responsibility for one another as possible. They are first and foremost individuals: to change what they do collectively first requires changing what each of them does separately.

What Huddleston at UNH seeks, indeed what Henry Rosovsky at Harvard was advocating, is a collective as well as a responsible faculty voice with which to share the risks and rewards of changing how the academy operates. In New Hampshire, the disruptive tactics of the union deny these university presidents a collective partner willing to engage in purposeful change. Across institutions without collective bargaining, the withering of the formal mechanisms of shared governance, along with the growing absence of an effective social contract binding the faculty to their institutions as well as to each other, has yielded faculty deliberations that are endlessly circular.

3

A Federalized Market with Little Incentive to Change

A sizeable portion of the American professoriate has a different explanation about what has gone wrong; in a Clintonesque moment they are ready, willing, and able to remind higher education's critics that "It's the market, stupid." Colleges and universities, professors remind all who will listen, are not businesses with a singular focus on their bottom line and therefore shouldn't be expected to achieve the kinds of efficiencies being demanded of them principally by legislators and congressmen. Instead of giving in to the antitax mantra and its consequences, higher education's leaders ought to be demanding sufficient funds to ensure the continued primacy of American higher education. The most disaffected and angry of these voices lament that the market has made learning a salable commodity by turning faculty into production workers and yielding control of the academy to cadres of well-paid, even coddled, collegiate administrators-turned-managers.

Such lamentations are not so much wrong as they mislead in their casting of the story as a conspiracy in which business-mogul trustees and aggrandizing presidents push aside the scholarly values and processes historically championed by the academy; in an age of markets and market-dominated politics, it is hard to imagine any cogent explanation of higher education's current travails that does not begin and end with market forces. The quite different reality, however, involves not a conspiracy, but rather the unintended entwining of market mechanisms and public policies put in place with the best of intentions.

A Twice-Told Tale

Most accounts of the federal government's support of higher education offer a tale with two beginnings. First, the Morrill Act of 1862 established a network of state-owned and state-operated land grant universities. Second, the G.I. Bill eased the demobilization of the country's armed forces following the Second World War. In the spring of 1972, the *New York Times* drew on both these iconic legislative beginnings to warn of an era of diminished opportunity if then current trends in higher education were to continue:

> For more than a century, American higher education has followed a consistent democratizing trend. Beginning with the Land Grant Act of 1862 and reinforced by the G.I. Bill of Rights after World War II, the colleges have been on a steady course toward greater egalitarianism. . . . Now for the first time, it's in danger of being turned around. The rising cost of going to college makes it increasingly difficult for all but the affluent or the completely subsidized poor to attend the expensive campuses. (*New York Times* 1972)

The trouble with such iconography is that it too freely mixes cause and effect. To be sure, the Morrill Act represented a precedent-setting federal investment in economic productivity, principally agricultural, and citizen education. The G.I. Bill eventually came to play the democratizing role the *Times* ascribed to it, but the tale is a more complicated story full of twists and turns that, over a forty-year span, has federalized the higher education market in truly unexpected ways.

That story begins in mid-1943 and the specter of a postwar America in which, as President Franklin Roosevelt warned, a victorious army was "demobilized into an environment of inflation and unemployment, to a place on a bread line or on a corner selling apples" (quoted in Haydock 1999). The antidote became the G.I. Bill of Rights, which Roosevelt signed into law on June 22, 1944, two weeks after the landings in Normandy.

The bill itself was a four-legged stool with a focus on protecting the labor market and providing an economic stimulus to spur the economy. The first leg promised veterans fifty-two weeks of unemployment compensation at the rate of $20 per week. The second guaranteed 50 percent of loans up to $2,000 for the purpose of buying a house or establishing a business. The third leg provided $500,000,000 for the construction of veterans' facilities, including hospitals. The fourth and final leg contained the educational benefits: grants of $500 a year for training and education, plus monthly living allowances of $50 a month for single and $75 a month for married veterans. In 1945, $500 in annual tuition and a $75 a month living allowance was roughly equal to a 2011 student aid grant of $6,065 and and an annual living allowance of just over $10,000 per year. Though relatively large in their own right, these sums cover a substantially smaller portion of the full cost of attending a college or university today than the original grants covered in the years immediately following World War II.

Though certainly generous, the inclusion of a higher education benefit was something of an afterthought. Most doubted that many veterans would want to avail themselves of the opportunity, and many thought that even those veterans who did participate would be primarily interested in vocational education—or as the *Saturday Evening Post* put it, having first reviewed a poll of returning veterans, "The guys aren't buying it." The two most famous naysayers were university presidents. The University of Chicago's Robert Hutchens argued that "colleges and universities will find themselves converted into educational hobo jungles. . . . [E]ducation is not a device for coping with mass unemployment." Harvard's James B. Conant lamented that the G.I. Bill failed "to distinguish between those who can profit most from advanced education and those who cannot," which led him to despair that "we may find the least capable among the war generation . . . flooding the facilities for advanced education."

They were wrong. The historian Michael Haydock neatly summarized just how the G.I. Bill contributed to the nation's stock of educated citizens: "By the time the last American World War II veteran was graduated in 1956, the United States was richer by 450,000 engineers; 238,000 teachers; 91,000 scientists; 67,000 doctors; 22,000 dentists; and more than a million other college-trained men and women, thanks largely to . . . 'the GI Bill'" (quoted in Haydock 1999).

Vouchers

Today the G.I. Bill's most important legacy is the precedent it created for having the federal government directly subsidize individuals in their pursuit of a collegiate degree. The first followup to the G.I. Bill was the National Defense Education Act of 1958, by which the federal government provided substantial capital to allow colleges and universities to make low-interest loans to students pursuing programs of study important to the security of the United States. Then in 1965, federal student aid became an integral part of the Great Society initiatives by which Lyndon Johnson sought to become known as the Education President. What heretofore had been the nearly exclusive domain of state and local governments became the subject of a broad range of initiatives promising federal funding without unnecessary federal oversight. Students without the means to pay for a college education, along with middle-class parents squeezed by the rising price of a college education, became the first beneficiaries of the Higher Education Act (HEA) of 1965. Lawrence Gladieux was to later note in what remains the single best timeline for charting the growth and changing nature of federal student aid:

> Colleges wishing to receive an allocation of funds under the new Educational Opportunity Grants program were required to make "vigorous" efforts to identify and recruit students with "exceptional financial need." Title IV of the law also included College Work-Study (another program first ushered in as part of the War on Poverty) to subsidize employment of needy students, and the Guaranteed Student Loan (GSL) program to ease the cash-flow problems of middle-income college students and their families. (Gladieux 1995)

The 1965 HEA made one additional contribution to the growth of federal student aid. Because the programs authorized by the act were set to expire in three years, Congress needed to reauthorize the act itself on a three-year cycle, though such reauthorizations in recent years have come on a less-than-regular basis. Besides ensuring that the subject of student financial aid would become a regular fixture of congressional deliberations, the term "reauthorization" has become a regular part of the student aid lexicon. The act's first reauthorization, in 1968, was largely a nonevent—a few tinkers and level appropriations.

By 1971, however, the world of American higher education had changed. College enrollments were set to drop precipitously as the generation of baby-boom students who swelled enrollments in the 1960s gave way to a baby-bust generation whose substantially reduced numbers had already led to the closing of primary and secondary schools and now threatened to do the same to the nation's colleges and universities.

The U.S. economy was also in the doldrums as runaway inflation coupled with little or no economic growth.

The 1971 reauthorization process kicked off with a strongly worded presidential statement—generally thought to have been written by Daniel Patrick Moynihan—embodying the coda that has since begun nearly every push for greater federal student aid: "No qualified student who wants to go to college should be barred for lack of money," an idea originally voiced by the Truman Commission as part of its 1947 report on American higher education. As the Nixon/Moynihan statement declared twenty-three years later, it was wrong that a middle-income student was nine times more likely to attend college than a student from a family with truly modest means. Something was "basically wrong with federal policy toward higher education" when "government programs spending 5.3 billion yearly have largely been disjointed, ill-directed and without a coherent long-range plan." It was wrong to ignore "the two-year community colleges so important to the careers of so many young people." To help right these wrongs and "spur reform and innovation throughout higher education," President Nixon proposed a series of initiatives that provided more direct aid to low-income students while allowing all students access to a federally guaranteed student loan (*New York Times* 1970).

This directive was not exactly what organized higher education wanted to hear. The emphasis on loans was at best unwelcome, and the administration's assumption, as reported by the *Times*'s Fred Hechinger, that the banks would "show their appreciation for the risk-free nature of the loans" by charging below-market interest rates was equally suspect. Organized higher education wanted not student aid but direct institutional aid to help them balance their budgets and stave off significant program cuts. Schools would, however, settle for a "student aid program that is accompanied—matched if possible—by grants to the institution which admit the aided student" (Hechinger 1971).

For a while it even looked as if the majority of college and university presidents who lobbied for direct subsidies to all colleges based only on enrollment would get what they sought. The House was the more sympathetic to this approach; the Senate and White House were decidedly cool. In the end, three substantive objections defeated the prospect of direct aid to colleges and universities: the budget realities demonstrated an inflationary cycle; a tangential imbroglio involved busing to achieve K–12 desegregation; and, as Fred Hechinger put it, those who opposed direct subsidies to colleges and universities were suspicious that the aid "would support the status quo, and reward all institutions alike, whether they were interested in self-improvement or not." In an aside that has proved depressingly prescient, Hechinger noted a lingering fear that direct grants to institutions "might create an excessive dependency on the federal Government and lead to weak colleges overcrowding their campuses to get more money."

Nonetheless, the 1972 reauthorization of the HEA was a significant achievement that deserved to be recognized as such. John Brademas, Democratic majority whip and later president of New York University, declared the reauthorization to be "the most significant higher education legislation since the Land Grant Act." Not to be outdone, Elliot Richardson, the administration's point person as secretary of health, education, and welfare, declared the final measure to be "truly a landmark in the history of higher education." And so it was, in ways I suspect that neither Brademas, nor Richardson, nor Hechinger (then the nation's leading reporter on higher education) ever imagined (Hechinger 1972).

The 1972 reauthorization created nothing less than a federally subsidized student market for higher education—one that over the course of the next forty years would help fund a cost/price spiral of now alarming proportions. In this respect the consequences of the 1972 reauthorization dwarf those of the Morrill Act and actually exceed the changes the G.I. Bill wrought in the American system of higher education. Without much debate—or I suspect without much intention—the legislation created a system of federal vouchers, on the one hand, and, on the other, hastened the time when institutions, in establishing their financial aid policies, would count on student and parental loans instead of savings to pay the increasing price of a college education.

A Changing Labor Market

The growing advantage a college education now confers in an evolving American labor market in which services have supplanted manufacturing just as in an earlier epoch manufacturing supplanted agriculture has been much discussed (some would say endlessly). Since the 1980s the college-to-high-school weekly wage premium has risen consistently—from a 50-percent premium in 1980, which meant college graduates earned half again as much as high school graduates, to a near 100-percent wage premium in 2008, which meant that, on average, college graduates were earning twice as much as high school graduates. These increased earnings made the decision to pursue a college degree that much more axiomatic.

Not surprising, then, increases in college participation rates mirrored the increases in the college-to-high-school wage premium for nearly everyone—men, women, whites, blacks, Hispanics, Asians—and for all income bands as well, regardless of parental college attendance. For example, the participation rate for all twenty- to twenty-one-year-olds increased from 31 percent to 50 percent between 1980 and 2008; the participation rate for high school graduates from families in the lowest income quartile increased from 34 percent in 1984 to 55 percent in 2008. Even the college participation rates of high school graduates from families in the highest income quartile increased from 72 to 80 percent between 1984 and 2008 (Baum, Ma, and Payea 2010).

Increased participation rates translated directly into increased enrollments. Between 1980 and 2009, total enrollments in degree-granting institutions of postsecondary education grew from 12 to 20.4 million; full-time enrollments expanded by the same proportion, from 7 million in 1980 to 12.7 million in 2009. The number of associate degrees conferred annually doubled, while the number of bachelor's degrees conferred annually soared by 80 percent, growing from 935,000 in 1980 to 1.6 million in 2010 (NCES 2010).

The Key Policy Question

The 1972 reauthorization put in place a package of federal programs that simply grew and then grew again, often by truly staggering proportions. From 1973, the first year of what became the new Pell Grant program, federal expenditures funding those grants increased from $234 million (in 2010 constant dollars) to about $35 billion by 2010. The number of recipients of Pell Grants increased over the same period of time from less than 2 million to more than 9 million. Federal student loans, including those guaranteed and subsidized, increased from $7.3 billion (again in constant 2010 dollars) to $104 billion. By 2010 the number of borrowers in these federal loan programs had exceeded 10 million, while the average student loan exceeded $8,000, and the average PLUS loan to parents was about $17,000. Over the past four decades, the number of full-time equivalent (FTE) students across all of postsecondary education has increased from 7.2 million to 15.4 million—that is roughly a doubling of the number of FTE students. The amount of federal grant aid over the same four decades has increased eightfold, and the amount of federal loans has increased nearly fifteenfold (Baum, Ma, and Payea 2010).

All these numbers are drawn from Sandy Baum's herculean compilations on behalf of the College Board to document the current trends in student aid. She would be the first to point out that all comparisons such as I have been making are inherently at risk of being misunderstood. For example, the growth in the total amount for federal aid is a function of the growth in the number of students being served, changes in the maximum amount of a Pell Grant, the availability of student loan funds, and, not to be minimized, the declining ability of students from families in the lowest economic quintile to pay for their college education. Those amounts, in different ways, are influenced by and at times are a function of the increases in the cost of attending an American college or university.

By 2010, one out of every three undergraduates at an American college or university had taken out a federal Stafford student loan either subsidized (5 percent), unsubsidized (4 percent), or both (25 percent). Ten years earlier, fewer than one in four American undergraduates had taken out a Stafford loan. By 2010, Baum and her colleagues at the College Board would report that more than half of all students who earned a bachelor's degree from a public college or university had used borrowed money to help pay for their undergraduate education. That proportion rises to two-thirds among students who earned a bachelor's degree from a private, not-for-profit college or university (Baum, Ma, and Payea 2010).

Aid aficionados often focus on the changing ratio between grants and loans to students receiving financial aid. Grants are good; they fulfill the promise to level the playing field so that those students with more limited financial resources pay no more for their college education in real terms than those whose families can simply write a check. Loans change that calculus, burdening aided students with an additional obligation to save after college in order to repay the loan funds they expended while in college. And in fact, since the broad-scale introduction of student loans after 1972, loans have provided an increasing share of the funds available to students and their families with which to fund their higher education. Twenty years ago, for example, students on average received $2 in grants for every $1 in loans they took out. In Baum's more recent calibration of trends in student financial aid, loan amounts come close to equaling grant award—42 versus 51 percent, with the balance accounted for by work-study jobs and tax credits (Baum, Ma, and Payea 2010).

Loans have generally substituted for savings. One irony of need-based financial aid is that savings reduce the student's financial need and hence eligibility for an institutional grant or scholarship. As more middle-income parents came to understand how this "savings penalty" worked to their disadvantage, financial aid offices began focusing instead on what came to be called the "expected family contribution," which, for the families of middle- or upper-income students, increasingly meant asking about the assets a family might borrow against to fund their children's college educations. In 1978, subsidized federal loans became briefly available to all families regardless of their income or other assets. Middle Income Student Assistance Act, or MISSA, provided lower-cost loans for which all students and their families were eligible; the federal government was obligated to make the interest payments on the loans as long as the student was enrolled full-time in an accredited college or university. Once the advantageousness of a MISSA loan for students from more well-to-do families became clear, the program was discontinued. Its legacy, however, helped make family borrowing an increasingly important source of educational capital with which to cover the rising cost of attending an American college or university.

Every institution and financial aid officer knows—and counts on— federal loans, to both students and parents, to supply an even more robust flow of educational capital. Through 2009, 45 percent of full-time, first-time students from families with an income of $92,000 or more who began their college education at a traditional four-year institution in 2003 had taken out a federal student loan. More than one-fourth of these cumulative loans were for $10,000 or more. As in the case of federal programs of direct student aid, federal loans were even more important for less affluent families attending a traditional four-year college or university. More than two-thirds of these students and their families had received cumulative federal loans totaling $10,000 or more. For students attending a private, not-for-profit, four-year institution fully one-third of the loans totaled $20,000 or more; the corresponding proportion for students attending a public four-year college or university was one-fourth. Price mattered as well. Once the annual cost of attendance reached or exceeded $20,000, 80 percent of full-time college students from families with an income less than $92,000 used federal loans to pay for their college education. Among more affluent families—with an income of $92,000 or more—whose children were attending an institution with an annual cost of attendance of at least $20,000, just less than half (49.2 percent) used federal loan funds to help defray the cost of their college education (Baum, Ma, and Payea 2010).

Today, nearly every college and university has made the ready availability of loans a key selling point in their marketing to new students. Institutions qualify students for loans, counsel them on the wisdom as well as the necessity of taking on educational debt, and now directly share in the penalties imposed on their students who default on their student loans. Among the most successful of these marketing strategies was the Penn Plan, created by the University of Pennsylvania in the 1980s, which made the university a partner in its students' and their families' quest for educational capital. The Penn Plan was an immediate marketing success, earning a coveted spot on the *Today Show* for Penn's president and a raft of institutional competitors who rapidly followed Penn's lead in developing comprehensive programs to aid students and families in securing their loans. To manage this new and constantly expanding function, Penn hired a banker with the unlikely name of Frank Claus, who, over the course of his twenty-plus years managing first the Penn Plan and later all of the university's financial aid programs, became a remarkable rainmaker; at one point he earned enough from his banking operations on behalf of the university to nearly cover the cost of operating the Student Financial Aid Office.

My colleague Ann Duffield, who in the 1970s headed Penn's publication office and in the 1980s all of University Relations, remembers her years in these two offices as the time when university marketing came of age—the birth of slick brochures, targeting search pieces, and increasingly the selling of the Penn Plan as a means of paying for an ever more expensive Penn education. William Ambler, who in the 1980s was celebrating thirty years as the dean of admissions at Haverford College, tells much the same story. When he started in admissions, Haverford "had a black and white view booklet with a plain gray Quaker cover. I was told that it was very expensive and that I should only give it to people who I was sure were going to enroll." By the mid-1980s all of that had changed. Ambler then headed a professional staff of four full-time admissions officers. He was mailing a four-color brochure to anyone who asked (and many who didn't). He had made a major investment in a video production, regularly cultivated more than 900 high school counselors, and ran "an overnight visitors service which at times threaten[ed] to turn the College into a motel." The change Bill was most proud of, however, was in the character of Haverford's applicant pool and resulting freshman class. While in the 1950s there had been slightly more than 500 applications for a class of 130:

> There are now a little more than 2100 [for a class of 287]. . . . Not
> only have the numbers increased, but the composition of the pool

has changed. In the late 1950s, more than a third of our applicants came from Pennsylvania; now, only about 10 percent come from Pennsylvania. Earlier, one-third of our applicants came from outside the middle Atlantic states; now, almost half of them do. In the late 1950s, we averaged about twelve minority applicants a year. This year there were 280. Of course, earlier there were no women in the applicant pool; this year there were 904 of them. These changes have made a difference in the composition of the entering classes. We have become a national institution. The numbers of students from New England, from states west of the hundredth meridian and from abroad have quadrupled. . . . Seven percent of this year's entering freshmen were foreign citizens. (quoted in Zemsky and Wegner 1987, 7)

Two Consequences

The dramatic increases in the demand for higher education, for the most part attributable to changes in the labor market and a culture that had come to value higher education as *the* means of achieving middle-class status, along with the emergence of the federal government as higher education's third-party payer changed the market for higher education forever. Two of those changes concern us here.

Compaction at the Top

Sandy Baum and Michael McPherson, both separately and together, have warned against thinking of the market for undergraduate education as a simple product market. Observing that in the admissions market there is competition both among institutions and among those institution's would-be students; one literally needs to be admitted to buy the product, and in that sense college admissions is a "matching market: more like [a] labor market or marriage market than [a] product market" (Baum and McPherson 2011). In many other ways, however, the admissions market is like other markets—the price an institution charges is a function of supply relative to demand, which in itself is highly correlated with the proportion of students from a given institution graduating in six years or less.

Recall that in the 1980s Bill Ambler could brag on Haverford College's behalf that his institution was then attracting more than 2,100 applicants for a class of 287 first-time, full-time students. At that time, tuition, room and board, and mandatory fees equaled $13,840 in current dollars and $27,990 in 2010 constant dollars. Twenty-five years later, Haverford enrolled 313 first-time, full-time students and charged them $55,250 for tuition, room and board, and mandatory fees. Haverford's price had *doubled* (in constant dollars). Just as important, the total number of students applying to Haverford increased by 60 percent, and the college's admit rate, the proportion of applicants it found worthy of admission, declined to 25 percent. What did not increase proportionally was its freshman class. While national FTE undergraduate enrollment increased 73 percent between 1985 and 2010, Haverford's freshman class was only 9 percent larger in 2010 than it had been in 1985 (NCES 2011).

Haverford's admission and enrollment statistics were true of all private, highly selective undergraduate institutions. Here the experiences of the thirty-one members of the Consortium on Financing Higher Education (COFHE) provide the best example of what has happened at the top of the undergraduate admissions market. Again, while the market as a whole increased by 73 percent, COFHE's collective freshman class was only 20 percent larger. The total number of applications received by COFHE institutions, at least a rough measure of the demand for a high-priced, highly selective undergraduate education, increased by nearly 50 percent between 2001 and 2010, the most recent years for which admission data for COFHE institutions is publicly available. Price increases across this segment of the market were equivalent to Haverford's increases in the total cost for a year of tuition, room and board, and mandatory fees—in short, a *doubling* of the annual cost of attendance between 1985 and 2010 in constant dollars (NCES 2011). The median income of families whose dependent children entered a highly selective college or university for the 2003–2004 academic year was $87,000 (slightly more than $100,000 in 2009 constant dollars), and the mean family income of this group was slightly less than $96,000 ($112,000 in constant 2009 dollars). Moreover, many of these families received financial aid packages that included institutionally funded scholarships and loans (NCES 2009).

That highly selective, high-priced private colleges and universities were increasingly becoming the preserve of the well-off is hardly news. The dramatic increases in demand, the shifts in the labor market, and this segment's market supply's only marginal increase are usually sufficient to explain what has happened during the last twenty or so years. But federally subsidized and guaranteed loans in particular also played a part by making sure that families who sought a prestigious degree for their children had sufficient access to educational capital to pay for the college education for which their children signed up. Across this segment of the market, 75 percent of all students enrolling in a private not-for-profit college or university availed themselves of a federal student loan, while just less than half of the dependent students from families earning $92,000 or more took out a federal loan (NCES 2009).

Less well understood, and less often commented on, has been a parallel shift in the undergraduate profiles of the nation's public flagship universities. Among the eleven top-ranked public flagship universities, the collective sizes of the freshman classes increased 41 percent, compared with the 20 percent increase for COFHE and the 73 percent for the market as a whole (NCES 2011).

Like their private research counterparts, public flagship universities now enroll substantially fewer recipients of Pell Grants. The families that send their sons and daughters to these universities are much more likely to have an annual income of $100,000 a year or more. These institutions are half as likely to enroll students of color as other colleges or universities, both public and private. Though these flagship institutions substantially increased the amount of institutionally funded aid they awarded, much more of these funds went to recruit students from families with a $100,000-plus income than to recruit students from low-income families. While institutionally funded financial aid to these low-income families actually decreased by 13 percent between 1995 and 2003, falling from $196.6 million to $171 million, institutionally funded aid to students from families with an annual income of $100,000 or more increased by 406 percent, rising from $50.8 million in 1995 to $257.3 million in 2003. That is, in 2003 the median income for families with children attending an American college or university full-time was $56,000, but the median family income for full-time students attending a highly selective public four-year university was $66,000 (Gerald and Haycock 2006).

Most of these comparative statistics were developed by the Educational Trust and included in its 2006 report, *Engines of Inequality: Diminishing Equity in the Nation's Premier Public Universities*. The report itself is a series of angry blasts in which its authors, Danette Gerald and Kati Haycock, charge the nation's flagship universities with having "broken" the compact that historically had placed "[them] atop . . . [the nation's] pyramid of opportunity, offering the hope that students from humble origins can learn alongside talented students from all backgrounds." That promise had now been replaced by a "relentless pursuit not of expanded opportunity, but of increased selectivity." Public flagships, like their private research counterparts, now seek to be "rated less for what they accomplish with the students they let in than by how many students they keep out," making these institutions "more and more enclaves for the most privileged of their state's young people" (Gerald and Haycock 2006, 3).

A Gaggle of Profitable Enterprises

A much more obvious shift in the market has been the rise of for-profit institutions. For-profit higher education has a long history, stretching back through the 1930s and, in a few cases, through the last decades of the nineteenth century. Typical were the launching of Monroe College and Berkeley College in the 1930s as family-owned enterprises that grew over the last decades of the twentieth century into multicampus enterprises in the New York and New Jersey metropolitan markets. DeVry, in many ways the grandfather of major for-profit institutions, began life as a training school, entered the corporate education and training enterprise, and officially became a university in 2002. The University of Phoenix, the name people most readily associate with for-profit higher education, began in 1976 and was followed by what I have elsewhere called "corporate network institutions" like Kaplan University, Strayer University, and Argosy University.

This market segment's extraordinary growth in the years following Phoenix's founding concerns us here. In 1977, the federal government recognized only 55 degree-granting, for-profit institutions providing undergraduate education; 40 offered two-year degrees, and another 15 offered four-year degrees. Three decades later, those counts had risen to 563 four-year institutions and 636 two-year institutions. In that year (2009), total enrollments in for-profit, degree-granting two- and four-year colleges exceeded 1.85 million students and accounted for 9 percent of all students enrolled in two- and four-year institutions (NCES 2010).

While increased demand for higher education in part explains the growth in both the numbers and enrollments across the for-profit market, what concerns most observers is the near-singular dependence on federal student aid that characterizes so many of these institutions. The numbers are so overwhelming that it has become impossible not to ask, "Were there no federal student aid, would there be such a robust market for for-profit higher education?" The facts do not paint a pretty picture. Students who started at a for-profit college or university in 2003 were twice as likely to have Pell Grants, three times as likely to have federal student loans, and, if they were borrowers, nearly four times as likely to be in default on their student loans in 2009 (U.S. Senate 2011, 3, 9).

That default rate has drawn ire—and at times the understandable wrath—of federal regulators and congressional committees. In 2010, the Senate Committee chaired by Tom Harkin of Iowa reported:

> The federal government and taxpayers are making a large and rap-
> idly growing investment in financial aid to for-profit schools, with
> few tools in place to gauge how well that money is being spent.
> Available data show that very few students are enrolling in for-
> profit schools without taking on debt, while a staggering number
> of students are leaving the schools, presumably many without
> completing a degree or certificate. . . . To ensure . . . increases, it is
> necessary for the schools to devote very large shares of Title IV
> dollars and other federal financial aid to marketing activities, not
> education. (U.S. Senate 2011, 11)

In the 1990s, the federal government sought to rein in the use of federal funds to underwrite for-profit higher education, principally through a 90/10 rule that limited to 90 percent the proportion of a for-profit college's or university's revenues that could come from federal student aid funds. Each year the Government Accountability Office (GAO) reports on the institutions that do not meet this standard—almost none so far— and in the process gives a snapshot of the revenue streams supporting for-profit higher education. Even the strongest of these institutions report heavy dependence on federal student aid funds. Most of the for-profit institutions I identified earlier in this chapter had significantly more than half of their revenues from programs of federal student aid: Monroe College, 78 percent; DeVry University, 77 percent; University of Phoenix, 82 percent; Kaplan University, 85 percent; and Strayer University, 77 percent. Only Berkeley College was close to the 50 percent mark at 53 percent. The sums were equally remarkable, particularly for the large corporate universities: Strayer took in $347 million, Kaplan $468 million, DeVry $594 million, and the granddaddy of them all, the University of Phoenix, took in a whopping $3.215 billion in federal student aid funds (FSA 2009).

In the most recent year for which data are available, private, for-profit institutions accounted for 25 percent of all Pell Grants and more than 25 percent of all federal loans. Of those students receiving Pell Grants, however, two-thirds (65.6 percent) had not earned a collegiate credential (certificate, associate's, or bachelor's degree) and were no longer enrolled six years after commencing their college educations; of those receiving federal loans, a similar proportion (63.3 percent) had not earned a collegiate credential six years after initial enrollment. In all, just 6.3 percent had earned a bachelor's degree. The comparison with traditional higher education hardly works to the advantage of the for-profit sector, where even the lowest six-year graduation rates cluster around 33 percent, and the median for public comprehensive institutions is in the 50 to 60 percent range. Among all students receiving a federal loan attending a public or private, not-for-profit institution, six years after initial enrollment, half had received a bachelor's degree and another 10 percent a certificate or associate's degree (NCES 2009).

In the hands of an angry polemicist, such numbers and practices make it easy to pillory the for-profit sector. For-profit institutions engage in near-predatory recruiting practices. They sacrifice educational quality on the altar of corporate profits. Many are little more than diploma mills selling credentials to those too busy or too lazy to earn degrees and certificates the old-fashioned way. The larger, almost never spoken charge is that making a profit from the provision of higher education is in itself morally suspect.

On the other side of the coin is the belief, trumpeted with equal fervor by the sector's champions, that for-profit higher education has discovered new ways of improving learning efficiency, gladly experimenting with different calendars, different curricula, and different ways of assessing student learning. The for-profit sector is best positioned to expand higher education's capacity to provide the increases in college graduates that a knowledge economy requires. There is more than a kernel of truth to such claims. Overall, for-profit higher education accounted for 36 percent of the increase in two-year degrees and certificates between 2001 and 2010 and 28 percent of the increase in bachelor's degrees over the same time period. The sector achieved these gains by doubling its granting of associate's degrees and more than quintupling its granting of bachelor's degrees. Still, the larger truth remains: only the ready availability of federal student aid made these gains possible (NCES 2011).

Why All This Matters

A nearly steady stream of lamentations notwithstanding, the four decades since the introduction of federal vouchers and the later expansion of the federal government's student and parent loan programs have seen a flourishing of American higher education. An evolving economy that came to emphasize service employment and new technologies substantially increased the demand for places in the nation's colleges and universities. New campuses opened, buildings were built, the participation rates of under-represented groups increased across the board, and a whole new segment of the market opened up and then expanded to further increase the supply of college graduates. It has also been four decades in which students and their families have consistently found the means to pay the ever-higher prices that colleges and universities have even more consistently been charging.

Those facts and the sheer size of the federal government's appropriations to fund student aid programs—more than $113 billion in the most recent year for which data are available—help explain why higher education has found change, not just unappealing, but in fact unnecessary. Even in the great recession of 2008–2009, enrollments continued to increase, as did the prices institutions charged. Indeed, except in those states with draconian budget deficits, most comprehensive public institutions actually saw their revenues grow modestly.

At the top of the market the rich got richer—a lot richer—with more applicants, more students, more federal grants for research, and, with the exception of 2008 and 2009, bigger endowments and increased donations. In general, institutions at the top used the increased demand to raise their prices rather than to increase the number of students they enrolled. The COFHE colleges and universities nearly doubled their prices in real terms while only marginally increasing the size of their freshman class. Public flagships followed a similar path, though they were more likely to increase both price and volume. While a majority of students entering highly selective, private, not-for-profit four-year institutions in 2003 received some form of aid, 20 percent were full-pays, and altogether one-third of the students received aid awards less than $10,400 against a cost of attendance that averaged just over $33,000. Among those in entering classes who were aided, the average federal aid component was slightly more than $8,300. At highly selective public universities in 2003, 22 percent were full-pays, while 55 percent received grants of less than $5,000 against an average cost of attendance of $16,500. Among those receiving aid, the average federal component was $6,000. Even at the top of the market, federal aid was an important price support, allowing the nation's highly selective institutions to proceed largely immune to the pressures for change that swirled about them (NCES 2009).

At the base of the market, federal aid played much the same role, but in a different, more all-embracing way. In a voucher system, like that operated by the federal government, enrollments matter most. All of the incentives are stacked on the side of enrolling more students, even students who are, at best, only marginally prepared to succeed. The particular—some would say the peculiar—shape of the for-profit market sector, with its high default and low completion rates, is testimony to the nature of the incentives the federal government has instituted. These same incentives have had a nearly equal impact on higher education's more traditional institutions, particularly those that enroll marginally prepared students. And as long as those incentives exist, there is little reason to invest in alternate programs of instruction or alternate calendars or, for that matter, any alternatives of any kind that might change an institution's basic production functions.

The sheer magnitude of federal funds and the fact that the federal government has become higher education's third-party payer have had one more impact on higher education's capacity to change itself. Willy-nilly the federal government has become the only game in town—the only set of agencies with sufficient power to compel higher education to change. That power is not legislative, but rather regulatory, derived from the fact that institutions whose students are not eligible for federal student aid are not sustainable. The trigger that makes an institution eligible is accreditation—a process the federal government sanctions but does not directly control. Over the last half decade, however, the U.S. Department of Education, under both Republican and Democratic auspices, has sought to change the accreditation process, not to promote either change or reform, but rather to scourge the for-profit sector and to more generally make all of higher education comply with the department's focus on measurable outcomes and improved graduation rates. Had they been introduced carefully, these initiatives might have promoted the kind of change the department said it sought; instead, the culture of compliance grows, and little, if any, change is likely to result. We turn next to that set of circumstances.

4 | A Regulatory Quagmire

In the spring of 2006, with his Spellings Commission still months away from making its final report, Charles Miller orchestrated a preemptive attack on the voluntary system by which American higher education had historically accredited its colleges and universities. First was a paper by Robert Dickeson, a former vice president of the Lumina Foundation and at the time a principal consultant to the commission. While Dickeson's title was modest enough—*The Need for Accreditation Reform*—what he produced at Miller's request, however, was a scathing report that argued "any serious analysis of accreditation as it is currently practiced results in the unmistakable conclusion that institutional purposes, rather than public purposes, predominate." Indeed, any "system that is created, maintained, paid for and governed by institutions is necessarily more likely to look out for institutional interests." With ill-disguised glee, *Inside Higher Ed*'s Doug Lederman reported that Dickeson's paper, along with a pack of similarly constructed briefing materials prepared for the commission and the press, was a clear signal of the "continued desire on the chairman's part to challenge college leaders to rethink how they operate."

Lederman described Miller's own contribution, a paper written with Geri H. Malandra, then associate vice chancellor for institutional planning at the University of Texas System, as "a sharply worded laundry list of many problems that Miller and . . . Malandra . . . say afflict

American higher education: a 'dangerous complacency about the real quality and impact' of the system, student outcomes that are of 'grave concern,' elitism and a growing chasm between college access for low- and higher-income students, and a 'gaping information void' about colleges' performance, to name just a few" (Lederman 2006a).

Although the heads of the accrediting agencies themselves were quick to cry foul, most of us on the commission and most observers of the commission's deliberations were more than a little puzzled as to what Miller and his acolytes were planning. Though accreditation per se found few champions within the commission, it was also the case that even fewer of us were convinced that a broad-scale attack on it would do much good. Former American Council on Education president Robert Atwell, though not a member of the commission, nicely summed up the ambivalence most of us felt when he told Lederman that the regional accrediting bodies "are very powerful when they decide to go to war" because "the institutions they accredit become their supporters." If the commission pushes a fight, then "there's going to be blood all over the floor" (Lederman 2006a).

An Emerging Plan B

Then in August 2006, on the eve of her commission's final report, Secretary Spellings took up that challenge. As we were putting the finishing touches on our report, the Department of Education announced a new round of "negotiated rulemaking," a complex, remarkably obscure federal process that gives the secretary of education considerable latitude in establishing federal regulations pertaining to higher education. What surprised higher education's lobbyists and policy wonks alike was the announcement that this time the process, in addition to drafting rules for implementing a pair of new federal statutes, would "examine whether any proposals made by higher education commission can be put in place through federal regulation." Again *Inside Higher Ed*'s Lederman best captured what became an unanticipated caper. In this case, Lederman used an interview with David Baime, vice president for governmental relations at the American Associations of Community Colleges, to establish the context for understanding what the secretary was proposing to do. Baime had been encouraged to say positive things about the commission's draft report and had done so, though now he felt more than a little betrayed: "So to pull out a section of the report and impose it upon us via the regulatory process certainly would violate the spirit of our statement of support. If the department is serious about applying the Spellings report ideas by the regulatory process, it would only be fair for them to also propose significant increases in need-based aid."

The rest of Lederman's story was a mix of concerns and cautions expressed by higher education's lobbying fraternity and his own surmise about the secretary's motives and intentions:

> The emphasis on accreditation particularly nettles college lobbyists. . . . The Spellings Commission's report takes broad shots at the perceived ineffectiveness and dysfunction of the system of voluntary regional and national accreditation, but offers relatively few firm proposals for transforming it. So while there are no obvious changes in accreditation that might emerge from regulatory negotiations, the department could see itself as having broad latitude to impose new requirements on accreditors and, in turn, on colleges, some observers speculate. (Lederman 2006b)

And so it went. In most public presentations, Spellings continued to sound conciliatory while Miller continued to be cast in the role of the bad cop. In November, Miller made clear just how little faith he had in what he described as the nongovernmental, largely volunteer system in which colleges and universities were responsible for accrediting one another. Accreditation, he said, was an "insiders' game" that focuses on inputs rather than outcomes and thus remains "one of the biggest barriers to innovation" (Blumenstyk 2006).

Then Spellings made explicit what she had only hinted at before, and this time the headline in the *Chronicle of Higher Education* told the tale: "Spellings Wants to Use Accreditation as a Cudgel." By then Spellings knew that with the Democrats in control of Congress there was little chance of pursuing a legislative strategy for enacting the commission's recommendations, beyond increasing the appropriation for Pell Grants, which historically had been a Democratic issue. It was also clear that her commission's report would not spark a general reform movement across higher education despite Miller's continued proclivity for what he repeatedly called "strong language." In fact the commission's report was already something of a dud. Accreditation and the largely untried strategy of using the accreditors' power to withhold accreditation were the only means left to the secretary and her department to compel institutions to do the secretary's bidding. The *Chronicle*'s Burton Bollag neatly summed up the state of the plan:

In the wake of the Democratic takeover of Congress, the accrediting system is one of the few vehicles Ms. Spellings almost totally
controls to drive her agenda. The Education Department reviews
accreditors every five years, an occasion the agency often uses to
persuade or cajole them to make changes in the way they operate.
Without the resulting recognition, accreditors lose an important
part of their utility to institutions: Students are eligible for federal
aid only if their institutions are approved by recognized accreditors. (Bollag 2006)

Although she would deny it was her intention, for the next nine
months Spellings's department pursued an aggressive campaign to federalize accreditation: accreditors that did not insist upon processes that
compelled colleges and universities to adopt measurable outcomes as the
basis for their reaccreditation faced the very real possibility of having
their federal charters revoked. The institutions those agencies accredited
would then face the possibility that their students would no longer be eligible for federally funded student financial aid. The foot soldiers in this
battle were the Department of Education staff members who oversaw the
negotiated rulemaking and provided support for the process by which
the federal government renewed the accreditors' charters.

Using the negotiated rule-making process to implement the recommendations of the Spellings Commission, particularly those that called
for increased metrics with which to measure outcomes, was an inside-
the-beltway story that, despite all the attention paid to it by both *Inside
Higher Ed* and the *Chronicle of Higher Education*, never seemed to matter except to those directly involved in the battle Spellings had will-
ingly provoked. In retrospect, two somewhat unexpected events can be
said to symbolize the problems facing Spellings and her staff. First,
Senator Lamar Alexander, the one Republican other than the president
whom Spellings could not ignore, issued a carefully worded warning.
Former governor, former secretary of education, former president of the
University of Tennessee, Alexander was perfectly willing to address
higher education's shortcomings, but not in the way Spellings was proceeding. In May, Alexander took to the Senate floor to declare, "The
department is proposing to restrict autonomy, choice, and competition." He continued: "Such changes are so fundamental that only
Congress should consider them. For that reason, if necessary, I will
offer an amendment to the Higher Education Act to prohibit the

department from issuing any final regulations on these issues until Congress acts. Congress needs to legislate first. Then the department can regulate" (Lederman 2007a).

Spellings back-pedaled. In December came a second event, a denouement at what was supposed to be a quiet session of the National Advisory Committee on Institutional Quality and Integrity (NACIQI), the federal panel charged with advising the secretary of education in general on accreditation and in particular on the fitness of specific accrediting agencies to assure the educational quality and integrity of the individual colleges and universities they accredited. Prior to Senator Alexander's warning, the line of attack the secretary had pursued was to have the Education Department, through the NACIQI process, deny recognition to those accreditors not prepared to force institutions to adopt standard metrics for measuring student outcomes and hence educational quality. By NACIQI's December sessions that strategy had been quietly set aside, and the expectation was that accreditors up for review would "win the panel's approval with barely a ripple of concern." Instead Anne D. Neal went off script—or, as *Inside Higher Ed* put it, "Someone Didn't Get the Memo." Neal, who by then had become something of a shill for Charles Miller (and vice versa), was a well-known critic of accreditation whom Spellings had added to the review panel the previous winter. At one of the panel's public sessions, Neal led Barbara Brittingham, director of New England's Commission on Institutions of Higher Education, through an interrogation that Neal would charitably describe as a colloquy.

> *Neal*: Tell me—how do you know that graduates of the institutions you accredit have achieved the standards of literacy to be informed citizens? Do you have a baseline set of standards you would like them to meet, or do you leave that up to the institutions?
>
> *Brittingham*: There is no accepted minimum standard.
>
> *Neal*: So basically, if an institution was having a 10 percent rate [of literacy] and thought that was good enough, that would be good enough for you?

At this point several participants tried to rescue the proceedings by stepping between Neal and Brittingham, but Neal would simply not be deterred. Having taken on literacy, she proceeded in the same vein to rail against grade inflation and the quality of math and science instruction before pausing to remark, "I'm trying to understand how it is you as accreditors are doing a quality job. If you have nothing but an institution's own sense of how it is doing, how does that help us?"

Here Neal crossed the line, raising a host of issues the department had more or less decided were not worth pursuing.

> *Neal*: I worry as I look at this application whether we are putting form over substance. I have some concerns, based on the colloquy we just had, that this application has produced a lot of paper that says we're assessing these [accrediting agencies], but it sounds very much like navel gazing to a layperson. I heard absolutely no standard that they deemed low enough to deny an organization accreditation. It seems to me that if we are responsible for being guarantors of quality, there is a need for these agencies to be able to show to us that they have some sense of what quality is. Other than self-reverential quality as defined by the institutions, I did not hear anything. (Lederman 2007b)

Prickly Accreditation

None of these contretemps should have mattered—but they did. Before Spellings, before Miller and the Secretary of Education's Commission on the Future of Higher Education, before Neal and those like her who used their critiques of the accreditation process to satirize higher education in general and elite higher education in particular, accreditation itself had become something of a sideshow. The only institutions that worried about the process were new or wanting to change or enlarge their missions or were in the kind of trouble that a shortage of students and excess debt inevitably brought. For most institutions, accreditation was a once-every-ten-years exercise that seldom if ever touched the sinews of the institution. The Spellings Commission was right in its description of accreditation:

> The large and complex public-private system of federal, state and private regulators, has significant shortcomings. Accreditation agencies play a gatekeeper role in determining the eligibility of

> institutions and programs to receive federal and state grants and
> loans. However, despite increased attention by accreditors to learn-
> ing assessments, they continue to play largely an internal role.
> Accreditation reviews are typically kept private, and those that are
> made public still focus on process reviews more than bottom-line
> results for learning or costs. (U.S. Department of Education 2006)

But nowhere in our final report, nor in any of the informal conversations in which I engaged as a commissioner, do I recall talking
about accreditation as the lever for federalizing the regulation of higher
education.

Judith Eaton, herself a former community college president as well
as a former head of a state system of higher education, captured the drift
of events in a commentary in *Inside Higher Ed* in which she looked back
at the years immediately following the Spellings Commission as though
she were writing in 2014, after the demise of what she called "self-
regulation through voluntary accreditation" in favor of "federal control
of thousands of U.S. colleges and universities." In her imaginary scenario, "the key element was the replacement of accreditation standards
with government standards for quality, comparable in a number of ways
to the 2001 No Child Left Behind Act that established government
expectations for success in elementary and middle schools." As institutions in general and college and university presidents in particular came
to understand that the old system of peer-centered voluntary assessments was simply extra work given the primacy of the new federal rules
then being expanded: "Accrediting bodies transformed themselves from
arbiters of higher education quality to providing audit and consulting
services to colleges and universities. They became enablers of government control of quality. Institutional accreditors assisted colleges and
universities in the data collection required by the federal government.
They provided advice to institutions about how to analyze and use these
data to showcase college and university efforts" (Eaton 2008).

As a matter of fact, such a transformation took considerably less
time than Eaton had imagined. Almost immediately accreditation
changed. Both irritated and alarmed, the accrediting agencies did what
bureaucracies under attack always do—they stiffened, making their
rules and procedures more formulaic, their dealings with the institutions they were charged with accrediting more by the book, and their
documentation of each of the steps more complete, as they sought to
demonstrate that they had put in place the new standards the U.S.

Department of Education was demanding. What the department was doing to the agencies, the agencies began doing to the colleges and universities they had hitherto seen as partners as opposed to petitioners.

Not wanting to be caught in a process they no longer owned nor necessarily understood, institutions about to be accredited became more wary, more conservative in terms of the educational initiatives they wanted the accreditation teams to review, and they were certainly less open to the kinds of exploratory dialogue that had once been a staple of the accreditation process. The safe way forward was to treat accreditation for what it had become—an audit process in which it was best to volunteer as little information as possible. Compliance became the new watchword.

Miller had been wrong in 2005 when he proclaimed that accreditation thwarted innovation. In a few cases, institutions being reviewed for reaccreditation would use the process to summon institutional energy in order to address the specific challenges and opportunities the institution itself had identified. All that changed, and not for the better, after Miller launched his attack and Spellings sought to use the mechanism of accreditation to federalize the regulation of higher education.

The Democrats Make Matters Worse

Underlying Miller's and the Republicans' assault on accreditation was a not too thinly veiled attack on the top of higher education's pecking order—the elites. Miller never resorted to talking about pointy-headed professors, but he came close in his attack on higher education's fondness for long-winded proclamations and meandering sentences. Almost always, Spellings was different, more congenial, more cordial, and certainly less confrontational. Near the end of her term as secretary of education, however, Spellings's frustration boiled over in an op-ed piece she wrote for *Politico.* What angered her was the ease with which the higher education establishment and its army of lobbyists had persuaded Congress to block her accreditation reform. Like most good headlines, the one topping Spellings's essay pretty much told the whole story: "Congress Digs a Moat Around Its Ivory Tower." The details conveyed her anger:

> Would the American people let powerful lobbying forces persuade Congress to handcuff the U.S. Securities and Exchange Commission from carrying out its responsibility for ensuring that consumers have the data they need to make informed decisions

about their investments, whether saving for a home, their retirement or their children's education? Of course not! Then why has Congress been persuaded to block the U.S. Department of Education from overseeing the quality of institutions of higher education by special interest forces determined to keep the accreditation process insular, clubby and accountable to no one but themselves? (Spellings 2008)

The Democrats who already controlled Congress and took control of the Department of Education in January 2009 offered different ideas and different targets: principally the bankers who feasted on their servicing of federal student loans and the for-profit enterprises whose business models made them unnaturally dependent on both the federal Pell Grants and guaranteed student loans. For these issues the key point person was Robert Shireman, a financial aid expert, veteran of the Clinton White House, and experienced Washington operative. After Shireman had helped steer through Congress the legislation by which the Direct Student Loan Program replaced the competing Federal Family Education Loan Program, thereby ending the guaranteed support for participating banks, he turned his attention to weeding out what the new secretary of education, Arne Duncan, had called the "bad apples" among the nation's for-profit higher education enterprises. So well known was Deputy Undersecretary Shireman's antipathy to the for-profit sector that the day after the announcement of his appointment, *Inside Higher Ed* reported that the stock prices of publicly traded higher education companies fell 5 to 10 percent in value (*Inside Higher Ed* 2009).

Shireman was also sympathetic to the use of the accreditation process to enforce federal regulations. In an interview with *Inside Higher Ed*, Shireman, lending more than moral support to Spellings's campaign to recast the purposes of accreditation, suggested that the secretary had not overstepped "her bounds in looking aggressively at what her options might be. That is what leaders should do: look for reasonable ways to accomplish their objectives" (Lederman 2006b).

One might be tempted to describe Miller and Shireman as regulatory bookends were the contrast between them not so stark. Charles Miller is an ever-present source of combustible energy—avuncular, larger than life, consistently entertaining. A multimillionaire investment banker, Miller is a Texas civic leader with a fondness for charter schools, an educational entrepreneur, an architect along with Margaret Spellings and others of George W. Bush's "No Child Left Behind" initiative in Texas, and a believer in performance metrics as a principal means for improving educational practices. The University of Texas System still lists the "Creation of State-of-the-Art Higher Education Accountability System" as the first of his many accomplishments as regent and board chair (UT System 2012).

Robert Shireman, however, is slight, ordinarily quiet, often pensive, and mostly content to let others have their say before setting them straight. A consummate insider, Shireman, like Miller, has an intrinsic interest in accountability, but where Miller focuses on metrics as a way of prodding recalcitrant educators to rethink both purposes and tasks, Shireman focuses on the rules and processes by which public agencies can achieve their goals. And while Miller and his Republican counterpart in the Senate, Iowa's Charles Grassley, directed most of their ire on higher education's elite, Shireman and his Democratic colleagues were equally focused on higher education's for-profit institutions and their growing dependence on federal student aid.

When the Democrats controlled both the Congress and the Department of Education the for-profit sector faced a three-pronged inquiry into the foibles of their industry. Iowa's other Senator, Tom Harkin, as chair of the Senate Committee on Health, Education, Labor and Pensions, conducted a series of hearings beginning in the summer of 2010, which put for-profit institutions on notice that they faced increased scrutiny. The titles that the committee gave to each of the five hearings pretty much told the story:

- Oversight Hearings of Federal Education Dollars at For-Profit Colleges (July 2010)
- The Student Recruitment Experience (August 2010)
- The Federal Investment in For-Profit Education: Are Students Succeeding? (October 2010)
- Bridgepoint Education, Inc.: A Case Study in For-Profit Education and Oversight (March 2011)
- Drowning in Debt: Financial Outcomes of Students at For-Profit Colleges (June 2011)

Inside Higher Ed simply described the Harkin hearings as "Shellacking the For-Profits" (Epstein 2010b). Indeed, not since John Dingle publicly skewered Stanford President Donald Kennedy twenty years earlier had a university or college president faced the kind of heated questioning Harkin and his staff now visited on the leaders of for-profit colleges and universities. There was simply nowhere to hide. The inquiry's level of intrusiveness became clear when the committee released the list of information it expected the presidents of the publicly traded institutions, as well as the leaders of fifteen privately held for-profits universities, to supply within the following six weeks. The "sample" of requested items *Inside Higher Ed* drew from the larger official request sent to the institutions scheduled to testify follows:

- Agendas, reports, financial statements and other documents provided to, or produced by, the college's board of directors or trustees.
- A spreadsheet with detailed school-by-school data on revenue from sources including Pell Grants, all federal student loan programs, Department of Defense tuition assistance benefits, vocational rehabilitation funds, private loans, institutional loans, state loans, state grants, student-paid tuition, employer-paid tuition, and any and all other sources.
- For the period July 1, 2007, to June 30, 2010, the number of students enrolled in online, in-person and hybrid programs; the number of new students enrolled each month by program, campus and mode of instruction; the total number of program completers each year; the total number who left by formally withdrawing or by stopping class attendance.
- Detailed information, with randomized identification numbers, for each student who entered the college between July 1, 2007, and June 30, 2009, including enrollment date and completion or graduation status.

Information due September 16 includes:

- A spreadsheet with detailed school-by-school annual expenditures since the start of fiscal 2006. The committee specifically asks for totals spent on various kinds of advertising, direct mail, telemarketing, compensation for admissions representatives and managers, faculty compensation, executive compensation, financial aid administration, educational facilities, equipment including computers and furniture, curriculum development, litigation expenses, corporate debt interest payments, private distributions to shareholders.

- Documents related to complaints from students and former students on admissions and enrollment, teaching, equipment, cost, financial aid, loans and debt, job placement, and school administration.
- All documents related to the possibility that a company or school is approaching or exceeding 90 percent of its revenue coming from the federal student aid program.
- All documents concerning tuition increases, including increases in credit hour costs and increases in the number of credits required to complete a degree.
- For the period January 1, 2009, to the present, all documents about lead generators including agreements and documents listing how many contacts were generated.
- Manuals, presentations, scripts and handouts used for training and supervising recruitment and admissions employees. Also, all materials used for training and supervising financial aid employees.
- All documents related to performance and compensation of all employees involved in recruiting, enrolling or admitting new students.
- All documents concerning recruiting in or near Department of Defense or Veterans Affairs rehabilitation facilities, wounded warrior transition units, homeless shelters, welfare and unemployment offices, or substance abuse and treatment facilities.
- Details of any use of a debt management or default consultant employed to help former students manage debt, including providing advice on loan forbearance, deferment and income-based repayment plans.
- All documents about the U.S. Department of Education's shift from monitoring two-year cohort default rates to three-year cohort default rates.
- All documents related to repayment of Title IV loans by the college to be replaced by institutional or private loans.
- Details of any institutional lending program.
- A document listing the name, address and phone number of all current and former presidents, deans or campus heads. The same information for the people in charge of recruiting, financial aid, student debt management, curriculum development, job placement, academics and marketing.

- For the period January 1, 2008, to the present, one copy of all written materials and disclosures provided to prospective students.
- Details of all policies, plans, practices and procedures for tracking and recording job placement, employment rates and salaries of former students. (Epstein 2010d)

I have included the *Inside Higher Ed* "sample" in its entirety in order to convey just how intrusive the Senate Committee was prepared to be and thus underscore just why the Harkin Committee was sending shivers through the ranks of organized higher education, public and private not-for-profit institutions as well as private for-profit entities.

The work of the Harkin Committee was the second prong of the Democrats' inquiries into how well the for-profit higher education industry was serving public purposes. The third prong was the Department of Justice's increasing willingness to join in whistle-blower suits charging for-profit colleges and universities with fraudulent actions, principally involving the compensation they paid their recruiters. In August 2011, the Department of Justice joined in charging that the Education Management Corporation (EDMC), the second largest for-profit in higher education and owner of the Art Institutes, Argosy University, Brown Mackie College, and South University, was not eligible for the $11 billion in state and federal financial aid it had received from July 2003 through June 2011. The scope of the Department of Justice's case against EDMC, like the Harkin Committee's list of requested documents, made clear just how serious the administration was in curtailing the activities of the for-profit sector. The *New York Times* quoted the former federal prosecutor who represented the two whistle-blowers in the case: "The depth and breadth of the fraud laid out in the complaint are astonishing. . . . It spans the entire company— from the ground level in over 100 separate institutions up to the most senior management—and accounts for nearly all the revenues the company has realized since 2003" (Lewin 2011).

Again not-for-profit higher education could only imagine what might happen if those same federal powers were brought to bear to change how traditional institutions recruited their students, rewarded their admissions and enrollment professionals, and assigned management responsibility for complying with federal regulations. And lest they forgot, the leaders of for-profit higher education were more than prepared to insist—in court, before Congress, and in the regulatory tribunals organized by the Department of Education—that what was good for the gander was necessarily good for the goose. The for-profit sector's new mantra became, "Apply to them the same rules you apply to us."

That even-handed defense became even more important as the for-profit sector confronted the regulatory pressures now being applied by the Democrats newly in control of the Department of Education. First, a "gainful employment" regulation was designed to ensure that graduates of accredited vocational programs earned sufficient salaries to reasonably repay their student loans. The department's mandate to develop regulations governing higher education was based on the need to provide operating procedures implementing the legislation that Congress passed and the president signed—most of that legislation was part of the triennial reauthorization process. The 1965 Higher Education Act made federal student aid available for programs that, in the words of the act, "prepare students for gainful employment in a recognized occupation." Through 2009 none of the ensuing six administrations had defined "gainful employment," a task the Obama administration and Robert Shireman now took up.

The process the Department of Education used to provide the regulations necessary to implement the Higher Education Act and its subsequent reauthorizations was known as "negotiated rulemaking." The department was to appoint a mixed panel of experts and practitioners to develop the necessary rules and regulations. Provided the panel reached a unanimous consensus on the form and function of the specifics, the department was pretty much required to accept the panel's recommendations. Whenever the panel disagreed, however, the department could follow its own lead, subject only to a mandatory review by the Office of Management and Budget and the White House. In December 2009, the department convened the requisite panel to develop rules for fourteen separate issues linked to the Higher Education Reauthorization Act passed earlier that year. One of those issues was the definition of "gainful employment" as applied to vocational programs and most for-profit enterprises. No one suggested the legislation itself required such a definition; rather, the department decided that the loosely worded phrase containing the term "gainful employment" required both a definition and a procedure for determining whether the colleges and universities covered by that phrase were in compliance with the legislation's intent.

Almost immediately the negotiated rulemaking sessions dealing with gainful employment became contentious. Initially the department proposed linking the prices charged for vocational programs, which included almost all for-profit providers and relatively few traditional public or private not-for-profit providers, to the expected earnings of workers in the field in which students were seeking either a degree or a certificate. The alternative was to calculate the ratio of student debt to expected earnings. In either approach the two quickest ways for an institution to avoid being cited for providing programs that did not lead to gainful employment would be to severely limit intake into such programs or, more likely, to limit the prices they charged.

In less than a nanosecond the for-profit industry charged that Shireman and his staff were seeking a program of price controls. Elaine Neely, senior vice president of regulatory affairs for Kaplan Higher Education, allowed that she was "flabbergasted" that the department "would impose price controls when clearly Congress itself has not been able to come to the decision to do that on higher education." And lest her counterparts in traditional higher education missed her point, Neeley went on to tell *Inside Higher Ed*, "This not only applies to private career schools, but to technical and vocational programs at non-profit institutions and would begin the descent down a 'slippery slope' toward price controls elsewhere in higher education" (Epstein 2009).

A month later the department, changing tack without really changing course, indicated that the better way to define "gainful employment" was to link expected earnings to anticipated debt. Again in the words of *Inside Higher Ed*, "The result of implementing a debt-to-income limit could be to weed out (or at least cut tuition at) vocational programs and institutions that don't yield their recent graduates in-field jobs that pay well enough for them to repay their student loan debt on a 10-year schedule" (Epstein 2010a).

The revision satisfied no one in the for-profit camp. First and foremost they wanted the continued absence of any formula defining "gainful employment" and, failing that, a long string of exemptions and alternate formulas that would leave most, if not all, of the for-profit industry unscathed. By April, unnamed Wall Street analysts were quoted as saying that just such exemptions were at hand, and by July, under the headline "Splitting the Difference on Gainful Employment," *Inside Higher Ed* reported that "striking a middle ground between aggressively attacking for-profit higher education and backing down under the sector's intense lobbying pressure, the [revised] rule creates multiple paths to eligibility and takes aim at only the most egregious of bad actors" (Epstein 2010c).

And so it went: thrust and counterthrust; claim and counterclaim; rhetorical outrage mixed with other forms of verbal fireworks. For nearly a year the discussion continued among those directly involved in the negotiated rulemaking, among a handful of congressional and department staff, and among the policy wonks and interested parties who regularly read higher education's two online dailies.

In September 2010, the department began a three-month process of collecting public comment on what had become the compromise—some said compromised—gainful employment rules. Then, for the second time, the department delayed issuing its final rule, choosing instead to schedule an additional two days of public hearings. Those sessions proved anticlimactic, at least in part because those lobbying on behalf of the for-profit industry had found a surprisingly bipartisan House of Representatives willing to block the department from putting the gainful employment rule into effect. That effort came to naught, however, when the following April, a House-Senate compromise temporarily ended the stalemate on federal spending and eliminated the provision blocking the implementation of the department's gainful employment rules. For those paying attention it was becoming abundantly clear just how much of a political football higher education and the rules governing federal student aid had become.

At last, in June 2011, the department published the final rules for gainful employment—an event that *Inside Higher Ed* marked under the headline, "Concessions or a Cave-In?" (Nelson 2011). The process had taken more than ten months and occasioned more than ninety thousand written comments along with a precedent-setting lobbying campaign and media blitz on the part of the for-profit higher education industry. As was often the case during the heyday of Charles Miller and the Spellings Commission, *Inside Higher Ed*'s Doug Lederman provided the best documentation of the extent to which the regulatory environment had changed:

> Largely lost in the instant analyses, pro and con, though, was the long-term significance of the department's actions. The "gainful employment" rules, as they have come to be known, represent a powerful and potentially game-changing shift in how the federal government looks at higher education. The agency has written into federal policy, for the first time, a direct (if crude) attempt to measure the *value* of an academic program, by linking a measure

of student expenditure (student loan debt burden) with an outcome measure (graduates' average income).

This current approach applies only to non-liberal arts programs at for-profit colleges and to vocational non-degree programs at public and private non-profit colleges—for the moment. But now that the federal government has such a tool, many observers agree, it's hard to imagine that it won't seek to apply it more broadly—if not this administration or Congress, then a future one. (Lederman 2011b)

Defining the Credit Hour

Given the vociferousness of the campaign for-profit higher education mounted against the Department of Education, it is little wonder that the proposed gainful employment rules dominated most discussions of the then-underway negotiated rulemaking process. Defining gainful employment, however, was but one task the process considered. Of equal importance was a new rule defining the credit hour, by which the department's Office of General Council, probably with the support of Shireman and his department colleagues, hoped to close down the for-profit institutions that were awarding college degrees for less than the requisite effort traditionally associated with their attainment. While the issue, like that of defining gainful employment, had simmered for a decade or more, the suspicion that for-profit higher education wanted to reduce costs and hence increase profit margins by reducing the amount of work required to earn a degree soon burst into the open. Kathleen Tighe, the Department of Education's inspector general, launched what Goldie Blumenstyk of the *Chronicle of Higher Education* described as a "stinging attack" on the Higher Learning Commission of the North Central Association of Colleges and Schools for its willingness to consider accrediting a for-profit provider with a questionable reputation for how it awarded credit for its distance education courses. Technically an "alert memorandum," the warning from the department's office of inspector general made clear that the commission's future status as a certified accreditor was now at risk (Blumenstyk 2010).

Not by coincidence, I suspect, in the same month the department moved to make defining the credit hour the business of the panel engaged in the negotiated rulemaking process. To standardize the basic unit by which American colleges and universities awarded academic credit, the department proposed a definition based on the Carnegie Unit, in which one credit equals one hour of class time or direct faculty instruction and two hours of out-of-class work per week for approximately fifteen weeks. The proposed rule allowed for a variety of exemptions provided they were approved by the institution's accreditor.

Here again the first targets of the proposed regulation were for-profit providers—and as expected they mounted a vigorous defense that essentially argued to let sleeping dogs lie. On this issue, however, traditional higher education could not remain on the sidelines. While neither as costly nor as slickly orchestrated as the assault the for-profits mounted against the gainful employment rules, the lobbying by higher education's traditional organizations was both organized and persistent. To begin, Molly Corbett Broad, American Council on Education (ACE) president, submitted a letter signed by more than seventy college associations and accrediting groups. Expressing its "grave concern," the group charged the department with having "federalized a basic academic concept and, at the same time, developed a complex, ambiguous and unworkable definition." Incorporating a definition of the credit hour in the federal regulatory code would "allow the Department of Education to micro-manage campus academic programs" (*Chronicle of Higher Education* 2011).

In March, the House of Representatives, now under Republican control, but also including a variety of Democratic friends of the for-profit industry, took up the issue in committee. Blair Dowden, the president of Huntington University in Indiana and a leader among private Christian colleges, testified that the department, in reaching a federal definition of the credit hour, was seeking to insert "the federal government into one of the most sacrosanct elements of higher education." But the crux of Dowden's testimony was that seeking a standard, one-size-fits-all definition of a credit hour was to thwart the very kinds of innovation higher education reformers were seeking: "A restrictive definition of 'credit hour' based on seat time alone would turn back the clock and discourage the kind of innovation that enables colleges and universities to serve these students. . . . It is one thing to measure how much time a student spends in a classroom; it is quite another to measure how much the student learned" (Moltz 2011).

Defending the administration's position again was Department of Education's Inspector General Kathleen Tighe, whose office had pushed the department into taking on the credit hour fight. Arguing that the new regulations were not only necessary for taxpayer oversight but also flexible enough to assuage many stated concerns, Tighe proclaimed, "The credit hour is the most basic unit for determining the amount of federal student aid provided to students and funded by taxpayers. . . . A credit hour is a proxy measure of a quantity of student learning in exchange for financial assistance. It is in the federal interest to ensure that students are receiving an appropriate amount of funding and instruction and that taxpayer money is being used properly" (Moltz 2011).

Here it helps to understand what was at stake. Federal financial aid rules had traditionally assumed a normal academic calendar—roughly two semesters plus two summer terms. To be eligible for federal aid, students were required to enroll in courses carrying, on average, nine credits per term. While this logic further assumed that the credit hour was in fact standard across higher education, the for-profit industry had championed the use of accelerated courses carrying extra credit presumably for extra work. The question was simple: was extra work really involved, or had the for-profit industry found a unique way to charge more for less, with the federal government picking up a large portion of the bill?

But for-profit institutions were not the only providers looking for new ways to speed up the education process. Many traditionally configured programs reaching out to adult learners were also interested in new ways to assign credits to courses. Others asked, What about credit by examination, no seat time involved? Still others championed the awarding of credit for learning experiences outside the classroom. A few hardy souls, myself included, began asking whether a bachelor's degree, for example, necessarily required 120 credits and/or four years to complete. To each of us, the credit hour rules the department was proposing became yet another barrier to purposeful change. When the *Chronicle*'s Blumenstyk asked Robert Mendenhall, the president of Western Governors University, the most written about of the publicly funded online providers, if he thought the credit hour had "become a relic," he responded that it "is the coin of the realm, but it's badly in need of an update." Mendenhall then added, "It's time we measured learning rather than time. . . . After all . . . the issue for governments is whether they are getting their money's worth. Ultimately they want to pay for learning, not for time. I don't know if they know that yet" (Blumenstyk 2010).

As if following up on Mendenhall's lament, the Gates Foundation, then in the process of approving a $4.5 million grant to Western Governors University, joined the fray. In a letter to Secretary Duncan, the Foundation's Director of Postsecondary Programs Hillary Pennington wrote:

> We fear that while the department says it does not mean to tram-
> ple on innovation, the practical effect of the credit hour regulation
> will be to reinforce the existing credit hour model. . . . For many of
> the colleges and grantees we support, how to measure and quan-
> tify student learning are areas they are trying to revolutionize, in
> order to break the supposed link between learning and a required
> number of credits or courses. (Field 2011)

The new rules defining the credit hour along with the rules defining gainful employment were in place by the opening of the 2011 fall term.

Examples of how all this regulatory drama played out on college and university campuses was reflected in a pair of events that tran-spired over the summer of 2011. The first, at the University of Pennsylvania, resulted in a memorandum from the provost to all deans, department chairs, and center directors—and in most cases for-warded via e-mails to those of us on the faculty. The Middle States Commission on Higher Education (MSCHE), Penn's accreditor working in conjunction with the Commonwealth of Pennsylvania's Department of Education, had noted that the university's academic calendar was short six days of instruction in the fall and one day in the spring. Because "compliance with these regulations is critical for Penn's reaccreditation and the MSCHE has indicated that definitions of 'aca-demic year' and 'credit hour' are important elements of their expand-ing role in ensuring compliance with state and federal policies," henceforth Penn's fall term would begin before rather than after Labor Day, a decision reached only after extensive discussion by the Council of Undergraduate Deans. No one had suggested that Penn's undergrad-uates needed to learn more or were being shortchanged, only that the new credit hour regulations indicated that there were not enough instructional days in the Penn academic calendar.

At about the same time Northern Kentucky University (NKU) and its accreditor, the Southern Association of Colleges and Schools (SACS) Commission on Colleges, found themselves in the hot water Penn was seeking to avoid. Two years earlier, NKU had revised its general educa-tion requirements so that students taking two foreign languages could fulfill the humanities requirement without taking any other course. The SACS accepted the change, but the NKU philosophy department cried foul and appealed to the SACS for help. When the accreditor declined to change its initial ruling, the disgruntled faculty appealed to the U.S. Department of Education and this time found a willing audience. The upshot was that the department formally chastised SACS for allowing what its staff ruled was a substantive change in NKU's general education requirement, which violated the SACS Commission on Colleges' own rules defining the role of the humanities in the college curriculum. As the *Chronicle of Higher Education* put it, "Federal officials also were not convinced that the Commission had used the correct process to review the new curriculum. It should have been treated as a 'substantive change,' the department said, defined as 'the addition of courses or programs that represent a significant departure from the existing offerings of educational programs'" (Kelderman 2011).

The NKU case sent two chilling messages to those people in higher education who were paying attention. First, the Department of Education was fully prepared to intervene on the basis of a complaint filed by a decided minority of the faculty. And second, the term "substantive change" had been redefined; now all changes were subject to review, not only by the accreditor, but also by Department of Education staff.

Assessing the Damage

Currently the talk among the accreditors, for the most part off the record and hence not for attribution, focuses on the growing volume of disconnected regulations and "Dear Colleague" letters, written from the Department of Education to the accrediting agencies, that are making less and less sense. While often conceding that the intent of the regulations is laudatory, the accrediting agencies are most concerned by the sheer tediousness and redundancy of a regulatory system that was too often a jumble of catch-22s. It starts with the 220-page manual describing the new regulations, to which were added the "Dear Colleague" letters. The letters, often unannounced as well as unexpected, offer what the department describes as interpretive guidelines, while the accreditors see them as subregulatory mandates that arrive without consultation and are not subject to appeal. Confusion bordering on chaos is often the description applied to the conflicting roster of offices within the department, each with its own notion as to which piece of the regulatory pie it owns.

Probably most irritating are the new rules governing substantive change, which the website for the Southern Association of Colleges and Schools (SACS) defines "as a significant modification or expansion in the nature and scope of an accredited institution" (SACS 2009).

Previously, most accreditors had assumed substantive change meant something major—a new program, a new campus, or the addition of an online entity. Substantive change now means any change at all, even a change of address. Expedited procedures had been in place to render the process of making the required changes easy and almost seamless, but, in the postregulatory frenzy sparked first by Miller and Spellings and later accelerated by Shireman, nothing is expedited, and even less is explained or adjusted. Everything takes more time, more forms, more outside consultants hired by the department to verify the procedures used and the data maintained by each accrediting agency. The irony, I suppose, is that a process created to speed adoption of learning modalities had itself become a caricature of what was supposed to be wrong with higher education.

In the midst of the negotiated rulemaking process that made all of this possible, Terry Hartle, for two decades higher education's leading Washington insider and advocate, noted that on the table was "'the most complicated regulatory package that the Department of Education has ever promulgated—this really is a brave new world'" (Epstein 2010c).

Often when in new, largely uncharted territory, the best survival strategy is to be still and quietly observant. "Do nothing that calls attention to yourself" becomes the mantra. Established bureaucracies are particularly good at observing this maxim, and colleges and universities along with the agencies that accredit them are nothing if not experienced bureaucracies. The irony, again, behind Charles Miller's oft-repeated charge that accreditation is stifling innovation across higher education is the reality that the Department of Education is now seeking to federalize accreditation. This quest has already created a climate discouraging all but the most foolhardy from trying anything too new. Though no one would have suspected it, the U.S. Department of Education has become the perfect partner for a professoriate still encamped just north of Armageddon and waiting for some other moment to take on the challenge of purposeful change.

5 | A Troublesome Fractiousness

Five years after the Spellings Commission issued its final report, American higher education could be forgiven for asking, "What happened?" Public colleges and universities have a right to feel particularly put upon. In that host of states whose economies and revenues have been ravaged by a debilitating recession, publicly funded institutions have cut programs, laid off faculty and staff, and instituted mandatory furloughs. Responding to diminished state appropriations, many of these same institutions have capped their enrollments, thereby sending significant numbers of students to both private and for-profit institutions. Gone from these institutions is that sense of security that was once a staple of the academy; now nothing remains certain, and nothing appears to be very promising.

Nonselective privates have fared only marginally better. Enrollments are up—thanks in part to the outflow of students from the public sector—but so is the discount rate reflected in the increasingly generous financial aid packages nonselective private institutions have felt compelled to offer. Somewhat belatedly, these institutions are coming to understand just how dependent they are on the continued flow of federal student aid dollars—and in some states, the continuation of almost as generous state financial aid programs—and the increasingly frightening prospect that reducing federal and state deficits will lead to a striking reduction in the monies made available to students to finance their college educations.

Even the for-profit sector now seems unsettled. The new federal regulation governing gainful employment is more than a nuisance, as is the continued beating the industry has taken from Tom Harkin's Senate hearings, the U.S. Department of Justice's new eagerness to support whistle-blower suits alleging the payment of illegal bounties to the for-profit recruiters, and the new scrutiny of for-profit institutions and practices by their accreditors.

Institutions at the top of the market, however, have largely weathered the recession and the continuing clamor for reform. Their enrollments have remained as strong as ever while their costs continue to escalate, as do the prices their students and families appear ready to pay. In public, the leaders of these institutions lament a collapse of equity prices that has diminished their endowments and placed a singular burden on them to provide sufficient financial aid to offset the high tuitions they have chosen to charge. To date, however, the most noticeable financial impact on these institutions has been a lessening of their willingness to offer financial aid packages that do not include loans to middle-income families, including those with an annual income between $120,000 and $180,000. At the same time, these institutions' fundraising programs are once again robust. The new gold standard for a major campaign has become $6 billion plus, thanks to the University of Southern California's eagerness to set that as its campaign goal.

Still, even in this sector there is now a palpable uneasiness among senior administrators, if not yet among the faculty. More and more of these leaders have become what might best be described as "defensive pessimists." The increasingly easy as well as politically advantageous tack is to imagine how much bad news lies just over the horizon—likely reductions in federal funds for research as well as student aid, more competition from abroad, and further escalation in the cost of doing the kind of big science on which the university's reputation depends. There has been, at least to date, little if any talk of recasting either the production functions or the business models that hitherto have accounted for so much of these institutions' market successes.

At the same time, the general questioning of higher education has crystallized around two dominant concerns: costs and outcomes. Today a nearly general consensus holds that American higher education is an expensive enterprise that lacks both the will and the know-how to do things differently. It is also an enterprise in which an embarrassingly large number of students start but do not finish a baccalaureate education, and completion rates all too often track the wealth, location, and ethnicity of enrolled students. The measure that best captures this concern is the six-year graduation rate for any institution, group of institutions, or group of students. The federal government, as well as the accreditors at the government's bidding, has set the rapid improvement of this measure as a national priority.

The focus on costs has similarly produced a too-simplified focus on the prices not-for-profit institutions find themselves charging to cover their ever-increasing operating costs. As I have argued before and am about to argue here, much discussion of the affordability of higher education has missed the mark: higher education has not actually become less affordable, as evidenced by increased enrollment rates for every segment of the population, including children from middle-income families; rather, the enterprise as a whole has become too expensive. Though individuals may still be able to afford the tariff, the nation as whole cannot—an insight I have gladly borrowed from Charles Miller. And every sector of higher education has discovered—with the singular exception of the large, for-profit providers—that these increases in operating costs have proved inexorable, given the inability of colleges and universities to do things differently.

A Different Proposition

Historically, these two concerns—disappointing attainment rates and escalating operating costs—have been treated as separate issues. This division of responsibility as well as blame mirrors higher education's view of itself as having a hard side where monies are concerned and a softer, more nurturing side when helping students achieve their academic ambitions.

In the spring of 2010, my colleague Joni Finney and I sought to change both the nature and tone of that discussion by asking: Are we sure these concerns have either separate causes or separate consequences? Is it not possible that controlling operating costs, encouraging more adaptable and nimble institutions, and achieving higher graduation rates require individually the same basic adjustment: the rethinking of a collegiate production function that has become both too expensive and too cumbersome to achieve the academic purposes expected of it?

The still dominant explanation for how and why colleges and universities cost so much remains Howard Bowen's classic observation that universities will raise all the money they can and then spend all the money they have raised. The way to excellence and reputation lies principally in having more money to spend on the good things colleges and universities want to achieve. Just as clearly, the quickest and easiest way to make colleges and universities cost less is to starve them of revenue—a proposition that the recession and state budget shortfalls are now testing with a vengeance.

Given the near absence of new monies and the looming presence of more economic bad news, higher education's leaders have come increasingly to portray themselves as being caught in what John Immerwahr of Public Agenda has described as an "Iron Triangle" (Immerwahr, Johnson, and Gasbarra 2008). Somehow they must find ways to simultaneously control costs, increase quality, and improve access—and that, they argue, is simply not possible.

State policymakers, barely persuaded by the presidents' arguments and newly frustrated by the universities' reluctance to change, have begun to experiment with strategies that use the power of the public purse to exact greater efficiencies from state public systems of higher education. The result can best be described as an operational cul-de-sac. Rhetorical tough love hasn't worked. Budget incentives have not changed educational processes. By reducing state appropriations and limiting tuition increases public colleges and universities spend less money without becoming either better or demonstrably different. Salaries can be reduced, positions left unfilled, perks and amenities eliminated, but the basic production functions that shape the enterprise's teaching and research missions remain unchanged.

This dismal prospect has led Finney and me to ask a different set of questions in our search for alternative strategies for controlling and improving graduation rates. We began with the question, "What costs the most money?" And we answer: the curriculum! To explain the link between the curriculum and higher education's escalating costs, we invoked a concept economists use to illustrate how perfectly rational actions on the part of individuals can, when summed, produce unintended and devastating consequences.

The "tragedy of the commons" tells the story of what happens when a community-owned pasture (or commons) is at or near its capacity in terms of the size of the herd that can be fed without destroying the pasture itself. Even then it remains in the interest of each farmer to increase the size of his own herd because he, like each of his neighbors, has a right to feed all the cattle he acquires on the same pasture where his as well as his neighbors' cows graze. The problem occurs when the total number of animals exceeds the pasture's grazing capacity; then the pasture begins to irreversibly decline. For economists, the moral of the tale is that a perfectly rational act (the individual sending just one more animal to graze on the commons) can have a devastating impact on the system as a whole (the withering of a productive pasture) (see Zemsky and Finney 2010).

In many ways the dilemma now facing higher education reflects the tragedy of the commons. Three decades of constantly adding new programs and more choices to the undergraduate curriculum have yielded colleges and universities that are economically unsustainable and educationally dysfunctional. To understand how this happened, we need to revisit a piece of curricular history that dates to the 1960s. Sparked by student revolts in Europe and a wave of student-led political protests in this country, American colleges and universities began granting students more personal freedom and adopting curricular changes that reduced both general education and graduation requirements. In time, the faculty, who had at first opposed student demands that they be allowed to "do their own thing," discovered that what was good for the goose was even better for the gander. Few faculty enjoyed either grading senior theses or comprehensive examinations or teaching the required course sequences that constitute major and pre-major programs at most institutions.

A laissez-faire environment emerged in which nearly every possible subject was admitted to the collegiate curriculum, provided the new course was taught by a fully qualified member of the faculty. Whole new disciplines and concentrations were similarly added, often in response to demands that full recognition be granted to specialties that previously had been considered outside the accepted canon. At the same time, except in the sciences, most courses became stand-alone experiences not requiring prerequisites or, in fact, much if any coordination among the faculty who taught similar courses in the same department or discipline.

For those of us on the faculty, the lessening and then the elimination of most requirements proved a bonanza. We could teach what we wanted—principally our own specialties—when we wanted, without having to worry too much about how or what our colleagues were teaching. Each course became a truly independent learning experience, and our principal responsibility was to absorb our fair share of the enrollments that were required to ensure that our department would not lose valuable faculty lines.

For students, this commitment to unfettered curricular choice proved more than appealing—a chance not only to do their own thing but also to change their minds, not just once but frequently. The curriculum became a vast smorgasbord of tempting offerings. Faculty seeking to ensure adequate enrollment were careful to tailor their requirements and expectations to meet student tastes. Students could design their own majors and concentrations. But, as has become increasingly obvious, too many students also got lost, unsure of what it took to graduate, on the one hand, or, on the other, of what was actually being asked of them in terms of either subject mastery or learning skills.

Institutions faced even greater problems, and here is the core of the financial side of our argument. The more open-ended the curriculum became—the more faculty and students were free to set their own schedules—the more resources, both financial and human, were required by the institution to meet its educational obligations. Adding more courses and majors to the curriculum forced the institution to spread its current faculty resources ever thinner, to increase the number of full-time faculty, or, as has proved most often the case, to hire more adjunct faculty.

The result is an almost endless series of undergraduate curricula in which "almost anything goes"—the observation that became the touchstone of *Integrity in the College Curriculum*. As I have already observed, what was true in 1905 is even more true today. Repeated calls for greater efficiency and the more parsimonious expenditure of public funds and tuition receipts have been rhetorically addressed and then largely ignored. In the meantime the fragmentation of the undergraduate curriculum has continued unimpeded.

And still, worries about the escalating cost of an undergraduate education, on the one hand, and, on the other, the large numbers of students who begin but do not finish a baccalaureate education have remained separate concerns. Those who focus on costs talk about outmoded work rules, including tenure, presidential salaries and perks, the avariciousness of athletic departments, and higher education's commitment to research always trumping its commitment to teaching. Those who worry about the curriculum continue to focus on its fragmentation, on a corresponding devaluing of the liberal arts, and on the continued sense that almost anything goes when it comes to approving new courses, new majors, even new disciplines.

A Sea of Reaction

In our original publication, "Changing the Subject: Costs, Graduation Rates, and the Importance of Rethinking the Undergraduate Curriculum," Finney and I argued that the way out of this box is to change the curriculum by productively constraining both student and faculty choice:

> We would start by having students choose not among an expanding menu of courses, but among a much shorter list of curricular pathways—that is, an ordered sequence of courses linked together by faculty design. This curricular structure would yield a much more efficient match between student needs and institutional resources. There would be fewer under-enrolled courses and, not so incidentally, more courses taught early in the day as well as on Mondays and Fridays (perhaps even on a Saturday morning). (Zemsky and Finney 2010, 4)

I don't think it is giving away the plot to indicate that an elaborated form of this proposition is one key solution this volume poses to fix what ails American higher education. My more immediate concern here, however, is with the reactions our argument encountered and what they tell us about the difficulty of implementing the kind of curricular reform we had in mind.

Simultaneous to the publication of "Changing the Subject," Finney and I began a series of conversations with the leaders of state systems of higher education made up of comprehensive institutions. We initially approached Charlie Reed of the California State University (CSU) system whose institutions, we believed, would welcome a strategy that allowed them to teach more students without a large increase in public appropriation using a process that the faculty would control. Next we talked to the leaders of the Minnesota State Colleges and Universities (MNSCU) and the Pennsylvania State System of Higher Education (PASSHE). Our conversations with the chancellors were cordial and supportive; each indicated they could be interested in having one or more of their institutions participate in a project designed to test the proposition that curricular simplification could reduce costs and increase graduation rates.

In Minnesota and Pennsylvania, the chancellors followed up by consulting their key constituencies, including the leaders of their faculty unions. In California, the faculty union, having been alerted to the project by its Pennsylvania counterpart, weighed in on its own. First to say "no thank you" was the Association of Pennsylvania State Colleges and Universities Faculties (APSCUF). In a detailed letter to PASSHE Chancellor John Cavanaugh, the union's president, Steve Hicks, documented his concerns: Finney and I had not understood the special context of the PASSHE environment; we were possessed of an "Ivy League Mentality"; he was not familiar with either Howard Bowen or *Integrity in the College Curriculum*; and he simply scoffed at the notion that there were under-enrolled courses.

Hicks described our proposal as involving an unsightly rush to implement a predetermined outcome: a reengineered curriculum of pathways, cohorts, and fewer electives. The result would be a devaluing of the liberal arts and a return to a past that was no longer appropriate. "I am amazed," Hicks wrote to Cavanaugh,

> at the trends shown in this proposal away from the kinds of institutions we became in the latter half of the twentieth century as we moved from normal schools to comprehensive four-year institutions. For years the argument for four-year comprehensive education has been that our graduates change careers an average of three times . . . many institutions trumpet "lifelong learning" as one of their missions; yet this idea undermines this notion by reducing the broader preparation in a trade-off for cost-savings and efficiency. Our mission isn't efficiency; it is to educate the Commonwealth in a way that provides them a lifetime of opportunity, not just a quick, affordable fix to their first job.

The cost savings we had promised would be by reduction:

> Sure, it's less expensive to provide a degree to someone if they take fewer credits to earn it—that math is unassailable. But to assume that just working in cohorts will provide the "value added" or make up for fewer gen ed credits is fallacious. There's a reason why the gen ed curriculum is the size it is and has been for at least a half a century: it prepares students well. (Hicks 2010)

Finally, our hypothesis that reengineering the curriculum to constrain both student and faculty choice, in Hicks's and his union's view, ran "counter to the currently established curricular approval structure." It was hard to see how the proposal could "operate within the confines of our system, especially as the autonomous units would need to work in coordination among the five selected schools" participating in the project. The project as outlined in our proposal "seems to undermine both the local process" and the "university autonomy presumption" embedded in the legislative act that had created the PASSHE itself. Or, as Hicks noted in the conclusion to his letter: "To turn to the Zemsky and Finney concept would be, to use their metaphor, to attempt to manage our pasture like their pasture. We have two very different pastures and two very different animals in it. As such, we have to be careful not to buy in to their concept and end up not with healthy cows but with our underfed hens" (Hicks 2010). In an end note to his letter Hicks told Cavanaugh he may have been wrong in his belief that the "Cal State system was 'on board.' I checked with them and the union is emphatically not." Hicks's checking with his counterparts in the California Faculty Association (CFA), the union representing CSU faculty, stirred up its own hornet's nest. Almost immediately, there began circulating among the local CFA chapters an e-mail warning that "Changing the Subject" presented yet "another new higher education restructuring initiative," this one calling for "sweeping and regressive changes to college curriculum." As is too often the case in such circumstances, rhetorical excess, this time tinged with the language of political correctness, became the instrument with which to bludgeon the proposal. Where Finney and I had noted that, starting in the 1960s, "whole new disciplines and concentrations were similarly added [to the curriculum], often in response to demands that full recognition be granted to specialties that previously had been considered outside the accepted canon," the CFA e-mail circular charged: "Their approach involves purging entire disciplines from the curriculum, particularly those that emerged since the Civil Rights movement of the 1960s and not central to the 'accepted canon' of that era" (E-mail shared with the author).

Later that spring, the CSU Academic Senate, having considered the project and met with Finney, decided it could not recommend that the system participate:

> The Zemsky-Finney paper enumerates many issues and challenges that face higher education; however, from an academic standpoint, the proposal shared with the ASCSU fails to provide any original evidence or a literature review justifying the research or supporting the assertions upon which it is based. In addition, the methodology suggested, though lacking in rigor and detail, exhibited methodological bias by suggesting potential changes to the CSU curriculum prior to the gathering of data. Such flaws

make it impossible for the Senate to support participation at this time. (Academic Senate of the California State University 2010)

In a preemptive strike, what had been presented as an interesting concept to be tested through subsequent data analysis and intensive conversations with faculty had been dismissed as a flawed research finding that lacked a literature review, statistical data, and good sense.

What is important to learn from these exchanges is not the willingness of the unions to engage in rhetorical combat to protect their members' right to resist change but rather what each union thought was the political high ground: we have a good product, don't mess with it, and don't tell us that protecting quality is not worth the fight. I suspect that in a growing number of states this high ground no longer matters.

Other Voices

About the same time as Finney was meeting with the CSU Academic Senate, I met with Marcia Welsh, then the provost at Towson University and subsequently its interim president. Welsh had read "Changing the Subject" and was intrigued by what it promised, but, like Steve Hicks in Pennsylvania, she thought the paper contained a fundamental flaw. "Bob," she said, "you're wrong. Towson doesn't have under-enrolled classes, it has over-enrolled students." She explained that at the previous week's commencement more than a third of the students whose hands she shook as they received their diplomas had earned more than 145 credits in a curriculum that only required 120 credits to graduate. Part of the problem was that some students frequently changed their major and hence were taking more courses and more time to graduate. It was also the case, she confirmed, that too many students were lost in a curriculum that had too many options as well as a bewildering set of requirements. The largest problem, however, was that too many of Towson's students were community college transfers who had arrived on campus with a year or more of credit that transferred but satisfied few if any of the university's general education and almost none of its premajor requirements.

Here was a different take on how and why the curriculum had become a principal driver of excessive operating costs—one that echoed the work of Jane Wellman and her colleague Nate Johnson at the Delta Cost Project who, in a 2009 paper analyzing data from the State University System of Florida, found that on average graduates of the system signed up and paid for extra credits that added as much as

50 percent to the cost of a college degree (see Johnson 2009). Wellman and Johnson were primarily concerned with the cost rather than the attainment side of the equations, though they did note that a fair amount of the extra costs involved students repeating courses.

Among the first discussions to make the connection between increased operating costs and baccalaureate completion rates was a faculty seminar I facilitated at the University of Wisconsin Oshkosh in the fall of 2010. The fifteen faculty members gathered around the table that fall were leaders in the university's efforts to make undergraduate education at Oshkosh more efficient as well as more learning-productive. About two-thirds of the way through the session one faculty member reported that he and a colleague, attending a faculty workshop at Fox River College the previous week (Fox River being Oshkosh's largest supplier of transfer students from a two-year institution) had been "booed." The reason why faculty from one institution should be booing faculty from another who in fact were invited guests was simple enough: "They are tired of us mistreating their students when they transfer to us." I was lost, having literally no idea what the problem was. So I asked, and the Oshkosh faculty member asked in return, "Have you seen our general education requirements?" Having allowed that I hadn't, he asked a colleague to hand me the sheet that described the current version of the requirements. I was next asked, "Do you know what you are looking at?" Jokingly I replied, "A badly written Fortran program with extra do-loops?" No, I was told, "What you are looking at is a peace treaty that is actually worse than the peace treaty that preceded it."

I did not need to ask who had been at war with whom; the answer was obvious. At Oshkosh, as at many—I think perhaps even most—institutions, the general education requirements are the result of a decades-long contest among the university's disciplinary departments, each seeking to ensure sufficient enrollments to justify current and future staffing levels. Every attempt to revise and modernize the university's general education requirements had fallen victim to this ongoing contest for academic resources at the department level. Given the deadly seriousness with which the faculty had engaged in this struggle, it had surprised no one at Oshkosh that afternoon that the result was a set of general education requirements both byzantine in construction and cumbersome in application. Transfers from two-year institutions were not being singled out; nearly all students were being affected by a set of general education requirements, rules really, that lacked both educational purpose and pedagogical design.

That same fall I facilitated a faculty roundtable at Northern Arizona University (NAU) in Flagstaff. Arizona's three public universities, like their California counterparts, were facing truly draconian budget cuts requiring each institution to find ways of doing more with less—a lot less. NAU faced the further challenge of being forever the state's third university, often seen as duplicating programs offered by the University of Arizona in Tucson and Arizona State University in Tempe. The fact that each year NAU lost 30 percent of its first-year class to attrition only added to the fear that eventually the system's Board of Regents would solve the budget problems by either reducing NAU to a glorified community college or simply eliminating programs of lesser market appeal.

NAU needed, the roundtable concluded, a set of strategies that made the curriculum more attractive, particularly to students who were better prepared, and less costly to deliver. In the end the faculty that afternoon came to focus on the need to approach questions of curricular change from a fundamentally different perspective. Curricular change had to proceed on a much faster pace, had to leave behind unspecified notions of academic standards, and, most important, had to depend on individual faculty working together in instructional teams. It was a faculty-centered conversation that explicitly embraced the idea that faculty could no longer act as if they were independent contractors uniquely responsible for their own students and their own courses. Required instead was the reemergence of a truly collaborative faculty culture. But, as we will see, moving from concept to changed practice is a path that very few institutions have navigated successfully.

Faculty and administrators at liberal arts colleges have had a slightly different take on the argument Finney and I put forth in "Changing the Subject." They were less concerned with questions of under-enrollment; small classes were considered essential elements of their branding. Presidents do talk about having a better mix of class sizes: most are small with a couple of big enrollment classes, but they often point out that the commitment to small classes is so engrained in their institutions' DNA that at many liberal arts colleges there are simply no large classrooms.

But "Changing the Subject" still resonated with many administrators and some faculty of these institutions. They worry about their graduation rates, particularly when less than 80 percent of their first-time full-time students graduate within six years. For these institutions, withdrawals prior to graduation are doubly costly in terms of the financial aid the institutions invest in the students who leave without graduating and in terms of the added marketing and recruitment costs that are required to replace nongraduating students. If they had a better gauge at the time of admission of which students in particular were most likely not to graduate, then they could make different admission and financial aid decisions. Indirectly, at least, presidents saw in the statistical analysis and curricular mapping called for in "Changing the Subject" a better way to understand attrition at their institutions.

Increasingly, as well, liberal arts colleges are sensing that their markets are changing to include more transfer students as well as traditional students seeking both a liberal arts education and a professional degree, probably at the master's level. Transfer students, especially those coming from a community college or a two-year technical school, represent a particular challenge because most liberal arts colleges are not prepared to enroll students who will begin as sophomores or juniors. In California, enrollment caps at CSU campuses and at the state's community colleges have meant a bonanza of new enrollments for California's often-beleaguered private liberal arts colleges.

Faculty reactions to these changing circumstances are often a mix of "I told you so" with a premonition that once again they will be asked to do more with less—to teach students that they didn't have the time or opportunity to properly advise and to teach larger classes even though they don't see themselves the beneficiaries of the added revenues the transfer students bring to their institution. In terms of establishing a context in which the faculty collectively become partners in the process of curriculum reform, faculty reactions often reflect a distaste with having to change what they truly believe they do well—the teaching of specialized classes to students who are both engaged in and academically prepared to benefit from the kind of learning experiences for which liberal arts colleges want to be known.

At the same time, faculty at liberal arts colleges are being asked to make other changes in their traditional ways of providing an undergraduate education. Often the most intriguing as well as remunerative options for these institutions is the introduction of a 3–2 learning sequence in which the student graduates in five years with both a solid grounding in the liberal arts and professional qualifications for a specialized career in either health care delivery or business services. Despite the financial resources such programs would likely bring their institutions, the prospect of offering a professional master's program in conjunction with a traditionally configured baccalaureate degree raises

the same questions: Why would we want to do this? Doesn't the introduction of one or more professional master's programs run counter to
our traditional liberal arts mission? Who will teach the new programs?
Aren't professional programs, particularly in the health sciences,
inherently more expensive to teach and won't offering them put our
institution at an even greater financial disadvantage? (In chapter 8, I
take up the tale of how one liberal arts institution, Whittier College in
California, answered these questions.)

The most vexing problem for liberal arts faculty—and indeed at all
institutions with a strong commitment to liberal learning—is what one
liberal arts college president characterized as the "propensity problem," being the propensity of academic institutions to constantly
expand their horizons, adding new courses, new majors, new specialties. It is a case of what goes up never seems to come down; the adding
of new initiatives is almost never matched with the removal of items of
declining value.

The segment of American higher education least affected by these
considerations is that of the nation's premier private colleges and
universities—the thirty-one COFHE institutions along with perhaps
two dozen more highly selective public and private universities. While
Henry Rosovsky's remonstrance to his colleagues on the Harvard faculty was, by intent, institution specific, it nonetheless characterized
faculty life at that set of institutions that historically sit atop American
higher education. Across these institutions faculty work just as hard as
before, but that work has increasingly become their property rather than
that of their institution. Faculty have truly become independent contractors for whom the propensity to constantly add more is not a problem
but an academic rallying cry. In these financially successful and academically prestigious institutions, there is no shortage of faculty to
provide the added coverage an ever-expanding curriculum requires, no
sustaining commitment to small classes, little reluctance to meld the
liberal arts and the professions, and almost no worry about whether
the institution is deviating from a historically prescribed mission.

And therein lies the problem. From the founding of Harvard in
1636 onward, the history of American higher education has been a
story of top-down change and innovation. A set of well-endowed
private colleges and universities, along with a limited number of state
flagship universities, has been responsible for most of the major
changes that have shaped the American collegiate experience. Never
more than a hundred institutions all told, collectively they have

created an American brand of graduate education and, in the process, cemented higher education's commitment to research as well as teaching. Their model of teaching dominates all of American higher education, even the instruction in traditional academic subjects at most community colleges. These institutions' definition of the faculty role permeates most of higher education. No more short of funds than they are of chutzpa, they have largely stood pat, letting those at what they consider the nation's lesser institutions debate the pros and cons of change, while their faculty remain camped just north of Armageddon waiting to see which way the winds of change are likely to blow.

Sorting Through the Pieces

Small wonder, then, that over the last thirty years the changes higher education ought to have made have remained just out of reach. The four strands that explain the why of this dilemma—a disengaged faculty, a federalized market for higher education, a regulatory quagmire, and a troubling fractiousness—are each important in their own right, but their entwining makes them truly debilitating. The weaving of these strands into a complex narrative begins in the 1980s when all the elements for an American reform agenda were seemingly in place.

My sorting through the pieces of this story begins with the faculty, who hold the key to a purposeful recasting of American higher education. Alas, too often they, or rather, we, have kept our distance. Having demonstrated little zest for confronting the changes that swirl around us, we have successfully put off recasting how and why we do what we do. The pertinent questions then become, "If not us, then who?" and "If not now, then when?" None of the ready answers to these two queries bodes well for American higher education: we're too busy; we're not sure that change is necessary; we are certain that doing nothing is better than doing something that will later prove to be wrong. It is more than twenty years since Rosovsky, in his second farewell address to the Harvard Faculty of Arts and Sciences, lamented the loss of the social contract that once bound faculty to one another and to the institutions that appoint and tenure us. Since then, few observers, informed or otherwise, have thought through how faculty might best discharge their obligations in a fundamentally changed world. How, in fact, like all other professionals, are we going to produce more with less?

In assigning responsibility for higher education's reluctance to change, we faculty come first, closely followed by an increasingly competitive market for students that has become federalized. Here most consequences fall into the "unintended" category, which makes them all the more debilitating because the academy has spent so little time understanding them. Put simply, the dramatic growth of federal student aid has created an intensely competitive market for undergraduate students, which has distorted the purpose of colleges and universities. At one time, competition was thought to be good. Competition among institutions for enrollments was once considered a welcome antidote to ever-rising prices and to higher education's reluctance to embrace new technologies and new ways of doing business.

Instead, the rich got richer, rankings flourished, and prices rose along with the public's discomfort with higher education as an industry. Not surprising, the growing importance of this federalized market has evoked calls for change from both within and outside the academy. This market at its base has made enrollments the currency of the realm. Almost universally, colleges and universities get paid according to the number of students they enroll rather than the learning they impart or the number of degrees they award. The direct federal student aid's voucher system simply reinforces the sense that what matters for most of American higher education is the sheer volume of students to whom an institution can send a tuition bill; the for-profit higher education industry learned this lesson well as it used the largesse of federal aid to underwrite its recruitment of students regardless of preparation or likely probability of success.

These markets have also spawned an American regulatory environment combining accreditation and federal oversight that seeks to control institutions while simultaneously ameliorating the consequences of unfettered competition. Though their claims of overregulation have largely fallen on deaf ears, American colleges and universities today suffer a host of conflicting and dysfunctional regulations that increase costs, freeze processes, and create a looming sense that to change is just to invite unwanted scrutiny.

Finally, across American higher education a learning environment has emerged that is increasingly fractured and, for that reason alone, is making less and less sense. The American public is just now beginning to discover that no one, either within or outside the academy, has any real evidence on what undergraduates are learning. While much of the focus has remained on what happens—and does not happen—within individual courses, the course-based curriculum itself is the problem.

A recasting as well as a streamlining of the curriculum is required to simultaneously control costs and increase graduation rates. A major problem remains: it is us the faculty who have the experience, authority, and practical know-how to recast the curriculum so we are back to square one, given that far too many faculty have decided to "sit this one out," not wanting to adopt curricular changes that will either constrain their choices about what and how they teach or reduce the number of faculty necessary to deliver a given curriculum.

Formulating the best response to the entwining of these four strands is the challenge I take up in the balance of this volume, all while keeping one eye on my faculty colleagues and the other on a set of circumstances that no one would have wished for but that, nonetheless, now holds American higher education hostage. Any good golfer will recognize the task I have set for myself—how to move forward without getting caught in one or more of those monster sand traps that time and circumstances have created for us.

6 A Disruptive Lexicon

Since 2010, at least, demanding that colleges and universities operate more efficiently has meant calling for fewer administrators, a less ready supply of student amenities, and a more flexible commitment to faculty autonomy in general and tenure in particular. Now, however, higher education's efficiency pundits are after much bigger game. Having decided to focus on how colleges and universities actually do their business, these critics now seek a recasting of those processes. Only fundamental changes, they argue, will yield the requisite combination of higher quality and greater affordability that a sustainable system of higher education demands.

Many of these analysts and policy wonks are attracted to the research and commentary of Clayton Christensen, a Harvard Business School professor who has contributed an increasingly complex and interrelated set of insights concerning the role that disruptive innovation can play in changing the market for complex products like computers. Not that long ago, the computer market was almost wholly owned by a limited number of major producers who supplied complicated products that were both expensive and inaccessible except to a small cadre of highly trained technicians. The disruptive innovation that changed the computer industry forever was the advent of microprocessors, which in relatively short order morphed first into the personal computer and thereafter into a bevy of tablets, smart phones, game boxes, and hand-held devices. Because these machines were convenient and affordable, they served an ever-expanding market of users with varying wealth, expertise, and age.

As the computer example suggests, a disruptive innovation targets not the sophisticated user but rather new customers with less complex needs and expectations. Why does the innovation succeed? As Christensen and his colleagues interested in higher education have observed, the innovation "redefines quality in a simple often disparaged application, then gradually improves such that it takes more and more market share over time as it becomes able to tackle more complicated problems." As a result, a new set of more affordable, higher quality products supplants those being produced by the industries that are losing market share (Christensen et al. 2011, 2).

To those attracted to Christensen's argument, American higher education requires a similar transformation. From their perspective, the most obvious analog to the revolution in personal computing is the emergence of an online distance education sector that is now being portrayed as having changed the shape of the higher education market by offering products that are more affordable, more focused on the needs of the student, and—given their highly structured delivery systems and commitment to competency-based models—better able to make a value-added contribution to their students' pursuit of purposeful careers.

My best guess, however, is that Christensen's most lasting contribution to the reform of higher education will derive from the terms and structure of his analyses rather than from his touting of the coming triumph of online distance education. If one follows Christensen's logic, then the inevitable conclusion is that colleges and universities need to change their business models, recast their production functions, and get serious about increasing their productivity. Indeed, in the decade ahead this new triad of terms—altered business models, recast production functions, and productivity gains—will likely dominate most research and policymaking that focuses on rendering higher education more sustainable.

Yes, Virginia, Colleges and Universities Have Business Models

In classic terms, the business model of a for-profit enterprise has four components. First comes the *value proposition* defining "a product that helps customers do more effectively, conveniently and affordably a job they've been trying to do." The value proposition helps determine the *resources* required to get the job done in terms of the necessary "people, technology, products, facilities, equipment." Next come the *processes*—what Christensen labels the "ways of working together to address the recurrent tasks in a consistent way: training, development, manufacturing, budgeting, planning, etc." The fourth component of a business model—the one outsiders too often focus on first—is the *profit formula,* or the "assets and fixed cost structure, and the margins and velocity required to cover them." The loop among the four components is then completed, by noting that the profit formula plays an important role in determining the value proposition (Christensen et al. 2011, 32).

Applying these terms to a college or university is one way to define the central problems a higher education reform agenda needs to address. From Christensen's perspective, higher education's value proposition clearly signals that the higher education customer—student, parent, locality, nation—matters most. That customer requires a product—degree, certificate, capacity, competency—that is convenient and affordable, that serves a documented need, and that meets well-established standards of quality. Defined in this manner, the value proposition for higher education pays little or no attention to the independent needs of the faculty or the maintenance of institutions or institutional forms that fail to attract sufficient customers.

The resources a Christensen college or university requires to produce products consistent with this value proposition are pretty much the same as in traditionally described institutions: the right people, productive technologies, ability to acquire useful products, and adequate facilities and equipment. The processes or production functions that the institution uses define what is to be taught, by whom, and when, and, most important, how what is taught will necessarily be different—more dependent on a host of new learning technologies as well as a tightly framed curriculum that reins in traditional higher education's propensity to continuously add new elements. Finally, the profit formula, even in a not-for-profit institution, is the means by which the institution garners sufficient revenues to cover its fixed and variable costs and a sufficiently robust operating margin such that it can invest in new products, processes, and markets.

Enterprises that fail do so, in large part, because they have failed to understand how their once successful business models have become broken, and, not so surprising, the charge that higher education's business model is broken is the new staple of presidential speeches, trade press commentaries, and policy blogs. When using that phrase most observers mean that colleges and universities cannot control their costs, are misaligned with the market, and employ pricing policies that mask the true cost of a college education. Prices are too high. Institutions rely too much on federal student aid. Too much of an institution's own scholarship funds go to merit aid, which is just a polite way of noticing that too many institutions actually buy their best students. As a result, the commentator concludes, higher education's business model is no longer sustainable.

Christensen and his colleagues mean something more when focusing on a higher education business model that is not so much broken as no longer appropriate. Higher education's business model might take only three basic forms. The most limited are "facilitated user networks in which participants exchange things with each other." Library consortia, as well as open-source software networks, are good higher education examples of what Christensen has in mind.

Much more important and numerous are "solution shops," whose business is the diagnosing and solving of unstructured problems. Such enterprises deliver value through the people they employ, and they derive their revenue from their ability to charge substantial fees for the services they provide. For American higher education the major research university, whose principal assets are the independent contractors it has attracted to its faculty, best exemplifies an educational enterprise that operates as a solution shop.

In this taxonomy of business models the third form—value-adding process businesses—best captures what most colleges and universities do most of the time when they are teaching students and awarding degrees and certificates. The change in the higher education business model that Christensen and his compatriots seek is one that more directly recognizes the task at hand as a conversion of inputs into outputs of higher value, principally in the form of more knowledgeable and skillful workers better prepared to take on the challenges of a twenty-first-century economy.

There is nothing wrong with that, but the problem is that higher education institutions as enterprises are not as neatly boxed as the value-adding process business model implies. Thinking about higher education's business models and how they might be changed, however, does provide an important analytic framework for asking about a higher education future in which colleges and universities are better aligned with the market, are more productive, and are better able to respond to demands for lower operating costs, more convenient programs, and greater accountability.

That reframing of higher education's future requires, in the first instance, recognition that most colleges and universities are sufficiently complex that they simultaneously contain elements of all three prototypical business models. Not just the sponsored research component of the university or college operates like a consulting firm organized as a solution shop. Institutions of all shapes, sizes, even missions have embedded within them organizations that operate just as consulting firms do—providing services, solving problems, offering customized instructional programs that are expected to earn sufficient revenues to cover their direct and indirect costs, plus an agreed-on margin that is expected to benefit the sponsoring institution. Many instructional programs operate as solution shops as well, in which an organized collection of independent contractors each teaches its own specialties and courses, having first counted on the sponsoring institution to provide students in sufficient numbers to cover the requisite direct and indirect costs, plus an acceptable margin. Although institutions still pay lip service to the need to teach subjects and specialties for which there is not sufficient demand, the inconvenient truth is that such offerings are increasingly few and far between—just ask retired professors of German or current professors of philosophy if their departments still have sufficient numbers of full-time, tenure-track faculty to mount credible programs and majors. Even facilitated user networks—as a business model—have begun to appear. In addition to library consortia and open-source networks, study-abroad programs are becoming facilitated networks, as are a variety of learning consortia that link students as well as faculty across a wide range of institutions.

The biggest problem may simply be the proliferation of quite different business models within a single institution—too much confusion, too much confounding of both ends and means, too little organizational flexibility to serve enterprises that are inherently different though they draw on the same pool of service providers. One attraction of online, distance, and for-profit programs to observers like Christensen and his colleagues is that they often have singular business models. The most successful of these enterprises, however, inevitably grow more complex, even convoluted as they grow more profitable. The Education Management Corporation (EDMC) is a good example of how mergers and acquisitions muddy the business models of even a successful disruptive innovation. Today EDMC provides the corporate umbrella structure linking the Art Institutes, Brown Mackie College, South University, and Argosy University, which itself grew out of a merger of three far-flung enterprises: the American School of Professional Psychology, the University of Sarasota, and the Medical Institute of Minnesota.

At the same time, none of the prototypical business model forms I have adopted from Christensen and his colleagues really fits most colleges and universities. These institutions provide a learning experience whose value is dependent first on the preparation and aptitude that the learners bring with them to the learning process. Poor preparation can be overcome, but, if it is not, how much the student is going to learn is tangibly limited. At the same time, the learner's motivation and work ethic play equally significant roles. The truth of the matter is that learning is a partnership linking the learner and the institution in a web of mutual responsibilities. If I can be forgiven a less than elegant analog illustrating how learning is a joint product equally dependent on the learner and the institution, it helps to think about the pricey resorts overweight people check into when they need to shed more than a few pounds. Several factors are important: the health of the guest on arrival, the level of excess weight, the guest's ability to handle a tough regimen, and the guest's metabolic proclivity toward easy weight loss. Once enrolled, the guest's diligence in observing the program's protocols goes a long way in determining how much actual weight is lost. Seeking a college degree is not very different whether the institution is a community college or a highly selective four-year college or university.

Because most traditionally configured colleges and universities are enterprises of long standing—with time-encrusted, often immutable to change, organizational layers—the rationalization of the enterprise's business models become much more difficult. And, as in the example of EDMC, even the brand-new, for-profit providers have often proved equally susceptible to this comingling of purposes that yields conflicting business models and disparate value propositions.

The need for appropriate business models for learning enterprises helps make clear just how anomalous traditional higher education's reliance on a workforce of independent contractors (often with tenure) is proving to be. While a solution shop business model, in which faculty are independent contractors, may work for research enterprises, it is hard to imagine that such a business model works well, or at all, in an enterprise where the product is student learning and the conditions for success are as dependent on the qualities of the student as on the adroitness of the instructor and organizational acumen of the enterprise itself. It's like asking patients in a hospital not to mind the fact that the physicians who treat them separately seldom talk to one another about the treatment modalities they are prescribing. Health care's answer to this dilemma is the "treatment team," which in itself requires a different kind of business model and a more collective understanding of what the business of the business really is.

Focusing on their business models ought to lead colleges and universities to ask similar questions. What is our value proposition? What is the minimum, as well as the ideal, set of resources—people, technology, and facilities—necessary to provide quality educational products? Do we have a profit or margin formula that will provide sufficient funds for reinvestment? And, no doubt the most important question of all, do we have in place the right processes to deliver the products we have promised our customers, be they students, parents, or governmental agencies?

It's the Curriculum

Indeed for the moment, focusing specifically on those processes that organize a college's production function offers the most ready strategy for making reform work. It really is the curriculum that matters most—what is taught, what is required, what is expected of both students and faculty. Here we must ask a host of questions: What is a curriculum designed to produce? Credits? Degrees? Jobs? Learning? Skills? Any or all of the above? Who owns the curriculum? Has the institution put in place well-conceived pathways for students to follow in pursuit of their goals as well as meeting the institution's definition of a qualified graduate? What role should electronically mediated instruction play in this process? How important is seat time? Experiential learning? Should credit by examination be an option? With so many undergraduates attending two or more institutions en route to their baccalaureate degrees, which credits deserve to be transferred following what kind of review and evaluation? And certainly not least, to what extent does curricular confusion and gridlock both add to the operating cost of an institution and discourage too many students from completing their baccalaureate educations?

These are all questions observers and critics both inside and outside the academy have been asking at least since the publication of *Integrity in the College Curriculum* in the 1980s. The basic building blocks of the curriculum have remained the same as well. Each semester full-time undergraduates register for an average of five three-credit courses, most of which will meet three times a week for fifteen weeks. Students are ready to graduate when they have successfully accumulated at least 120 credits (roughly the equivalent of forty courses spread over four years). In theory students can shorten the time to graduation by taking Advanced Placement (AP) credits in high school, by attending summer sessions, and by enrolling in more than five courses a semester. In fact, however, many students take longer to graduate, amass more than 120 credits, and often have to repeat courses because they have not earned the requisite grade required by their major. This perspective defines undergraduate education largely in terms of seat time, required courses satisfying a general education requirement—that is, boxes to be checked—and a sufficient number of advanced courses to satisfy the requirements of the major the student has chosen. For the most part, the courses students take reflect a mix of faculty and student interest; faculty members have learned they cannot offer courses in which there is not sufficient enrollment. Outside a limited number of professional programs—engineering and nursing come most readily to mind—there is actually little discernible shape to the curriculum. At most institutions today, I am sad to report, the undergraduate curriculum is just as *Integrity in the College Curriculum* described the collegiate curriculum more than two decades ago.

Some have argued that the success of for-profit institutions, particularly the large publicly held enterprises like the University of Phoenix and Kaplan, is due to their ability to design and offer much more focused curricula—fewer choices, more design, more structure, more coherence, and better, more imaginative uses of technology. Closer examination, however, suggests that the for-profits owe much more of their success to their ability to teach would-be students how to acquire federal student aid funds with which to pay their bills than to any imaginative recasting of the undergraduate education production function, beyond the heavier reliance on technology-based delivery systems. Even that aspect pales somewhat on closer examination because most online distance education courses are electronic workbooks rather than electronically mediated learning environments.

The Association of American Colleges and Universities (AAC&U), in pursuit of revitalized undergraduate curricula that stress liberal learning, has had considerably more direct impact on the nature and shape of collegiate curricula in general and that portion focusing on the general education component in particular. A decade of staying on message and the convening of literally hundreds of conferences, colloquia, and workshops has substantially added to the lexicon of undergraduate reform. The five high-impact educational practices promoted through AAC&U's Liberal Education and America's Promise (LEAP) initiative—first-year seminars, learning communities, service learning, undergraduate research, and capstone experiences—have become standard elements in most accrediting reports in which the institution under review is expected to focus on student learning and its assessment.

What the AAC&U initiatives have yet to tackle is the basic redesign of the curriculum. Symptomatic of the association's response to proposals to change the education production function underlying most undergraduate curricula was the statement by AAC&U President Carol Geary Schneider that spelled out the association's opposition to a three-year baccalaureate degree:

> AAC&U is concerned about shortsighted and simplistic proposals to reduce the number of credits required to complete the bachelor's degree. We are especially concerned about the idea—already gaining some traction in media and even policy circles—that the United States can save a significant amount of money on higher education by just cutting the number of expected years and credit hours—from, say, 120 hours to 90 hours. We also are concerned about the companion idea—now touted by some prominent leaders—that, "since the senior year in high school is wasted," students should just skip it and proceed directly to college. Either way, students will be shortchanged, and many will end up unprepared for success. (Schneider 2010)

From my perspective AAC&U ought to have been in the lead in thinking about how to simplify and redesign the undergraduate curriculum. Instead, Schneider offered a defense of the status quo. Underlying Schneider's opposition was an old argument: spending more time in college would enable students to learn more of what they need to be of service to themselves and the nation. Seat time was, after all, still more important than learning outcomes.

More purposeful and, in the end, more sustainable has been the work of Carol Twigg and her National Center for Academic Transformation (NCAT). Operating with a multiyear grant from the Pew Charitable Trusts, NCAT developed a four-step process leading to what Twigg calls course redesign, which requires a faculty team to first analyze how a high-enrollment and expensive-to-deliver course is currently being taught. In quick succession the team is expected to define a clear set of learning objectives, specify the content linked to those objectives, define a set of teaching and learning activities that will produce the objectives as cost-effectively as possible, and finally make operational a set of assessment procedures that will allow the faculty responsible for the course to measure how well they are meeting their intended learning objectives.

Twigg, who has regularly reported on the progress of these efforts, is justifiably proud that significant cost reductions have been achieved while simultaneously improving the ability of the course to achieve its stated learning objectives. Although the use of technology is not required, in almost all cases the imaginative use of electronically mediated instruction has been a key component of the redesigned course.

The other big project promoting major curricular change is the Open Learning Initiative (OLI), developed by Carnegie Mellon University (CMU) and funded by the current "big four" among foundations promoting a higher education change agenda: Hewlett, Gates, Lumina, and Kresge. OLI works within course structures to develop technology-intensive learning objectives that, once embedded within a course or across a curriculum, produce a stream of data that drive what OLI defines as four powerful feedback loops for continuous evaluation and improvement: feedback to students; feedback to instructors; feedback to course designers; and feedback to learning science researchers. As instruction is being delivered, the web-based modality being employed simultaneously collects real-time data, charting how students both process and proceed through the learning objective. Learning is continuous, but so is change. The more a specific learning objective is used by different students, the more the analytic program learns about what works and what doesn't and about the kinds of alternatives that the objective's designers might include in future releases. This collective enterprise takes its cue from CMU's Herbert Simon, who consistently pitched the idea that "Improvement in Postsecondary Education will require converting teaching from a 'solo sport' to a community-based research activity" (OLI 2012).

For Now, Taking a Pass on Productivity Gains

While discussions of new business models and recast production functions have become more common, the need for

increased productivity occupies the foreground in nearly every critique of higher education. Is the public, the critics ask, really getting
enough value for the additional funds that higher education has
received? If, in real terms, operating costs have risen steadily over the
last half-century, have the benefits provided increased commensu-
rately to both individuals and the public writ large? Or is the nation
simply paying more for products that used to cost less?

Productivity is one concept most people simply assume they
understand. Productivity is the ratio of inputs to outputs; a productivity
gain is achieved when inputs are held constant while outputs increase,
when inputs are reduced while holding outputs constant, or when
inputs decrease while outputs increase. More precisely, a gain in productivity is achieved when the quantity of the outputs relative to the
quantity of inputs increases, provided that the quality of both remains
constant or increases.

Currently higher education is awash in different ways to measure
the productivity of the nation's colleges and universities. As policy
discussions have renewed attention on the gap between college participation and attainment rates, higher education is being asked to be
more productive by increasing the proportion of the population with a
collegiate degree. Public agencies want an increase in output without a
corresponding increase in public appropriation or tuition revenue—in
short, a true productivity gain, provided that the resulting degrees
maintain their value in terms of both the skills graduates acquire and
the wage premiums they receive.

More often than not, today's policy discussions also focus on more
detailed measures of productivity from the faculty. Here the aggregate
gauge is usually average student credit hours per full-time instructor,
both adjunct and tenure track. Occasionally current discussions of
higher education's productivity venture even into the realms of learning and the curriculum, a conversation that allows conjecture about
how to increase the productivity of a given course of study by limiting
operating costs as well as the time necessary to earn a degree or certificate. Proposals to make the standard BA degree a three-year program
requiring 90 rather than the current 120 credits (or more) are within
one category of ideas promoting increased productivity by limiting the
time and hence the costs associated with an undergraduate degree.

Among those now addressing questions of productivity, William
Massy is one of the more thoughtful as well as optimistic analysts.
Higher education's attempts to define productivity once evaporated in

a fog of complexity, but Massy has helped introduce conversations that explore the metrics for measuring productivity gains along with the strategies for their achievements. Massy's work builds from the proposition that increases in educational productivity will require more than the trimming of administrative fat. Having argued that traditional universities must become more productive, Massy observes that "a glance at their cost structure shows that the improvement must include the academic areas—that is to say, teaching and learning" and then concludes:

> The universities and their professors are trapped by the very strengths that sustain their quality. Getting out of the trap requires, . . . to quote Christensen and [his co-author Henry] Eyring, that the changes "be thorough-going, a matter not of belt-tightening but of genetic reengineering." Failure to set academic productivity on an improvement trajectory will expose schools with little or no endowment (that is to say, most schools) to both price and quality competition from the industrialized sector, plus a continuing loss of government subsidy as their performance lags and more cost-effective alternatives present themselves. The result will be stranded human and physical capital and, worst of all, a massive loss of capacity for "classic" undergraduate education. (Massy 2011, 2)

Massy argues that the advent of reliable data measuring productivity will spur changes at three basic levels—macro, micro, and nano; if implemented appropriately, these changes will maintain, perhaps even enhance, quality, while simultaneously lowering the operating costs associated with the production of college degrees. "Program rationalization" at the macrolevel can be achieved, for example, by streamlining the curriculum (think three-year degree) and/or by relieving bottlenecks in the curriculum (principally by making certain that the courses students need to graduate are available when students need to take them). At the microlevel, Massy believes that the course redesign as championed by Twigg offers a demonstrated means of substantially reducing educational costs while simultaneously increasing student output in the form of successfully completed courses. Here the striking feature is the imaginative use of technology, not for technology's sake but in pursuit of well-documented educational outcomes.

Drawing on the work of OLI's Candace Thille, Massy calls the nanolevel the location of the "learning episodes" that "produce the new connections in student brains we call 'learning.'" The collegiate curriculum of the future will draw on our "increasing understanding of how these cognitive episodes work or fail to work, and the ways they can be managed for optimal performance. . . . As experience accumulates, it seems likely that more and more professors will master . . . [the principles of the new learning science such] that most course redesign initiatives will adopt the science-based and technology-facilitated nano approach" (Massy 2011, 5). In part, Massy has in mind here the "course objects" that are now the standard elements of most electronically mediated college courses.

Thus far Massy and I have in mind pretty much the same methods as well as goals—not so surprising given our past collaborations. Each of us wants to increase educational productivity such that more students who begin college finish with a degree and requisite work skills; and we have each argued that the means to that end involves a substantial reengineering of the college curriculum. Thereafter, however, our paths diverge in an interesting and illustrative way.

Massy believes the way forward is to specify a data framework making possible analytic models of sufficient power by which faculty, in particular, can evaluate alternate paths to increased productivity. He begins with higher education's standard "credit hour system . . . [that] a century or so ago produced a common quantity measure that has ever since been taken as 'the' measure of educational production" (Massy 2011, 3). The problem, as Massy notes, is that using the credit hour alone as the measure of output yields misleading conclusions. Productivity thus measured can be increased by having larger classes, fewer seminars, higher faculty teaching loads or, as is most often the case in administrative or politically driven processes designed to increase productivity, all of the above. Missing, however, is a corresponding notion of quality. An increase in output of lesser quality is not an increase in productivity, or as Massy observes: "Productivity judgments depend crucially on inferences about quality, and these inferences need to be made apparent to people at multiple levels both inside and outside the academy. The challenge is to design a model that can provide snapshots of instructional activity and resource consumption with enough resolution to enable inferences about quality" (Massy 2011, 8).

Massy testifies to the fact that quality has been ignored because there is no generally accepted measure, "and it is this shortfall that has given productivity improvement a bad name" (Massy 2011, 3).

For Massy the resolution lies in adopting a strategy for the present that still uses "student throughput" as the basic output measure but breaks down the kinds of learning exposures into a matrix of instructional activities that can serve as surrogates for educational quality. As a first cut, he suggests three such surrogates: class size, adjunct vs. regular faculty usage, and faculty teaching load. Productivity increases could result, for example, from adopting a portfolio strategy for class sizes that increases the numbers of seminars and other small courses in areas where active learning and faculty mentoring are essential, while "'paying' for these by boosting the number and size of high-enrollment courses in areas where quality effects would be the least onerous" (Massy 2011, 10). At a minimum, the use of the quality surrogates would eliminate the possibility of believing that increases in output could be achieved without first reengineering the basic production functions that make up the curriculum at the department or program level.

My quarrel with Massy's approach is somewhat unexpected. His analysis and resulting model keep in place the basic production terminology that now organizes undergraduate education: courses, credit hours, faculty teaching loads, and average class sizes. At the same time, his discussion stays clear of substituting student learning for the credit hour as the unit of educational production except to assume that his surrogates—smaller classes, more seminars, fewer adjuncts, and reduced faculty teaching loads—promote student learning. Massy would respond that reform should not be held hostage to the development of reliable measures of either student learning or educational quality. Useful measures of productivity gains are actually possible, he argues, by using the current curricular frameworks: "For the foreseeable future, therefore, productivity tracking will require inferences derivable from information that can be collected routinely from today's data systems—which do not include quality measures. These inferences won't be as accurate as valid direct measures, were such to become available, but they will be much better than no quality adjustment at all" (Massy 2011, 7).

My concern is easily explained: the information that is readily available in 2013 is almost exclusively derived from an educational production function that presumes standard semesters or quarters, a catalog of individual courses, and curricular rules that determine both the number and distribution of courses students must complete in order to graduate. My proposition is that the productivity gains Massy

seeks will only be possible if that curricular structure itself is fundamentally changed. From this perspective, the way forward is to focus
on reengineering higher education's production functions—including
the building of learning pathways that are not defined as a sum of individual courses—and, where most needed, on recasting the enterprise's
dominant business models. If successful, operating costs will be
reduced, with more students graduating in less time. As to questions of
quality, I would trust the faculty's sense of pride and purpose to sustain the quality of the products in the immediate future as they have in
the past.

The questions to ask now are roughly the same questions Massy
asks: Are there useful examples pointing to an alternate future based on
changing production functions and business models? Are there true
harbingers of sustainable change out there? I believe these exist. In
chapters 7, 8, and 9, I discuss the stories of three institutions that have
directly tackled the issues I have raised here.

First, the University of Minnesota at Rochester (UMR), now six
years old, offers a host of lessons that focus on a limited business
model and an equally constrained educational agenda to convey sustainable advantage. UMR, precisely because it is a new institution, has
been able to chart a different course, one that stresses the importance of
collective faculty behaviors, on the one hand, and, on the other, the
imaginative use of technology to change what is taught and how it is
taught.

Whittier College faces the future that haunts almost all liberal arts
colleges—a workable but financially unsustainable educational model.
Whittier's challenge, which it is confronting in imaginative ways, is to
find a business model that will allow it to remain mostly as it wants to
be, while simultaneously providing an infusion of funds that will come
from doing other things differently.

Finally, the University of Wisconsin Oshkosh has launched a general education reform that builds on the premise that curricular design,
more than curricular choice, holds the best promise of increased graduation rates along with constrained increases in operating costs. Even
as it changes its curricula, UW Oshkosh knows its future depends on
reining in a commitment to educational propensity that the university
can no longer afford.

7

A Different Footprint

The explosive growth of American higher education since the Second World War notwithstanding, the founding of a new research university has not proved to be a common occurrence. With few exceptions, the more than fifteen hundred new or transformed institutions created after the war were either community colleges, public comprehensive universities newly founded or converted from state normal institutions, or for-profit entities that made no claim to research proficiency. There have been no new private liberal arts colleges to speak of, only a few new private comprehensive universities, and just a handful, literally, of new public research universities: two in New York if one counts the conversions of the University of Buffalo to the State University of New York (SUNY) Buffalo along with SUNY Stony Brook; and six in California if one counts the University of California (UC) Riverside, which was first a Citrus Experiment Station and only after World War II a full-fledged UC campus.

The University of California Merced—A New Public Research University

The sixth new UC campus—the University of California Merced—can rightly boast of being "the first new American research university in the 21st century" (UC Merced 2012). Its history also offers something of a morality tale about why so few new research universities have begun over the last six-and-a-half decades in the United States. The founding of UC Merced is a testament to California's enduring faith in the power of its universities to transform both people and landscapes. By the 1980s the state's agricultural midlands, having long chafed at the absence of a major UC campus in their midst, had the political clout to lay claim to a campus of their own. The effort's political godfather was probably Cruz Bustamante, in the 1990s the powerful speaker of the State Assembly who, as *Inside Higher Ed* later reported, "cajoled, pushed [and] arm twisted the university president into making . . . [a central valley campus] a [UC] priority." Bustamante and his colleague Dennis Cardoza, having eventually realized that appealing to UC's sense of political correctness could overcome most arguments against establishing a new UC campus so far removed from the state's major population centers, simply would not take no for an answer. Serving the Central Valley and California's agricultural hinterlands, they regularly pointed out, would mean serving a population of substantially Latino and first-generation college-going students.

UC Merced remained a tough sell that triumphed only because UC's leadership felt boxed in by a political calculus that threatened to hold the UC system hostage. As Andrew Scull, chair of the department of sociology at UC San Diego, succinctly observed to *Inside Higher Ed*, "I think the university caved on the politics of [creating Merced], and thought if they didn't agree to this their budget would be punished. . . . I think many people, even at the time that Merced was just a figment in some planner's eye, were very, very concerned" (Stripling 2009). Probably the most consistent as well as vocal critic of establishing the Merced campus was Patrick Callan, president of the National Center for Public Policy and Higher Education, by then best known as the publisher of *Measuring Up,* the biennial report card measuring the effectiveness of state systems of higher education. As the Merced campus set out to recruit its first class of students in the spring of 2005, Callan told the *Chronicle of Higher Education*, "If there were no such thing as opportunity costs, if we had money to do everything, how could anyone be against this?" The inconvenient truth of the matter, Callan observed, is that "we have been squeezing people at the bottom and turning people away at community colleges at the same time we're investing in this. The tragedy of Merced is that we never did have that debate about what we need to do to provide opportunities for Californians" (Hebel 2005).

The last real opportunity to substantially delay operating the Merced campus came in 2003 when California faced a $38-billion budget deficit and an unpopular governor who was about to be recalled from office. The legislature put off the official opening of the campus for a year while most of California waited for the dust to settle from the political wrangling that accompanied Governor Gray Davis's attempts to solve the budget crisis. A long-time supporter of the Merced campus, Arnold Schwarzenegger replaced Davis in the fall of 2003. Almost immediately the new governor signaled that the Merced campus would open in 2005, just a year later than originally planned. It was, he said, a way to "expand the dream of college," and his budget would include $24 million for the first year's operating costs (Hebel 2005).

By then California had already made a significant capital investment in the new campus—$269 million, or roughly $20 million more than the planners had initially envisioned in the first phases of construction. Part of the cost, as well as of the delay, was the result of initially acquiring land for the campus that served as a habitat for a rare breed of crustaceans that are an important link in the food chain. By 2009, however, the new campus could claim that the state's capital outlays were $85.6 million short of what had originally been called for— to which the state could reply, yes, but the campus was also accommodating two thousand fewer students, six hundred fewer staff, and eighty-five fewer faculty than had originally been projected.

UC Merced's signal achievements were basic: it had opened its doors more or less on schedule and had attracted some interesting faculty, many of whom were committed to interdisciplinary research and teaching. But the campus has not proved a magnet for bringing students or business from outside the valley to Merced, has not proved more attractive to minority students than other UC campuses, and has not sparked a renaissance of local pride and purpose across the valley. A series of headlines in *Inside Higher Ed* and the *Chronicle of Higher Education* pretty much told the story: "The Hard Birth of a Research University" (*Chronicle of Higher Education,* April 2005); "New California Campus Struggles for Respect" (*Chronicle of Higher Education,* November 2006); "Buyer's Remorse" (*Inside Higher Ed,* August 2009); and "U. of California at Merced Turns 5 Amid Growing Pains" (*Chronicle of Higher Education,* November 2010). Again Callan best summed up the Merced dilemma: "There's a kind of hubris" at work, Callan told *Inside Higher Ed.* The leaders of the UC System "believe they are the best public university in the world and all you had to do was hang out a sign that said 'University of California' and students and faculty would come running. Now they're under-enrolled and it's hugely expensive. . . . The university would like to have you think they were innocent bystanders, but for decades they stoked all this. . . . Nobody is clean on this one. This is a bad decision for the state" (Stripling 2009). The school represented not just wasted money, but a wasted opportunity. The *Chronicle of Higher Education* observed on UC Merced's fifth anniversary:

> When Merced was in its planning stages, the campus's advocates and other higher-education leaders hoped it would be a model for future research universities, with its focus on interdisciplinary research and the integration of technology into everyday teaching. But the current campus looks less radical than some had expected. In fact, it looks a lot like the system campuses built in the 1960s and earlier. While those are not bad company to be in, some outsiders say Merced lacks originality.

Callan added: "Wouldn't you think that, here in California, home of Silicon Valley, we would do something to knock everybody away. . . . There was much more innovation when people were thinking about what the last batch of new campuses should look like than went into the design of Merced" (Kiley 2010).

University of Minnesota Rochester— Starting with a Clean Slate

I do not mean to add to UC Merced's travail, although I agree with Callan's notion that it was the wrong kind of institution in the wrong place but at the right time. The sad truth is that the next decade will likely see few new institutions, and those that are founded are more likely to be for-profit enterprises or the providers of on-line postsecondary education, or both. The United States needs new institutions, places starting with clean slates that have both the resources and energy to do things differently in a big way. Though UC Merced does not provide that model, it nonetheless offers an important counterpoint to a new institution that is just as grand an experiment at a fraction of the cost, with little of the political overhead that continues to plague Merced. That institution is the University of Minnesota Rochester (UMR).

In one important way, however, the creation of a new University of Minnesota campus in Rochester mirrors the early history of the efforts to bring a University of California campus to the Central Valley; in both cases, local business interests played an important role in getting the parent university system to take their needs more seriously. Located eighty-five miles due south of the Twin Cities, Rochester is the home of both the Mayo Clinic and a major IBM facility housed in an Eero Saarinen edifice affectionately known as the Big Blue Zoo. The Mayo Clinic and IBM are Rochester's dominant employers, each with a highly educated workforce and a well-developed sense of civic responsibility. Mayo Clinic currently employs more than thirty thousand people in Rochester, including physicians, scientists, residents and fellows, and allied health staff in its clinics and hospitals. IBM Rochester's employee count is now down to less than five thousand, though the Big Blue Zoo remains IBM's largest manufacturing facility under one roof.

In partnership with Rochester's political leadership, the Mayo Clinic and IBM-Rochester have waged a campaign for more than forty years to increase the availability of postsecondary education offerings in the Rochester area. In the 1960s the University of Minnesota (U of M) began offering specialized engineering, education, and math courses that by the 1990s had been substantially augmented by the founding of the University Center Rochester—an educational coalition joining the efforts of the U of M Rochester Community and Technical College and Winona State University–Rochester.

The civic leaders of Rochester, like their California counterparts, wanted, however, a real university, preferably one that was an integral part of the state's public flagship U of M. Though the leadership of the U of M was less than enthusiastic about opening a new campus, the Rochester campaign kept chipping away. In 1998 the legislature officially recognized Rochester as a branch campus that, after 2000, was to be presided over by a provost responsible for what many hoped would be a growing operation. Five years later, then Governor Tim Pawlenty gave Rochester what it wanted—a Rochester Higher Education Development Committee specifically charged with developing a plan to redress southern Minnesota's historical lack of educational opportunities commensurate with those of the rest of the state in general and the Twin Cities in particular. The result was the designation in 2006 of UMR as a "full and official coordinate campus of the University of Minnesota system." UMR was to have its own downtown campus, nestled in among Mayo's hospitals and clinics, and, most important, its own chancellor reporting directly to the university's president. In the summer of 2007 the University of Missouri's senior vice president for academic affairs, Stephen Lehmkuhle, was named UMR's first chancellor (UMR 2012).

Still, Minnesotans were imagining, even as late as Lehmkuhle's appointment, a relatively low-key operation—an education outlet that borrowed courses from other U of M campuses while conveniently offering them at the new UMR facility at University Square in downtown Rochester. Lehmkuhle wasn't buying. Lehmkuhle, by training a psychologist interested in how people learn, wanted to try something new; he wanted to prove, really, that there were better as well as different ways of teaching critical skills and values. Under little pressure to build enrollment quickly and in charge of a physical facility that had required no major capital investments, he could take his time coming to better understand what Rochester really needed while simultaneously looking for an academic partner that shared his interest in doing something different.

Literally surrounded by Mayo—its clinics, thirty thousand employees, and a variety of hotels serving Mayo's patients and their families—it did not take long for the chancellor to decide that Mayo's needs and interests held the key to his challenge. The Mayo Clinic is by every measure a distinctly different enterprise. It has championed the team approach to medicine and wellness—what is sometimes referred to as the Mayo way—in which the organization itself is the star, rather than individual physicians or practices. Much of Mayo's interest in having a U of M presence in Rochester centered on the need to have a sufficient supply of well-trained allied health professionals who make the hospitals and clinics special places. Already Mayo was offering a variety of certificate programs in conjunction with the educational providers in the area. The leadership of Mayo understood, however, that the future success of their allied health workforce was in university-trained and credentialed professionals—that is, men and women with baccalaureate degrees.

Keeping It Simple

Mayo's needs provided Lehmkuhle with the focus his new enterprise required. Unlike UC Merced, UMR would not be a comprehensive, soup-to-nuts research university. Rather, for the time being—and that time span might be a decade or more—it would offer but a single undergraduate degree program leading to a Bachelor of Science in Health Sciences (BSHS). Just as important, it would be a truly integrated as well as integrative program—not a series of specialized silos, but a comprehensive space in which would-be health care and wellness professions of nearly every stripe learned together, sharing insights and experiences as well as tough lessons garnered through actual practice.

The idea was simplicity personified: just a single degree program for undergraduates with a professional focus for which there is growing demand—now, and in the foreseeable future. Enrollments could be concentrated instead of dispersed across a varying curriculum. The program's small size would allow for the marshaling of students along a limited number of curricular pathways that combined basic skill courses in core subjects with a variety of laboratory experiences and internships, many of them at Mayo itself. As increasingly in real life, future health care professionals would share common experiences, whether they were heading for medical school, graduate school, or a specialized program leading to an allied health master's or doctoral degree. Mayo would provide the context for the program, but here UMR needed to be mindful of just how brand-conscious Mayo was— willing to collaborate but not co-brand.

The single degree program allowed for a simplified business model that limited the number of curricular options to be offered on a regular basis; at the same time the sole path substantially reduced the probability of having under-enrolled classes. A single degree program would also allow for a greater degree of commonality among faculty specialties, thus further facilitating the development of faculty instructional teams.

UMR's lower-division curricular requirement largely reflected changes that had already been put in place at the U of M Twin City campus, ensuring that UMR first- and second-year students would receive an adequate grounding in the humanities and social sciences as well as the STEM disciplines in which UMR students were expected to concentrate. Starting in their first semester, full-time students are expected to take four to five courses per semester. Statistics and Calculus are required of all students, though most take the former before the latter as a means of increasing the probability of successfully passing Calculus before beginning their more specialized training in their junior year. Each semester every student takes a Center for Learning Innovation (CLI) designated course developed and delivered by the university's student-life professionals. The first of these one-unit courses focused on college readiness. Later CLI designated units to introduce students to career choices and subsequently the capstone experience that, for most, will occupy their entire senior year.

Two basic science courses anchor the students' first year at UMR: organic chemistry and integrative biology. Similarly required are introductory courses in philosophy/ethics and sociology. About 80 percent of the students take a pre-calculus mathematics course in the second semester of their first year, to be followed by calculus itself in the first semester of their sophomore year. The other 20 percent proceed directly from statistics to calculus; these students have the option of taking a second semester post-calculus mathematics course during their sophomore year.

Each semester of their first year students also take a writing studio with a strong digital component that complements the one-on-one work of a cadre of writing instructors. Writing studios are linked to various substantive courses, including some in the sciences, in which students learn how to express complex ideas in accessible formats.

The second year moves the students closer to the study of health care and policy. Most students, particularly those not taking the physics II elective, will continue their science training by taking a required course in anatomy and physiology. For all students there is also a required course in public health. Subsequently elective courses in public health focus on epidemiology, the international dimensions of public health, and environmental issues. Most students will take at least two of these additional courses, and some take all three. At the same time, students are required to start a four-semester Spanish language sequence, with the expectation that graduates of the program will be comfortable enough in the language to work in health care environments where Spanish dominates. For many students, the second year provides the introduction to general chemistry as well. As in the case with statistics preceding calculus as a means of ensuring all students can pass calculus, the general chemistry follows rather than precedes organic chemistry, given the conviction that studying organic chemistry first improves the success rates of students studying general chemistry.

Throughout the first two years and extending into the third, students take a variety of history, literature, and social science courses en route to satisfying the U of M general education requirements. All of these courses are thematic, however, since none has to double as a pre-major requirement. At UMR there is but one major and one degree program for students who matriculate as first-year students.

From the minute a student begins his or her first semester at UMR, the focus is on degree completion. The required one-unit courses the students take with the CLI designation begin the process by laying out in sequential order the importance of understanding what the students want to get out of their college experience, exploring a variety of possible health sciences career paths and then choosing one, and finally organizing their senior Capstone Experience, which can easily absorb the students' final thirty units at UMR. The experience can be singular (a major research project) or eclectic (a mix of elective courses and internships, either of which can be taken at UMR or another institution). The key is that the Capstone is an exercise in curricular design in which the students, having spent most of their time in very ordered pathways, are turned loose to pursue their own interests, provided there is both logic and rationale to what becomes part of each student's Capstone Experience. Students, starting sometimes as soon as sophomore year, though more likely in the junior year, develop a proposal so that there is a work plan along with a set of explicitly stated outcomes and a strategy for assessment.

The result is a truly compact curriculum that students navigate as part of the cohort of new students who begin their studies each fall. There is not a great variety of courses, and most of those offered enroll the expected number of students. Indeed, because choice is limited, matching student demand to curricular supply is a reasonably straightforward exercise in arithmetic. Through at least the first three semesters, most students take the same courses; only as specific career paths are chosen in the fourth semester and beyond do students have divergent experiences within the broad field of health sciences.

UMR's fall 2011 enrollment was just 250 students. UMR antici- pates that by 2016 enrollment in the BSHS degree program will increase to one thousand students. The university is also developing a bachelor's degree program that includes a Mayo Clinic certificate in a limited number of allied health specialties. Because these students will enter as juniors, they will have quite different experiences from the BSHS students because Mayo clinicians teach most of their courses within Mayo Clinic facilities. It will also be possible for students who start in the BSHS program to transfer into one of the BS plus profes- sional certificate options, though currently not many students are expected to avail themselves of this opportunity. Finally, UMR remains the institution of record for a number of small extension programs that echo the institution's past.

New Standards for Tenure

The core academic programs at UMR belong to the CLI, which is presided over by a director, Claudia Neuhauser, who is also UMR's vice chancellor for academic affairs—or more simply, the vice chancellor. The faculty of the CLI fall into two classifications: twenty student instruction faculty, half of whom have PhDs and play much the same role that section instructors play at large universities; and eleven tenure-track faculty (fall 2011 census), who have been designated as design faculty with principal responsibility for designing the UMR curriculum and being its lead instructors. Even before the first faculty were appointed, Lehmkuhle and Neuhauser had developed a tenure policy that in several important ways reflected the revised tenure processes of the U of M Department of Ecology, Evolution and Behavior, which Neuhauser led prior to joining Lehmkuhle at UMR. Besides defining the rules that were to govern the tenure review process for the design faculty, the tenure policy statement describes what UMR is about, beginning with the CLI, in another statement that meant to convince as well as govern:

> The CLI is an administrative structure designed to promote a learner-centered, competency-based learning environment in which ongoing assessment guides and monitors student learning and is the basis for data-driven research on learning. The Center seeks to bring insights from the cognitive sciences to bear on student learning. It leads the development of an integrated curriculum for a baccalaureate degree in the health sciences where the classroom extends beyond the four walls of a lecture hall and will serve as a laboratory for learning.

The center's mission statement has, in fact, become the mantra with which UMR and its CLI define as well as talk about themselves:

> The vision of the Center is to advance learner-centered, technology-enhanced, concept-based, assessment-driven, and community-integrated education in the health sciences through cognitive science-based, innovative learning approaches.
>
> When making tenure decisions it is this mission that establishes the necessary criteria. At UMR the tenured faculty will be those whose teaching and research make significant contributions to the academy's understanding of the learning and assessment processes that best promote career-based learning in the health sciences.

Its self-congratulatory tone aside, the teaching standards embedded in UMR's tenure policy statement offer a model of what probationary candidates for tenure ought to meet generally across American higher education:

> The evaluation of probationary faculty will include a summary of the candidate's teaching assignments, evaluation of learning modules and their assessment components, and the candidate's ability to integrate curricular materials across the curriculum. The Center for Learning Innovation requires student evaluations of each course by its faculty. Senior faculty will provide regular feedback on teaching, including but not limited to classroom performance. (CLI 2009)

Put succinctly, successful teaching—the kind that merits tenure—is teaching that yields measurable gains in student learning.

It is in the definition of what constitutes research that UMR most obviously breaks new ground for an institution with a strong research mission. Like faculty everywhere, those at UMR are expected to be subject-matter experts whose research makes significant contributions to a relevant knowledge base. Only in the case of UMR, the faculty member is expected to be a subject-matter expert twice over: first in the cognitive processes that promote learning in their disciplines, and second in the knowledge base of that or a related discipline. The focus of the research shifts in the UMR statement, but not the standards for evaluating whether the faculty member has made a significant contribution.

A Sustaining Commitment to Pedagogical Research

Just how serious UMR is about making its mark as a national leader in research that documents effective teaching practices and learning strategies is reflected in its investment in a home-grown course management system called Intelligent System for Education Assessment and Learning (iSEAL). This system is in the process of becoming a data cache that resembles Carnegie Mellon's Open Learning Initiative (OLI) and its focus on building a "nano-database" that can be data-mined. The program expects that design faculty will use the data collected in iSEAL to build their research portfolios. The iSeal system builds on a distinction learning researchers have begun to make between learning analytics and academic or institutional analytics. The latter produces data that describe learning across the institution, most often using categories and terminology derived from administrative and institutional practices. Academic analytics produce the data that smart marketers use to capture new markets and retain old ones. Academic analytics similarly produce the data institutions use when defending themselves politically or seeking to compare themselves with other either more or less successful institutions. How institutions and higher education critics now use data drawn from the National Survey of Student Engagement (NSSE) and the Collegiate Learning Assessment (CLA) are good examples of the new kinds of academic analytics that seek to describe learning across institutions rather than at the level of individual learners. The data drawn from the federal government's Integrated Postsecondary Education Data System (IPEDS) similarly yield analyses that fall under the rubric of academic analytics.

Learning analytics, however, are both more detailed and more explicitly focused on the behaviors of individual students. Learning analytics will likely provide the analysis and define the data conventions that make possible research that focuses on learning processes, the curriculum, and the roles and responsibilities faculty have as instructional mentors and guides. The problem is that, while the concepts underlying learning analytics are becoming clearer, the necessary data have yet to be produced. An imaginative attempt to produce those data essential to CLI's research mission, iSEAL simultaneously provides the utilities students have come to expect from course management systems like Blackboard and Moodle. In fact, the designers envision a massive data-mining exercise in which all the artifacts a curriculum regularly generates at the course level—course readings and problem sets, quizzes, student papers, exams, and questions, along with faculty lectures and lecture notes—are tagged and available for detailed analysis.

The faculty does the tagging in terms of identifying key concepts, learning outcomes, and learning objects in the courses for which they are the responsible instructors. For the tagging to work faculty members must share a sense of definition that derives in part from continuing conversation and analysis and in part from UMR's commitment to shared and joint teaching responsibilities. The more the faculty tag, the more data become available for comparing experiences and outcomes across the UMR curriculum. The result, yet to be fully realized, is real-time data the faculty can use when designing new or revising established courses and for evaluating the overall effectiveness of the curriculum in terms of the learning outcomes that are expected to be the hallmarks of UMR's success. Just as important, the iSEAL data make possible the research on learning and pedagogy that is required of all tenured and tenure-eligible faculty.

When asked if the resources UMR is pouring into iSEAL are returning a commensurate benefit, the chancellor responded, "I sure hope so. We really do need to know if by teaching differently we are also teaching better in the sense that the students are both learning more and are able to do more with what they have learned" (confidential conversation with the author).

Not Exactly a Blank Slate

Still, in focusing on how UMR is different, it is easy to lose sight of the fact that its CLI is delivering a curriculum that in many ways is quite traditional: four years in length, roughly 120 units, many of which are required; recognizable majors; and courses whose learning outcomes stress both skills and competencies, along with subject matter knowledge and the values of a liberal education. The vice chancellor has also been known to chide me publicly for linking UMR's willingness to be different to the fact that it was beginning with what I had labeled in *Making Reform Work* "a blank slate," which enabled Lehmkuhle and Neuhauser to build an institution that would take full advantage of the new learning technologies, creating in the process a roster of learning programs that were to be twenty-first century in both their focus and their organization" (Zemsky 2009, 157). "Not exactly," the vice chancellor responds. If the administrative structure of UMR is different—no departments, a single academic unit organized as a Center for Learning Innovation led by the vice chancellor herself, and a faculty organized much as a major research institute would be organized—the faculty members themselves are nonetheless traditionally trained professionals in pursuit of academic careers that include the ability to begin at one institution and then move to another. No one wants to be labeled an academic zombie who, in search of a new beginning, gives up all that brought him or her into the academy in the first place. UMR is not necessarily that conservative, but it certainly is in the broad middle of the academic spectrum.

That said, however, where UMR's academic programs are different they are truly different. There is, to begin with, a sustaining commitment to shared responsibility and collective action. UMR faculty are less likely to talk about "my course" or "my students" because both are readily shared across the curriculum. Team teaching, which might better be described as "joint teaching," is the norm. Students are encouraged to share responsibilities and to engage in project work that is collaborative rather than individualistic. Emerging within the program's core courses is a heady experiment: having students take part of their exams in groups rather than as individuals. Posted to the UMR website is a pair of announcements directing surfers to two NPR podcasts explaining how and why UMR is a different kind of institution. The first, "DON'T LECTURE ME: Rethinking the Way College Students Learn," documents the interactive learning practices that have become standard features of the UMR curriculum. The second, "GROUP LEARNING," talks about how "at the University of Minnesota Rochester, group work is a core part of the curriculum." A part of the program follows several students who have, as a group, taken the last section of an exam worth 10 percent of the grade. They discover that, having first worked alone and then as a group, they have a more robust understanding of the concepts being tested on the exam (American Radio Works 2011).

Micromodels as Vehicles for Changing Higher Education

In two quite different ways, UMR suggests how higher education might best be changed over the next decades. Its educational innovations—a focused as well as compact curriculum, faculty who serve as members of learning teams, students who are collectively responsible for their learning, fully specified links to careers in the health sciences, course management systems that make possible the analysis of complex learning outcomes, and imaginative uses of the new electronic learning technologies—are, each in its own way, important demonstration projects that can reject as well as validate alternative instructional strategies and practices.

The larger importance of UMR will likely be the scale of the effort. UMR has succeeded because it is compact and focused and does not require massive capital investments, while UC Merced still occasions doubts. UC Merced owes its founding to a different era and different sensibilities. For more than a half-century, the UC system has responded to the demand that it teach more students by building complete campuses, with a full range of disciplines, majors, and research programs. This inherently expensive proposition has, in the past, paid off handsomely for the state: nine major public research universities exist, six of which—Berkeley, Los Angeles, Davis, Santa Barbara, Irvine, and San Diego—are full-fledged members of the Association of American Universities (AAU). No other state comes close to matching California's total of nine AAU members when the state's private research universities—Stanford, the California Institute of Technology, and the University of Southern California—are included. New York has five (three private and two public), Pennsylvania has four (two private and two public), and Texas has three (one private and two public). California's investment in public research universities has brought the state a visible edge in the competition for economic as well as academic distinction. But as Pat Callan has pointed out, continuing to invest in full-service research universities will not yield new educational models, nor will such investments result in better rates of student participation or student attainment.

The UMR experiment promises both, though it, like UC Merced, will be open to and appeal to that segment of the undergraduate admissions market that is prepared for the kind of undergraduate experience only a research-intensive faculty can deliver. UMR's competitive advantage is that it is a small, compact, noncapital intensive micromodel that is developing and testing alternate modes of instruction and, because it is a narrowly focused educational institution, is proving the value of implementing a noticeably different business model. It will likely succeed in doing things differently precisely because it will not be saddled with the propensity to constantly add new programs or degrees and because its tenure-track faculty members, now numbering less than fifteen, have collectively embraced UMR's commitment to research programs that test the effectiveness of the new learning modalities they are putting in place.

It is worth asking, at least rhetorically, whether California and higher education would have been better served if the UC system had invested in twenty-five such micromodels instead of building yet another full-service research campus. Could California have become the national center for educational experimentation, as it was briefly in the years following World War II when its system of mostly new community colleges served as a national model for other states seeking to rapidly expand educational opportunity?

In the late 1940s and 1950s the emphasis had been on building big. In the twenty-first century, the emphasis ought to be on building smart and building small. It is critical that the pace of creating new institutions capable of doing things differently again quickens. At the moment the for-profit sector has been most responsible for creating new institutions that have substantially expanded the capacity of the nation's postsecondary institutions to enroll those students who, in the past, have eschewed seeking a postsecondary degree in general and a baccalaureate degree in particular. Some educators will want to argue that the for-profit-sector has also been responsible for much if not most of the educational experiments that are increasing higher education's capacity to respond to changing economic circumstances. The better lesson to be drawn from the success of the for-profit sector is the sheer importance of new beginnings. In the past the United States has enjoyed, and in the future will require, a reliable supply of new institutions or agencies capable of doing things differently by virtue of the fact that they are starting from scratch.

And that ultimately is why UMR is such an important harbinger of a better, more productive and responsive future for American higher education. The new institutions that I have imagined will, like UMR, have to be seen and will have to see themselves as integral parts of an expanding system of postsecondary education that prizes diversity of form as well as diversity of people. By establishing micromodels like UMR, expanding systems of public higher education will be able to afford—both economically and educationally—the sustained experimentation that a more robust and flexible postsecondary system will require. The unacceptable alternative is for states to shy away from establishing new institutions and hence promoting educational experimentation because the cost, as in the case of the University of California Merced, has come to seem prohibitive. Micromodels work; they are affordable, and they are relatively easy to establish, as the University of Minnesota Rochester has demonstrated.

8 | A Liberal Arts Conundrum

In 1994, David Breneman, already a scholarly rarity in that he was both a noted economist focusing on higher education and the past president of a liberal arts college, posed the central question then vexing what had once been the crown jewel of American higher education: *Liberal Arts Colleges—Thriving, Surviving, or Endangered?* He opened his volume bearing that title with a recitation of the unsettling statistics that had necessarily begged the question. To set the tone Breneman used David Starr Jordon's 1903 prediction: "as time goes on the college will disappear, in fact if not in name. The best will become universities, the rest will return to their places as academies." Then Breneman told the story of the numbers:

> In 1955 liberal arts colleges still accounted for nearly 40 percent of all institutions—732 private colleges . . . enrolled only 7.6 percent of all students. By 1987, the Carnegie Foundation identified 540 out of 3,389 institutions (16 percent) as private liberal arts colleges, with only 4.4 percent of total enrollments. While the apocalyptic vision of the early university presidents did not come to pass, it is hard to argue with the judgment that, by 1990, the small private college had become a much diminished part of the educational landscape. (Breneman 1994, 21)

Today that diminishing continues. Liberal arts colleges account for substantially less than 2 percent of all undergraduate enrollments, and, as Breneman noted nearly two decades ago, liberal arts colleges, in substantial numbers, have survived by becoming something else: comprehensive master's degree institutions with a growing array of professional programs requiring advanced study and specialization.

To better understand how these trends and forces now shape the future of the four-year, residential liberal arts college, one needs to know what they look like today, up close and personal. Although I have spent my career at the University of Pennsylvania, much of my professional and family history reflects a sustaining attachment to liberal arts colleges. I am now a trustee of three such institutions: Franklin and Marshall College (where I have served on the board as both an active and emeritus trustee for nearly thirty years), the Sage Colleges in Troy and Albany, New York, and Whittier College, my own alma mater. Two of my three children attended Carleton College in Minnesota, and I have been a regular visitor, facilitator, and expounder at more than two dozen other liberal arts colleges. All of these institutions are today surviving, to use Breneman's classification, but nearly all face a tough struggle that is getting tougher.

Why? There are various explanations. A really good liberal arts college is an expensive operation—small classes, a constantly expanding knowledge base that somehow needs to be taught, a business model that often requires draconian investments of merit-based student financial aid, and a sense on the part of the students they most want to attract that a small, residential college is too confining. But, as is so often the case, the devil really is in the details. Each institution that I have come to know well has had to face both tough choices and hard times, all the while seeking to remain true to its mission and, at the same time, learning how to become market smart.

Among these, the institution I now know best is Whittier College, where I am in my fifth year as a continuing trustee. Whittier College is an interesting amalgam of old ideas, new realities, periods of strong presidential leadership interspersed with a few disastrous choices, and the always looming disruptions of a California economy and political climate that appear to go from bad to worse on a weekly basis. By ancestry, Whittier is a Quaker college founded in 1887. It is Richard Nixon's alma mater, but it is also the only liberal arts college in America that has been officially designated by the federal government as a Hispanic-Serving Institution. It is residential, neatly nestled in a southern California community whose stock of small, California bungalows gives the town the appearance of a still-intact movie set.

As its website makes clear, what the college most likes to boast about, is its sense of itself as a place distinguished "by its small size, pioneering faculty, and nationally recognized curriculum. Facilities rival those at large public institutions, but ours is an intimate setting where students and professors unite in an ongoing pursuit of knowledge" (Whittier College 2012). The college was one of the first to have a campus-abroad program, which opened in Copenhagen, Denmark, in 1959. It pioneered a pattern in which faculty from different disciplines co-taught a series of paired courses combining, for example, the insights of French literature and the social realities of modern-day Paris, linked the study of children's literature with how social work theories focus on the welfare of children, and coordinated the science behind obesity and the sociology of health and medicine. For nearly two decades, Whittier students have been required to take two such paired courses (a total of twelve credits), which, in addition to having faculty learn from one another, create mini-cohorts that help Whittier students bond with each other as well as with the institution.

The Wabash Study Comes to Campus

More recently Whittier has become something of a poster child for the efforts by a variety of organizations that have sought to bolster the fortunes of liberal arts colleges by demonstrating the superiority of their learning outcomes. Often in the forefront of these efforts have been the Council of Independent Colleges (CIC) and its president, Richard Ekman. CIC has officially and wholeheartedly embraced the National Survey of Student Engagement (NSSE) and the Collegiate Learning Assessment (CLA) as means of demonstrating that graduating from a liberal arts college is a smart investment—one that both saves money and delivers impressive learning outcomes. More than 80 percent of CIC institutions have used the NSSE, and, with a grant from the Teagle Foundation, the CIC has formed an active partnership with the CLA under the banner of the "CIC/CLA Consortium," which has played a major role in testing the validity of the CLA as a direct measure of student learning. Ekman trumpets these efforts as part of an integrated campaign to reintroduce American families to the value of a liberal arts education at a true liberal arts college. As he told *Inside Higher Ed*'s Doug Lederman in the fall of 2011, "We didn't need mandates or government pressure to explore ways to improve teaching and learning on our campuses. Our institutions are interested in getting it right, and they have embraced the use of data to diagnose what is and isn't working and then changing their practices" (Lederman 2011a).

The Wabash Study, hosted by Wabash College in Indiana and funded by the Lumina Foundation, takes the argument one step further: over the long run the study requires a willingness and a capacity to collect data measuring learning outcomes and turns them into action plans that are more than puff pieces telling prospective first-year students how good the college is. So far, forty-nine liberal arts colleges have submitted themselves to the regime the Wabash study imposes— systematic testing, on-campus interviews, and pointed reports detailing the actual progress a participating institution has made, as opposed to rhetorical claims of what it has accomplished.

Whittier is one of the forty-nine institutions participating in the Wabash Study and, like the other forty-eight, waited with bated breath for its results. Whittier need not have worried. Just before Christmas 2010, the Wabash Study staff informed Whittier that, as a result of its on-campus interviews, the responses of Whittier students on the NSSE survey, and the CLA testing, the college could be proud of the learning outcomes it had promoted in its students.

Whittier's results were conveyed using the study's standard template reporting measures of growth in student outcomes during a four-year span by using twelve key indicators presented as belonging to three clusters (four indicators each):

A. Moral Reasoning, Critical Thinking, Socially Responsible
   Leadership, Need for Cognition
B. Psychological Well-being, Universality-Diversity Awareness,
   Political and Social Involvements, Openness to Diversity and
   Challenge
C. Positive Attitudes toward Literacy, Contribution to the Arts,
   Contribution to the Sciences, Academic Motivation

With the exception of two categories in Cluster C (Contribution to the Sciences and Contribution to the Arts), Whittier students evidenced substantial growth in six measures (Moral Reasoning, Psychological Well-being, Socially Responsible Leadership, Critical Thinking, Universality-Diversity Awareness, Need for Cognition) and moderate growth in the four remaining measures. At the same time, in nearly every measure Whittier students showed more growth than the average for all liberal arts college students in the Wabash Study. Along three measures the differences between Whittier student scores and average liberal arts college student scores were substantial and significant: Moral Reasoning, Universality-Diversity Awareness, and Openness to Diversity and Challenge—a finding that neatly jibes with the Quaker values Whittier seeks to promote.

At the same time, the Wabash Study team reported to Whittier on the qualities that made real the college's commitment to good teaching: faculty interest in teaching and student development, prompt feedback, teaching clarity and organization, academic challenge and effort, frequent higher-order exams and assignments, challenging ideas and high faculty expectation, integrating ideas, information and experiences, and meaningful interactions with diverse peoples. It was a report card that warmed the heart of a president striving to make Whittier both better and more distinctive. In an email to her trustees previewing the Wabash Study results, Sharon Herzberger, Whittier's president, could brag: "Over the last four years Whittier participated in the Wabash Study of Liberal Arts Education, and just this weekend we received reports of this project. The results echo what we have known for years: a Whittier education is extraordinary." In quick succession the president recited the study's two specific findings:

- Measured from their first year to the end of their senior year at Whittier, our students showed greater growth than students in the comparison group on many dimensions including moral reasoning, socially responsible leadership, psychological well-being, and awareness of and openness to diversity.
- Whittier students also reported experiencing more "high impact practices" than students at other colleges. High impact practices—such things as quality interactions with faculty, high expectations for students, and experiences with diversity—are known to produce greater levels of intellectual and personal growth over the college years.

Herzberger concluded with the boast that has eluded almost all college and university presidents: "We've always known that we are transforming lives; now we have more data to prove it" (Sharon Herzberger, in an e-mail to the Whittier Community, December 1, 2010).

The Rest of the Story

And yet, like almost every other liberal arts college, Whittier worries—about next year's enrollment, about less than robust fundraising and a diminished endowment, about the need to make major capital investments in the campus starting with a new $40-million-plus science building, and above all about a spiraling discount rate that makes Whittier's net price substantially less than its sticker price. The details of Whittier's financial condition are regularly presented by the college's chief financial officer, James Dunkelman, a recent addition to the college's senior staff. Tall and taciturn, Dunkelman speaks from authority, often invoking his experiences as a financial officer at one of Whittier's better-off competitors. He hasn't wanted to panic the board, though he knows that the tough sledding ahead requires a better understanding of the college's current circumstances.

Almost always, Dunkelman begins with the college's enrollment history and the fact that it has grown substantially, if unevenly, since 2005. Total undergraduate enrollment has increased from 1,325 students in 2005 to 1,643 in 2012—almost all of it full-time and residential. A variety of circumstances account for this 24-percent increase in the size of the Whittier student body: the capping of enrollments at California's public institutions and the generally bad press this sector has received as the state struggles with a draconian budget deficit; a successful revamping of the admissions function—and not incidentally, continuing improvements in the rate at which the college retains and then graduates students; and a new capacity to recruit and then retain community college transfer students.

This enrollment growth has stabilized Whittier's finances. In 2003, the rolling three-year average operating margin at all institutions with an A rating from Moody's was 2.7 percent; the three-year rolling average operating margin at institutions with a Baa rating from Moody's was 3.1 percent; Whittier's three-year average operating margin was 4 percent. For the five-year period 2003 through 2008, Whittier had averaged a heady 8-percent net operating ratio; then circumstances changed just about the time Dunkelman arrived on campus. In 2010 the college's rolling three-year average operating margin was a meager 2.6 percent—just over half the averages for institutions with either an A or Baa rating from Moody's. By 2011 the college's rolling three-year average operating margin was back to 4 percent, roughly on a par with the rest of the industry. That result was achieved by a further increase in full-time undergraduate enrollments and some modest belt tightening, including delayed salary increases.

The problem, as Dunkelman now regularly reported to the board, was that the college was required to increase the discounts it offered prospective students in order to secure their matriculations. When financial aid was awarded on the basis of need, students that an institution wanted would pay the amount of tuition determined by a calculation that took into account both the cost of attendance and the student/family's financial resources. By the 1990s, however, the competition for students among the nation's private colleges and universities had created yet another, market-based form of aid—an amount that represented what the student/family determined was necessary to win their matriculation. Colleges still published sticker prices and escalated them significantly faster than inflation; however, the real number became, not the sticker price, but the net tuition—that is, the amount of money each student was actually expected to pay. Although the sticker price was the same for everyone, the net price varied widely, depending on each student's attractiveness to the institution, the family's assets, and the degree of external financial aid available to the student, principally through federal grants and loans along with state grants.

Starting in the 1990s, as the scramble for qualified students intensified and liberal arts colleges like Whittier again felt under the gun, the discount rates at all liberal arts colleges, save those perched in the rarified air of institutions belonging to the Consortium on Financing Higher Education (COFHE), began to increase substantially faster than the posted increases in sticker prices. At Whittier, the discount rate increased from 40 percent in 2003 to 45 percent in 2011, having first dropped to 34 percent in 2007 on the eve of the "great recession." Over that same period, total net revenues from tuition increases kept rising, going from $24 million in 2007 to $29 million in 2011. Although enrollment increases accounted for most of the $5 million in new monies, relatively little was invested in new tenure-track faculty positions; instead, most of the new faculty—added to maintain small class sizes—were given multiyear contracts instead.

The enrollment analyses Dunkelman annually presented to the trustees had a second, in many ways more disturbing, message. Traditionally Whittier had divided its admitted applicants into five quintiles, ranging from least attractive to the college to most attractive. Students in the lowest quintile received much less advantageous financial aid packages, and more than a few received no financial aid at all. Students in the top quintile received the largest awards, often requiring substantially lower amounts of either student or parent loans. Students in that quintile, on average, supplied only half as much net revenue per student as students in the lowest quintile—$13,000 per student versus $26,000 per student.

The point Dunkelman made was simple and direct: as long as the discount rate increased and student enrollment did not, Whittier would be unable to meet its aspirations to pay higher salaries to faculty and to create a capital renewal budget fully addressing Whittier's older buildings. Whittier, however, was operating at full capacity; there were no more beds in the dorms, and no additional faculty available to teach the curriculum that had allowed Whittier to excel as a learning laboratory.

If the short-term enrollment/revenue dilemma weren't painful enough, Dunkelman would, when asked and sometimes just to satisfy his sense of keeping the board properly informed, remind us of his longer-term worries. His primary concern was Whittier students' considerable dependency on governmentally supplied student aid grants and loans. The college received $2.7 million annually in federal Pell Grants and another $3.2 million in State of California CAL Grants. These two programs together, though they represented aid to students, supplied 20 percent of the college's net revenue, and, given the budget frenzies in Washington and Sacramento, those programs were now at risk.

On a regular basis Dunkelman's reports to the board summarized Whittier's financial struggles using an analytic Tool Kit developed by KPMG LLP, Prager, Sealy & Co. LLC, and Attain LLC, under the sponsorship of the KPMG Government Institute. Now a standard tool readily available through the National Association of College and University Business Officers (NACUBO), Strategic Financial Analysis for Higher Education identifies key financial operating and capital risks and highlights methods to address these risks. The Tool Kit's key indicator is a Composite Financial Index (CFI) that ranges from 1 (institution under financial stress), through 3 (modest ability to access capital and address financial challenges), and finally to 10 (financial returns provide resources to experiment with and support new initiatives). In the fall of 2011, Dunkelman reported to the board that Whittier's five-year rolling average CFI was 3.4—just barely above the Threshold Score of 3, which the Tool Kit identified as an institution that retained a modest ability to address its financial challenges. Dunkelman's particular concern was that the college's CFI had steadily declined during the previous five years and faced the very real possibility of falling below the threshold score in the not too distant future.

On occasion Dunkelman provided a more operational context for understanding what his analysis was teaching him and what he hoped the board was coming to understand. What would it take, he asked, for the college to truly secure its future? The answer prescribed that Whittier do three things: keep the promise to its faculty and staff to bring their salaries up to par with the college's peer institutions; significantly increase investment in its physical plant, principally by budgeting funds for depreciation; and realistically plan for increased funding for student financial aid. To fully fund each item would require an additional $4.35 million in annual operating expense—an amount just over 10 percent of the college's current operating budget. His analysis also made clear that for most of the previous decade Whittier had met its budgets by relying on unbudgeted revenues, principally from increased enrollments and gifts. And even then, faculty and staff salaries had remained below those of the college's peer institutions, though still substantially higher than most similarly constituted liberal arts colleges. At the same time, the infrastructure supporting the Whittier campus continued to age and, in some cases, decay.

A Dilemma Explained but Not Resolved

The dilemma Whittier faces—and by extension the dilemma faced by most successful liberal arts colleges—is neatly framed by the president's enthusiasm for what Whittier accomplishes educationally, on the one hand, and, on the other, by the set of financial circumstances her CFO has identified as adding up to as much as a 10-percent budget problem through 2020 at least. Make no mistake—Whittier succeeds educationally, providing good value at a still remarkably low net price. It is an institution that provides access, particularly to young Latinos. Its educational programs are models of innovation. Its faculty is both engaged and collaborative. When challenged to respond to those critiques of higher education that focus on low completion rates, faculty-centric cultures, and an absence of student learning, the Whittier community can rightly claim that the critique does not apply in its own case. And when that same community is faced with the financial reality of Dunkelman's analysis, it has an equal right to feel betrayed, not by Dunkelman to be sure, but by that set of financial circumstances that seem to devalue the college's very real achievements and the quality of the education it continues to offer. What hurts the most, I suspect, is the simplistic response that says to succeed in an increasingly uncertain future, you will have to learn to do more with less—or to do less well by teaching more students in larger courses—because overall the Whittier faculty and staff would have to shrink relative to student body size in order to meet the financial circumstances it is likely to face.

At many liberal arts colleges today, the exact same medicine is being prescribed: increase enrollments but not the size of the tenure-track faculty; hire more adjuncts; make better use of technology in general and online education in particular, perhaps even outsourcing some instruction to those for-profit entities that have mastered the web as a learning platform. An alternative strategy converts the liberal arts college into a small, presumably nimble professional school offering master's degrees in those specialties for which there is a growing promise of gainful employment—principally health care and business services. Or still another strategy allows the institution to develop an export brand that takes advantage of the growing demand for higher education across Asia and the Middle East. As long as the institution's network of branch campuses abroad sends its profits home, that home campus can survive, provided that the flow of funds is sustainable and the home campus does not become an empty shell.

Herzberger, Dunkelman, and their senior colleagues have considered each of these alternatives, briefed the board as to what may prove necessary, if not necessarily palatable, and gingerly looked for ways to engage the Whittier faculty in a discussion of the long-run sustainability of the current Whittier model. Ultimately, however, Herzberger chose another strategy, one that sought to preserve Whittier's core strengths while augmenting them with a portfolio of new programs that promised sufficient net revenue to ensure that the college thrived as well as survived. Together that alternative strategy and Herzberger's campaign of shared responsibility make the Whittier story an important harbinger of how productive change might alter higher education.

The president's first challenge was the faculty, who, like faculty nearly everywhere, were not convinced that doing something differently was better than doing nothing, given there was every possibility that what was being bruited about would likely prove either impractical or logistically impossible. Here a piece of Whittier's recent past reinforced faculty skepticism. In the 1970s, Whittier had acquired a stand-alone law school, then located in east Los Angeles about twenty miles from the Whittier campus. Ten years later, the college moved its law school to Orange County, convinced that the explosive growth there would assure the law school's success. People, particularly those on the Whittier Campus, expected that the law school would take care of itself while simultaneously providing an infusion of much-needed cash to the undergraduate institution. For a while, the plan seemed to be working, but then enrollments flattened, and the American Bar

Association (ABA) put the law school on probation because too few of its graduates passed the bar exam on their initial try. The result was a host of bad publicity and a wounded entity that increasingly absorbed the time and energy of the college's senior staff and principal trustees. Much, perhaps even most, of Herzberger's first two years as president were devoted to orchestrating the winning campaign that improved the school's bar pass rates, forced the ABA to lift its suspension, and scaled back the law school's faculty and staff to better match the school's revenue.

When the president and others began talking about the need for a diversified revenue mix to be achieved by launching new programs, faculty leaders could be forgiven for rolling their eyes as they reminded their colleagues that Whittier did not need another venture like the law school. In this case nothing ventured could in fact turn out to be something gained. Still Herzberger persisted, arguing that the college's current business model was not sustainable and that the result of doing nothing would be a Whittier College of which few could be proud. She also changed tactics. Where initially she had challenged the faculty to rapidly consider a host of alternative programs, she now put in place a pair of committees that drew on her senior staff, the elected faculty leadership, and a handful of trustees with business and higher education experience.

A trustee committee focusing on new initiatives quickly identified a range of possibilities, each pushed by one group or another prepared to argue that its proposal would prove practical enough to gain real traction. In the fall of 2011, Herzberger submitted a list of such possibilities to the full board, including a number of partnerships with other small colleges as well as a local hospital, a variety of short-term academic programs drawing on Whittier's current strengths (for example, a Los Angeles intensive arts program for both students and others interested in spending a week, a January term, or a semester studying in LA), and finally a series of new professional master's programs (for example, master's programs in documentary films, international policy and management, and nutrition/dietetics, as well as a limited number of new teaching credentials, adding to Whittier's portfolio of educational programs).

The second committee was charged with developing both a process and a framework for the college's consideration of these and other new business ventures. Dunkelman was a member, along with senior staff from admissions and the academic dean's office. Newly elected faculty leaders were also members, along with three trustees whom Herzberger hoped would contribute special insights into the changing market for higher education both here and abroad. One was Edwin Keh, who until 2010 was chief operating officer and senior vice president of Wal-Mart Global Procurement. Keh knew China, knew the market for business education, and through his connection to Penn's Wharton School, understood the dynamics of business programs that attract an international clientele. The second trustee was Kristine Dillon, since 2003 the president of COFHE. A researcher and a seasoned administrator at both the University of Southern California and Tufts University, Dillon was a long-serving trustee who, despite the fact that Whittier was not in COFHE's sights, brought to the discussion a nuanced understanding of the changing market for private higher education. I was the third trustee on the committee, having already pushed for a more tractable process for considering what many in the college community thought was beyond consideration.

The work of this committee provided the breakthrough process that change required. It began by affirming what both the faculty and Herzberger each embraced: Whittier was a special place that needed to be preserved, not recast. At its core, the committee said, Whittier needed to succeed as a residential liberal arts college of roughly fifteen to sixteen hundred students who were taught in small classes by full-time faculty committed to a curriculum that stressed student engagement and exploration.

That, however, was still the business model Dunkelman and Herzberger knew was not sustainable. To preserve this core, the college needed to augment its mission while carefully considering each option the new business ventures committee was simultaneously exploring. Those ventures need not generate exaggerated margins, but they did need to cover a proportional share of the college's fixed and central operating costs. No one program could provide that much margin, but collectively they just might, and, if they did, then the core undergraduate program in its present form would be sustainable into the indefinite future. It was also possible that the success of these master's degree and related programs would, in time, suggest how the undergraduate core of the college could improve its offerings. Were all of these dreams to be realized, Dunkelman would have the funds that maintaining the physical plant required, while faculty and staff salaries could be expected to rise to match the salaries at the institutions Whittier saw as its principal competitors. It was a bargain the faculty leaders said they could recommend to their colleagues.

What allowed the process to be successful—and remember the process is of principal interest here—was at least in part a function of the mix of trustees that Herzberger recruited to her two committees. On each were trustees who knew academic institutions well and understood, but more important appreciated, faculty prerogatives and perspectives. The trustees she recruited were unlikely to stamp their feet, either individually or collectively, and demand the faculty become more businesslike or work harder or diminish their interest in research and publication.

Implicit in each committee's deliberations was the notion that the new programs had to fit and had to draw on the expertise the college already possessed without absorbing resources, faculty time in particular, needed by the core undergraduate program. In the beginning, at least, the college would have to invest some discretionary revenues to get the programs started—discretionary revenue that had to come either from philanthropy or from a partner organization with deep enough pockets to cover start-up costs, directly or indirectly. Hence, it was important to build programs that appealed to China, with its increasing demand for postsecondary options for its citizenry. Whittier had already hosted an American immersion program that involved providing language instruction and enrichment experiences, in which the sponsoring Chinese partner had covered all the costs of mounting the program, including the provision of residential and instructional spaces. Provided the contracts for this kind of hosting program were properly negotiated, the goal of earning revenues in excess of direct costs would be within reach.

Also being explored was a long-term partnership with a nearby hospital that had both needs and resources, including the ability to build new facilities and a professional staff, many of whom were qualified to teach their specialties. This potential partnership just might prove a match not unlike that between the Mayo Clinic and the University of Minnesota Rochester (UMR). With both parties interested, the challenge becomes one of developing a portfolio of joint initiatives that serve both the hospital and Whittier.

Making the Case

The parallel between UMR's partnership with the Mayo Clinic and Whittier's interests in building a hospital partnership raises the question of whether there are other similarities, either shared experiences or comparable challenges. Though the comparison is tempting, the two harbingers are more important for their differences than their similarities. UMR is a public institution attached to a major research university that gives it immediate recognition. Few doubt its sustainability over the long run. It has the advantage of public subsidy, which may well diminish, but which will, into the indefinite future, allow it to charge a lower tuition than its private or independent competitors. The real difference, however, is the singularity of its business model: one basic product, one dominant degree.

Whittier, however, is exploring options that may move it in the opposite direction. In the future will the college offer more degrees, more specialties, less singular focus? As it moves to execute its strategy of exploring and then building a portfolio of programs, even if those programs adhere reasonably well with one another, it runs the risk of losing its identity in an increasingly cluttered market in which niche branding is becoming something of a fetish. Whittier does not have a public subsidy, knows that the CAL Grants its students receive are now at risk, and faces the prospect of not being able to assume greater debt in order to finance its entrance into the professional master's degree market. At the same time, Whittier will continue to struggle with the propensity problem—the need to constantly add new fields and disciplines to an already cluttered curriculum—that UMR's singular focus on the health sciences has allowed it to sidestep. To repeat an observation made earlier, the small, focused model UMR champions is more likely to win the day than the inclusive strategies of the big research and comprehensive institutions or the mixed-methods models to which liberal arts colleges like Whittier may be tempted to turn.

Liberal arts colleges that adopt a mixed-methods model, particularly those that call for partnerships with larger, often for-profit entities, face at least one additional challenge: enterprises that contribute substantially to an institution's financial stability and well-being occasionally become less inclined to contribute in this way if they perceive they can be equally or more successful on their own. In time they bristle at what they come to perceive is a subordinate position within the partnership. The demise of Antioch College, for example, is a story in which the auxiliary campuses ultimately overcame the college itself. The liberal arts college, which originally oversaw each of its adult education campuses around the country, in time became but one of several reports to the university chancellor. The lesson is clear: how best to make certain that the benefit to the partners is reciprocal and has the flexibility to evolve over time.

Nor, for that matter, would Whittier's success be assured if it took this route. Key questions abound. Where will the start-up funds necessary for launching the new programs Whittier wants to explore come from? How much does the college, or for that matter anyone else, really know about the markets for professional master's programs? Isn't it at least possible that the for-profit institutions, with their more efficient production functions and commitment to online education, will prove more adept at mounting and sustaining the programs that capture this segment of the market?

As both an alum and a trustee, however, I am betting this strategy will work—that Whittier will prove an important harbinger by demonstrating that its faculty, administration, and trustees, working together, can build an enterprise model that allows it to have *both* a true liberal arts core and a more entrepreneurial outer shell. Each party will have to be careful, prudent really, and learn to resist in the process those proposals that offer a quick path to the extra revenue the college seeks. Together they will need to understand which of Whittier's current strengths and specialties offer the best foundations for building an expanded portfolio of professional programs. Together they will have to draw more directly on the energies and judgments of the faculty as the college combines new and old ways of doing business. For Whittier, then, success at a minimum requires a redoubling of its commitment to collective endeavors that, by design, involve the many as opposed to the few.

9 | A New Peace Treaty

I have already told the story of the faculty delegation from the University of Wisconsin Oshkosh
journeying to a neighboring two-year institution that annually supplies
the largest number of Oshkosh's transfer students. Invited to participate
in a faculty and staff workshop, the Oshkosh delegation was greeted,
not with the polite applause they expected, but with a robust round of
boos. When they tentatively inquired about the unfriendly welcome,
they were told, frankly, that the college was tired of the mistreatment
being dished out to the students it encouraged to transfer to Oshkosh to
complete their collegiate educations. Too often, they were told, Oshkosh
faculty treated the transferring students as if they had wasted their time
at the two-year college, denied them credit for the general education
courses they had taken before transferring, and more generally delivered
a curriculum that few could complete in a timely and efficient manner.

However unpleasant, as well as unexpected, that altercation had
been, it was but one more warning that the university needed to
address a host of educational problems. Among the more pithy obser-
vations then making the rounds at Oshkosh was a remark by a senior
member of the provost's staff: "At Oshkosh, we don't have a general
education curriculum, we have gen-eds instead," by which she meant
there's not much logic to what is required, just an endless list of
detached courses that are designated as satisfying some element of the
general education requirement (confidential conversation with the

author). The university had actually been on notice for nearly a decade that its general education requirements needed attention. As part of its review for reaccrediting the university in 1997, the Higher Learning Commission (HLC), the accrediting arm of the North Central Association of Colleges and Schools (NCA), made clear what needed to be changed sooner rather than later:

- Greater coherence in the general education curriculum is sorely needed.
- General education needs to have "a coherent, integrated focus," as "it lacks clear definition and does not clearly address the need to stimulate and examine values or to promote intellectual inquiry."
- A systematic plan for assessing general education must be devised to coincide with a revised general education program.
- The number of general education courses needs to be reduced.

Ten years later, the HLC was back with a longer list suggesting that not much had changed—or improved:

- Reconsider the policy that all natural science and social science courses count for general education.
- Reduce the number of courses that count for general education.
- Reconfigure the general education program so that there is a practical way to assess whether the goals of the program are being met.
- Put into place a review process for individual general education courses to assure that they continue to meet the goals of the general education program.
- Put assessment strategies in place that will allow for not only collecting but also disseminating to the University information on whether the goals and objectives of the general education program are being met.
- Consider ways to integrate the "sustainability initiative" into the design and assessment of general education.
- Make information regarding the general education program available to faculty and students (currently the only, and limited, information is in the *Bulletin*). (USP 2012, 25)

As a result, the chancellor and provost committed themselves and the university to a painstaking—some would now add a painfully slow—review process that by the spring of 2012 had produced a radically different approach to general education: one that was noticeably less of a peace treaty among departments competing for enrollments and, instead, offered the vision of a substantially different general education program. As a prelude to the reform process, the provost had both funded and politically supported a program that had Oshkosh faculty, in substantial numbers, joining in the reform conversations the American Association of Colleges & Universities (AAC&U) had launched with its LEAP campaign in 2005. In time, much of the AAC&U reform vocabulary became a standard reference point for those the provost had charged with making sure Oshkosh did not come up short on the next HLC review. While the LEAP campaign promoted the values AAC&U had been championing for a decade or more—a focus on learning outcomes, authentic assessments, and inclusive excellence—Oshkosh came to pay equal attention to the ten High-Impact Educational Practices that George Kuh from the National Survey of Student Engagement (NSSE) identified largely at the behest of AAC&U:

- First-Year Seminars and Experiences
- Common Intellectual Experiences
- Learning Communities
- Writing-Intensive Courses
- Collaborative Assignments and Projects
- Undergraduate Research
- Diversity/Global Learning
- Service Learning, Community-Based Learning
- Internships
- Capstone Courses and Projects (USP 2012, 27)

From AAC&U's perspective, and now increasingly from Oshkosh's perspective as well, the ten High-Impact Educational Practices provided a means of making real the promise of an effective education fully informed by the values and precepts of a liberal education. For Oshkosh the values embedded in the LEAP campaign and the practical focus embedded in the list of High-Impact Practices became the building blocks of the five-year process that was expected to culminate in a revamped program of general education at the university.

That process was, in turn, fueled by a growing consensus that too many students who began as first-time, full-time first-year students at Oshkosh were not graduating—not in four years, six years, or even eight years. Too many simply disappeared, not to be heard from again. At the same time, the concerns of the unhappy transfer students were given voice by the faculty at the neighboring two-year college: too many requirements, not enough flexibility, not enough advising, not enough coherence in what they were being asked to accomplish.

Mapping Attrition and Graduation

And that was how I was first introduced to the University of Wisconsin Oshkosh.

It was the fall of 2009. The previous spring, Joni Finney and I had published "Changing the Subject," in which we argued that a convoluted, and often fractious, curriculum was responsible for both the inexorable increase in operating costs and the lower completion rates that had come to describe higher education across the United States. We sought that fall a limited set of institutions that would be interested in our developing detailed curricular maps documenting when and how their students earned sufficient course credits to satisfy the requirement for a baccalaureate degree. Eventually we had a conversation with the president and senior vice president for academic and student affairs of the University of Wisconsin System who, in turn, set up a conference call of campus leaders from across the system. On the phone that afternoon were Lane Earns, Oshkosh's provost and vice chancellor for academic affairs, and Lori Carrell, an Oshkosh professor of communication and director of its Center for Excellence in Teaching and Learning (CETL), who would first help facilitate the general education reform process before ultimately assuming responsibility for managing the university's review of the proposed changes to the general education curriculum. Leaders from other universities in the system participated on the call, but only Earns and Carrell understood what we were after and, more important, how a detailed curricular map might help them sustain a process focusing on curricular reform.

In time, we successfully recruited three more institutions: Towson University in Maryland (like Oshkosh, a public comprehensive university), and two midwestern liberal arts colleges, Alma in Michigan and Augustana in Illinois. Grants from the Spencer and the Teagle foundations funded our work, which was expected to produce what Spencer president Michael McPherson called a "Proof of Concept" paper—that is, a paper that either did or did not demonstrate that the shape and functioning of the curriculum itself contributed to both escalating costs and lower completion rates. Drawing the curricular map for Oshkosh was our first order of business.

In the fall of 2004, the University of Wisconsin Oshkosh enrolled 1,520 new, first-time first-year students into what would nominally be labeled the class of 2008. In fact, 245, or just over 16 percent, of these first-year students graduated in the spring of 2008, with a larger block—443, or nearly 30 percent of the class—graduating the following year. All told, by the spring of 2011, just over 55 percent of the class of 2008 had received a baccalaureate degree from the University of Wisconsin Oshkosh.

To understand how new students progress through the Oshkosh curriculum, it is best to start with the four colleges in which first-year students provisionally enroll upon matriculation: Business, Education and Human Services, Letters and Sciences, and Nursing. The College of Business has the best track record, a six-year graduation rate of 67 percent. Business was also a net gainer of internal transfers. Of the 164 first-time first-year students who graduated from the College of Business in 2011, 68 began their undergraduate careers in another Oshkosh college.

The next best six-year graduation rate, 58 percent, belonged to the College of Education and Human Services. Because the college's curriculum is a five-year course of study leading to professional certification, just a handful of first-year students from the Class of 2008 graduated that spring. The following year, however, 33 percent of the college's initial first-year students received their baccalaureate degrees, with another 15 percent (58 percent overall) receiving their degrees through the spring of 2011. Education and Human Services was a modest net loser of internal transfer students, principally to and from the College of Letters and Sciences.

Oshkosh's largest college, Letters and Sciences, had just an 18 percent four-year graduation rate, though its seven-year graduation rate, at 54 percent, was roughly the same as the university's overall rate. The college lost a substantial number of students to both the College of Business and the College of Education and Human Services, though in the latter case it picked up more internal transfers than it lost.

Finally, students who started at the College of Nursing had just a 13-percent four-year graduation rate and an overall graduation rate of 49 percent. Nursing has a stiff set of requirements, which many of the students preliminarily admitted to Nursing fail to complete. In Nursing's case, most of those students leave Oshkosh to seek nursing education at another institution, often at a lower level.

In fact, significant numbers of students who leave Oshkosh without a degree enroll in other colleges and universities (for the most part public) across Wisconsin. It was possible to trace the subsequent educational careers of 640 (out of a total of 652) students who first matriculated as first-year students in the fall of 2004. Just over three-fourths of these students enrolled in another college or university subsequent to leaving Oshkosh; of these, 193 earned a baccalaureate degree elsewhere, bringing the overall completion rate (Oshkosh plus another institution) to 68 percent. Another 55 former Oshkosh students earned an associate's degree or its equivalent after leaving Oshkosh.

While the College of Nursing lost two-thirds of its initial enrollment to attrition and transfer, more than 90 percent of these students continued their education elsewhere; the average for Oshkosh's other three colleges was 74 percent of students who continued their studies at another college or university. Of the former Oshkosh nursing students who transferred, however, only 43 percent eventually earned a baccalaureate or associate degree; the average for Oshkosh's other three colleges was an even lower 38 percent.

Altogether, 25 percent of the original 2004 first-year student cohort left higher education without earning any degree, and 10 percent left and did not enroll in any college or university, at least through the spring of 2011. It is a case of the glass being three-fourths full, one-fourth empty, though the fact remains that more than 40 percent of those who initially chose Oshkosh left the institution without a degree. And it did not take the students long to make the decision to leave. One-fourth of those who left did so by the end of their first semester; another fourth left at the end of their first year, and a third fourth left sometime during their second (sophomore) year. Further attrition after that point was limited, suggesting that for the remaining students who left, personal factors and circumstances were probably the cause.

At this point the key analytic question becomes, "Why did Oshkosh lose so many of its first-year class in their first year of attendance?" While no one actually told the first-year students on the first day of classes, "Look to your left and look to you right, half of you will not graduate and a third of you will be gone from Oshkosh within the next year!" it is a bromide that would have rung remarkably true. In part, attrition at Oshkosh reflected the under-preparedness of some in the first-year class, but that was not the whole story. While the first-year students who dropped out had a lower grade-point average (GPA) at the time of their departure than their classmates who stayed, the differences were not that great—a solid B average for those who persisted (GPA = 3.1) and a B−/C+ for those who did not stay (GPA = 2.5). Moreover, on average one-fourth of the students who left Oshkosh without a degree earned either an A or a B in one or more of eight tough "barrier courses" (discussed below) that then dominated the first-year curriculum at Oshkosh. While on average three-fourths of these A or B students would enroll at another college or university once they left Oshkosh, one-fourth did not, which suggests that they had never been committed to earning a degree, that something in their Oshkosh experience discouraged further enrollment, or that they did not have the financial resources to continue their college educations. And of those A and B students who did enroll at another institution, about the same percentage (51 percent) earned a subsequent degree as those who stayed the course at Oshkosh. To repeat, the lack of preparation no doubt played a role in determining who was likely to depart the university without having earned a degree, but that, in itself, cannot explain the fact that each year Oshkosh loses one-fourth of its first-year class to attrition.

Another, in many ways more striking, clue is the fact that the nonpersisters began to drop courses early on, thus ensuring that they would not have earned enough course credits to graduate on time (that is, at the end of four years or eight semesters). At the end of the first semester, the nonpersisters, on average, were already short nearly a course worth of credits—a gap that grew to more than a course worth of credits by the end of these students' first year. Nonpersisters also had more trouble with a set of courses we have identified as "barrier courses"—large courses (at least 100 students) taken in the first year in which 20 percent or more of the students who enrolled either withdrew from the course or received a D or an F. In all, fifteen courses met this criterion: three introductory mathematics courses, three introductory history courses, a pair of religious study courses, and a variety of introductory social science and humanities courses that doubled as introductions to the major and as courses satisfying a general education requirement. Missing from this list were most courses in the sciences as well as courses in writing and composition, although they were standard elements of Oshkosh's first-year curriculum.

These barrier courses were just that, and they affected the course-taking patterns of students who did graduate and of those who left the institution without earning a degree. As in the case of GPA and credits earned, those who graduated did significantly better—that is, they were more likely to complete the barrier course rather than withdrawing or receiving a D or an F—than those who would not earn an Oshkosh degree. On average, across all fifteen barrier courses, there was a 15-percentage-point gap between the experiences of persisters and nonpersisters in terms of the proportion of each group that withdrew or received a D or an F.

One principal lesson this analysis of Oshkosh course-taking patterns teaches is that these barrier courses were but part of a larger problem embedded within the curriculum. In its shape and form the Oshkosh undergraduate curriculum then resembled what can be found in most public comprehensive universities: a menu of courses that can satisfy one or more aspects of the general education requirements; a series of degree requirements, for the most part a second list of courses or subjects a student must master en route to graduation; and finally, a set of major requirements starting with a list of courses and the minimum grades that need to be earned in those courses before the student can be admitted to the major.

Over time, however, the requirements at Oshkosh had become entangled with one another—so much so that some courses could be counted double and in a few cases triple in relation to fulfilling the requirements. While the courses satisfying the general education requirement were expected to meet a set of stated outcomes, they had become, for the most part, courses whose principal purposes were ensuring that the departments offering them continued to attract sufficient enrollment to justify the number of faculty appointments to which the department was entitled. Faculty, like the students they were expected to advise, had trouble keeping track of which courses satisfied which set of requirements. They simply began lumping the general education and degree requirements together, though they were, in fact, quite separate and called for different student enrollment strategies. Finally, the major requirements were idiosyncratic. Knowing the general form of what one major required was of little help in guessing what a different major might require.

Over time, confusion had trumped cohesion. The university's undergraduate curriculum was largely—some would say wholly—without design, and Oshkosh's students knew it. In February 2012, as part of the university's consideration of a new general education curriculum, undergraduates were asked to comment on both the new and the old sets of requirements. Most of the three hundred-plus who responded to the survey had little understanding of what was being proposed, but they knew exactly what was wrong with the general education requirements to which they had been subjected.

Just half of those who responded said that general education at Oshkosh was a "valuable component." Even fewer said that the general education curriculum provided a "foundation for success in my major." Perhaps in the unkindest cut of all, less than half agreed with the statement that the university's general education requirements were "clearly understood and explained by academic advisers across campus" (confidential e-mail to the author).

The most specific as well as most repeated comment (and the one that most clearly echoed the argument Finney and I made in "Changing the Subject") was that the general education curriculum was "a waste of time and money." The second most common complaint was that the general education requirement "is very disorganized and does not link to a major." Some student comments were wonderfully prescient in their estimate of the faculty's commitment to a well-formed introduction to the liberal arts. As one student put it, too much of general education at Oshkosh does nothing "more than keep particularly irrelevant courses funded and tired faculty continually employed." Or, as another student put it, "there needs to be more communication among departments and advisors. It is very frustrating as a student to be told one thing by a professor, another by an advisor, and yet another by department faculty" (confidential e-mail to the author).

The third most common complaints were that the faculty did not understand the requirements, which helped explain why advising too often left students taking the wrong road to graduation, and that "a lot of the professors who teach the general education requirements seem to not really care about what they are teaching." At least one student found a way to encapsulate all these concerns in a single comment:

> It was not brought up to my junior year on how many "upper level" courses I needed. Therefore, I am now going a WHOLE extra semester because my advisor, when I was a freshman, did not help plan for that. Also I am in my 4th semester of Spanish, which is extremely hard because I did not come from high school with Spanish background. It has brought down my GPA, I think it's ridiculous that I am taking this much Spanish when I could be taking more things that pertain towards what I am actually going to school for. (confidential e-mail to the author)

At least some of the responding students were aware of the fact that one could pursue other pathways to earn an Oshkosh baccalaureate.

From this perspective, the best way to avoid the time and money sink that the general education curriculum had become was to begin in a two-year college or technical institution:

> We have way too many general education requirements that make going to a four-year school into a five- or six-year school and most of the gen. ed. classes are completely useless to our field in life. If I could redo my college experience I would have gone to a two-year school because I feel the gen. eds. made me waste my time and money. (confidential e-mail to the author)

And in fact, large numbers of Oshkosh students come to the university as transfers, principally from the University of Wisconsin System's two-year colleges and the state's two-year technical colleges. The Oshkosh class of 2008, that is, the class of first-year students in the fall of 2004, began with 1,520 full-time, first-time students. Even during that first year, however, the class received an infusion of 155 transfers who entered with first-year standing and 28 with sophomore standing. The next year brought an additional 115 transfers entering with sophomore standing and 60 with junior status. During the next two years, an additional 160 students entered with either junior or senior standing. In sum, then, the composite class of 2008 numbered 1,520 students who entered as full-time, first-time students and 478 transfers, or roughly 25 percent of a total class of 1,998 students.

Again, academic preparation does not appear to have played a major role in determining who persisted to graduation and who did not. Among first-year and sophomore transfers, on average those who left had achieved after their first two Oshkosh semesters a B−/C+ GPA, just a notch below the B/B− GPA of the persisters.

At the same time, the survival rate for these transfers generally mirrored the rates of their classmates who were not transfers. Of those who transferred to Oshkosh with junior or senior standing, 78.3 percent would graduate. The graduation rate among sophomore transfers was 64.3 percent, but for first-year transfers, the graduation rate was just 51 percent. As in the case of the Oshkosh first-year students who left the university without having earned a baccalaureate degree, most departures happened early. Of the first-year transfer students who did not persist, 56.6 percent left during their first three semesters. Two-thirds (63.8 percent) of the sophomore transfers who did not persist left during their first three semesters at the university. The fact that so many of those students left early reinforces the conclusion that Oshkosh's general education curriculum lacked the stickiness that in other, more selective institutions, converts first-year students and sophomores first into upperclassmen and later into graduates.

Time to Graduation

The other issue roiling student opinion was time to the degree. In this respect, the University of Wisconsin Oshkosh can be thought of as a poster child for the morphing of the traditional four-year undergraduate course of study into a five- or six-year experience that, as a student plaintively observed, "made me waste my time and money." Excluding from the analysis those students graduating from the College of Education and Human Services, which operates a five-year curriculum leading to certification and a master's degree, less than one-third of the full-time, first-time students who entered in the fall of 2004 and graduated did so in four years. Half of the graduates completed their degree sometime during their fifth year at Oshkosh, and the remaining 18 percent who graduated did so during their sixth year.

In part, students who changed their major or college of enrollment took somewhat longer to graduate, but changing one's educational goals was at best a partial explanation of what had gone awry at Oshkosh. More telling was the total number of credits students earned en route to graduation. Again excluding the graduates of the College of Education and Human Services, more than one-fourth of the graduates had accumulated more than 140 credits in a nominally 120-credit curriculum—more than an extra semester, which those students paid for and the university funded as part of its instructional budget. Of these graduates 20 percent accumulated between 130 and 140 credits— roughly an extra half-semester or more. Just over half of the students managed to graduate having earned fewer than 130 credits. None of these totals include the number of courses these students withdrew from or those in which they received a grade of F. The more credits a student earned, the longer that student took to graduate with a baccalaureate degree.

Two drivers accounted for most of the excess credits Oshkosh students were accumulating en route to graduation. The first was the temptation to double major. Students talked about the necessity of hedging one's bets in the job market. If one major was good, then two majors were twice as good. At Oshkosh, as at many four-year public comprehensive universities, majors, minors, specialties, and certificates were pursued much as boy scouts and girl scouts pursue merit badges—though the educational pursuit inevitably involved more courses, more time, and more money.

The second set of drivers involved the needs and ambitions of the departments offering the major. More students taking more courses over an extended period of time meant better coverage of an ever-expanding knowledge base and, not so coincidentally, more filled seats in the advanced courses that the faculty wanted most to teach. We were able to track the credit accumulations of students who graduated with one of the nineteen most popular majors. Again, we have excluded the Education and Human Services majors, all of whom required substantially more than the standard 120 credits over eight semesters.

The most popular majors produce, by all accounts, an odd list. In six majors—accounting, music education, art education, English, biology, and physical education—more than one-third of the graduates accumulated more than 140 credits en route to graduation. Among nursing and journalism majors, more than one-fourth of the graduates accumulated more than 140 credits. At the other end of the spectrum were six departments—human resources management, psychology, human services leadership, finance, criminal justice, and history—with fewer than 15 percent of their majors accumulating more than 140 credits en route to graduation.

There is no real pattern in this list, with the possible exception of the inclusion of various College of Business majors among those students who regularly graduated without having accumulated 140 credits or more. The explanation that best fits the idiosyncratic nature of the data is simply that departments felt relatively unconstrained in determining the requirements of their majors. From a student perspective, the apparent randomness of these requirements further added to the students' sense of confusion about how best to navigate the Oshkosh curriculum.

Making Reform Work

In the fall of 2011, we began sharing these results with the Oshkosh community. By then, however, a growing portion of both the faculty and the staff had come to the conclusion that something was basically wrong with Oshkosh's undergraduate curriculum. Most understood that the numbers didn't add up: too many first-year students who started at the university did not graduate, and too many of those who did took too long to qualify for an Oshkosh degree. The apparent eagerness of the university's accreditor, the HLC, to hold

Oshkosh accountable helped create a sense of urgency, but fundamentally a gnawing feeling that the university simply had to do better drove the reform effort.

Starting in the late 1990s, a growing number of faculty and staff supported by the provost began to think through how Oshkosh might better introduce its first-year students to both the university and the liberal arts. As in most successful campaigns there was an important set of benchmarks, starting with the chancellor and provost's charge to the university's Liberal Education Reform Team (LERT) in 2007, following another reminder from its accreditor that the university had to develop a more coherent general education program. The faculty and staff who joined LERT helped shape the campus dialogue surrounding many of the broader concepts and much of the language used to inform the campus about general education reform. LERT's first major recommendation provided essential learning outcomes, which the university adopted in 2008. In the spring of 2009, Lori Carrell, in her role as the director of CETL, began facilitating parallel discussions of both the means and the ends that would ultimately be embedded in the reform of the general education curriculum

The step-by-step reform campaign at UW Oshkosh teaches two important lessons about how American colleges and universities might best go about the business of reforming their curricula (and hence their production functions). First, haste truly makes waste. In the beginning there were neither bold announcements nor rhetorical flourishes summoning the campus to action. Outside the barbed recommendations of the HLC, there was little drama. Instead, the chancellor and the provost convened a series of quiet conversations asking the university what it knew about doing its work better. Small teams were dispatched to a variety of conferences and workshops, more than a few sponsored by AAC&U, though on returning to campus these first adopters were cautioned against engaging in too much "AAC&U-speak." Oshkosh's Center for Excellence in Teaching and Learning (CETL) received an infusion of new resources. With the provost's support and encouragement, Carrell launched a series of initiatives, including an annual Teaching and Learning Summit and, more important, a variety of small experimental courses that would become the testing ground for the reform effort that was beginning to gather momentum.

Carrell also exemplified the second lesson that Oshkosh's reform campaign teaches. Changing the curriculum is first and foremost a faculty responsibility. A communications specialist with twenty-plus years on the Oshkosh faculty and a full professor since 2002, Carrell understood from the outset that the kind of changes she, the provost, and others had come to pursue were not going to be put in place by administrative fiat. Indeed from the outset, the provost and his key decanal partners kept purposely in the background, with both leadership and worker-bee roles being performed by faculty remarkably like Carrell herself—good teachers, successful researchers, and quiet advocates. New monies supplied by the university's central administration, along with financial support from the University of Wisconsin System, helped fund the experimental courses, on the one hand, and on the other to send Oshkosh faculty and staff to conferences and workshops where they could size up other campuses' experiments. A steady stream of national teaching and learning experts, brought to campus by the campaign, often complemented these activities.

More reports followed using Carrell's Center as the repository of what was becoming an increasingly complex and intertwined set of proposals, suggestions, and cautions. The obligatory website was created complete with a discussion board. Summer workshops and task forces did much of the work, often with support, but not direction, from the office of the provost. In an appendix to the proposal that was ultimately put before the faculty in early 2012, Carrell and her colleagues reminded the campus of just how much consultation had occurred since 2008: "hundreds of members of the UW Oshkosh community have provided input to this reform process through dialogues, departmental meetings, online discussions, workshops, CETL book clubs, sessions during the Provost's Teaching and Learning Summit, e-mail, and conversations" (USP 2012, 30).

The big push came over the summer and fall of 2011, when the provost created a General Education Reform Team with thirty-two members, all but two of whom were regular members of the faculty, and a Leadership Team numbering just seven regular faculty members. Taking the Essential Learning Outcomes (2008) and the General Education Reform Framework approved by the Faculty Senate in 2011, the Leadership Team guided their colleagues through what at the time appeared to be an exhaustive process, intended to produce a detailed proposal to lay before the Faculty Senate and its two key committees focusing on educational policy and the curriculum.

Most of the work was done in the open, with drafts of proposals being posted on the CETL website and periodically summarized in meetings with the Faculty Senate and its committees by Carrell and others from the Leadership Team. Members of the Leadership Team also met with every unit on campus and conducted a number of small-group or one-on-one discussion sessions. Collectively, these efforts became a campaign—not unlike those waged in pursuit of policy goals in the public arena—in which key leaders and opinion makers within the faculty were both targeted and listened to and in which words and voices took on particular meanings. Here it is important to note that Carrell has written extensively on the role sermons and, by extension, preachers play in teaching a community to speak collectively. From the beginning, Carrell and the Leadership Team took note of not just who said what, but how they said it; then the team found ways to harvest those opinions to help establish a critical mass of faculty who were prepared to speak out, both proclaiming the need for change and supporting the specific proposals the larger faculty community was just beginning to consider.

My sense as a visitor to the campus during this period was that though Carrell and her colleagues consistently assumed their plans and proposals would be the subject of an expanding faculty dialogue, some within the faculty (how big a proportion was never clear) hadn't been paying attention and, as a result, believed they had been blindsided. A number of the faculty voiced this theme of surprise when given the opportunity to respond to a web-based survey of faculty opinion regarding the proposed USP:

> I am not entirely convinced that the current general education format needs to be changed. The problem is settling on goals and objectives. It seems as if we are changing the whole approach before we have even agreed on goals and objectives. How can you figure out how to do something before you have figured out what you are trying to accomplish? Even a cursory discussion among the faculty (if such a thing was actually allowed to occur) would reveal deep, deep, deep divisions, such as the very important distinction between HOW and WHY questions. For instance, consider the difference between these two questions: 1) How do we do more with less? 2) Why should we do more with less? See why this is important? Many of us feel as if decisions are being made, and this process advanced, without our input and concerns being taken into account. Every few minutes, the formulation changes, and we don't know how or why this has happened. (confidential e-mail to the author)

Another, more succinct version of this lament simply noted:

> I have been quite unconcerned and uninterested in our general education requirements until now. Perhaps that is a failing of mine but I think it is typical. We are so focused on doing well in our own area that there has been little attention paid to the common experience until now. (confidential e-mail to the author)

Among the truly harsh comments, about a handful in all, was one with the kind of critique the Leadership Team had feared all along:

> The new proposal is largely a collection of things the administration has been pushing for years plus a pet cause of some. It is incompatible with curriculum being the primary responsibility of faculty. It is obese on skills and raising student self-esteem with disciplinary content on a starvation diet. It needs considerable work just to simplify it. (confidential e-mail to the author)

Some of the faculty, who began feeling that they had been left out of the loop, eventually decided, however, that in fact an ongoing conversation was actually moving in the right direction—or as one faculty member put it: "In my experience it takes several conversations with those in the know to really begin to understand the proposed changes. But once understood, the rationale for the changes is arguable" (confidential e-mail to the author).

The majority of the faculty commentary was more supportive, including a gushing congratulation that managed a succinct summary of what the reform team had asked the faculty to endorse:

> This proposal is amazing, and I can't quite believe people have put together something this good at this University. I love the way it builds distinctive campus initiatives (particularly Sustainability, Intercultural Knowledge, and Civic Learning) into the curriculum; I love the learning communities for first-year students; I love that there is a mechanism built into the program (the advanced writing course) to enable students to synthesize their "University Studies" experience. This is a coherent, purposeful program. While it seems to maintain some or most of the breadth of the old check-box model (requiring students to take courses in a variety of disciplines), it is also far more purposeful and focused, and really, really distinctive. Bravo! (confidential e-mail to the author)

The faculty survey was conducted just after the Teaching and Learning Summit that presented the proposal and just before Carrell and her colleagues began their final push to ensure a positive response from the Faculty Senate. First, the Senate's Academic Policy General Education Subcommittee met to grill Carrell and wanted to be certain that the interests and concerns of the faculty writ large had been taken into account. Next came the Senate's Academic Policy Committee and another session focusing on the process of approval and implementation. Both committees voted unanimously in favor of the proposal. The discussion by the full Senate raised no new questions or concerns. On March 13 the CETL website gave a simple denouement proclaiming: "This proposal for the reform of general education at UW Oshkosh was approved by the Faculty Senate on Tuesday afternoon, March 13, 2012" (CETL 2012). In a subsequent phone call, Carrell reported that Senate approval had come with but a single dissenting vote.

The Importance of Being Earnest

I have focused on the process by which Carrell and the Leadership Team persuaded not just a majority but, in fact, nearly all of their colleagues that it was time to break the logjam of the past that too often resulted in universitywide curriculum initiatives that offered little more than negotiated peace treaties in which departments sought to garner sufficient enrollments to justify their faculty lines. The content of the reform proposal, however, is itself a significant achievement, echoing many concepts and strategies that I have made an integral part of my own Checklist for Change. Like Gaul, Oshkosh's new University Studies Program curriculum (the new label replaces the former general education designation) can be divided into three parts: Question, Exploration, and Connection.

In the Question part of the new curriculum first-year students enrolling at Oshkosh would begin their collegiate education by taking a three-course sequence in which each course would address a different signature question:

> *Focus*:   Sustainability
> *Question*:   How do people understand and create a more sustainable world?
> *Focus*:   Civic Knowledge and Engagement
> *Question*:   How do people understand and engage in community life?

> *Focus*: Intercultural Knowledge and Competence
> *Question*: How do people understand and bridge cultural differences? (USP 2012, 5–7)

The first of these signature questions was, to some degree, already infused in Oshkosh's undergraduate curriculum. The focus on civic engagement includes an effort to have the university better connect with the Oshkosh community. The signature question focusing on intercultural knowledge is part of a continuing effort by a university, with little cultural or ethnic diversity, to have its students better prepared for the reality of a multicultural world. The first Quest course a first-year student takes will be limited to twenty-five students; thereafter, the remaining two Quest courses will be limited to fifty students each. There will also be a pairing of the first two Quest courses a student takes with a course in either writing or communication such that, each semester, first-year students will take 40 percent of their courses with the same group of students, thus forming a mini-cohort or learning community. Finally, the students' initial Quest course is also expected to address issues of acculturation to the university and the strategies students will require to successfully make it to graduation, hopefully in just four years at Oshkosh.

The Exploration component of the USP curriculum will comprise a menu of courses in three clusters: Culture (humanities and the performing arts); Nature (mathematics and two lab science courses); and Society (social sciences). As the comment I quoted above suggests, this part of the reform package looked pretty much the same as the bulk of the old general education curriculum, but there is an important exception. While introduction to the major courses could qualify as Exploration courses (on occasion even a Quest Course, if it fulfilled the matched criteria), the proposal promised renewed scrutiny of all University Studies courses to make sure that they were providing the Essential Learning Outcomes that AAC&U had developed in the 1990s and Oshkosh had modified and then adopted in 2008.

The Connection component of the Universities Studies requirement will be a three-credit course, most likely taken in the second semester of the sophomore year, in which one of the three signature questions addressed earlier becomes the focus of an advanced writing course. Here the stated purpose is to integrate and synthesize the knowledge and skills acquired throughout the University Studies curriculum.

To this outsider, most striking about the new Universities Studies curriculum and the process used to secure its adoption was the role that normative judgments played in shaping the reform movement. My sense was that the Leadership Team, in particular, through conversations and visits to campuses elsewhere, had developed a well-articulated theory as to what would work best at Oshkosh. While the members of the team in general, and Lori Carrell in particular, talked about their reforms deriving from "research-based teaching," they had proceeded largely with beliefs that what they were proposing was right—and that it would necessarily succeed. One reason they were eager to have the Penn research team involved, even late in the day, was their sense that sooner or later they would need to be able to better document the problem they hoped the new University Studies curriculum would help solve. But they had not begun with those problems; rather they had proceeded, as faculty have historically proceeded, by assuming they knew what would work and why.

And that is the third and final lesson the Oshkosh experience teaches. Almost all reform movements intent on reshaping academic processes and outcomes face the irony that detailed evidence of an existing problem has seldom proved sufficiently motivating. Rather, faculty will proclaim that they do what is right—what their experience, training, and interaction with both students and their research tell them to do. In too many cases today, however, doing what is right means sitting tight. The faculty at the University of Wisconsin Oshkosh exemplified an important exception. The card Carrell and the Leadership Team played most often was the faculty's sense that they could do better—for their students and for themselves. What was involved was not so much data or evidence as pride—pride of place and pride of scholarship. It was a pride not unlike that expressed by the Whittier faculty as they struggled to shore up the financial core of their college. And it was a pride not unlike that of the faculty at the University of Minnesota Rochester as they sought to develop new teaching and learning strategies in order to better achieve the learning outcomes they sought to define for their new campus.

10 | A Stronger Faculty Voice

Despite my fondness for the Ecclesiastes metaphor, American higher education may at last have reached a moment of inflection—or as Robert Reich would want to say, "It's just possible, maybe even this year, that American colleges and universities will have to change." To be sure, I have made such predictions before, only to have the moment come and go, leaving things pretty much as they were before.

Here are the three reasons why change may finally be upon us—change that can either rejuvenate the academy or transform it in ways we would neither recognize nor celebrate.

On Being Lost in a Financial Desert

In the 1980s, D. Bruce Johnstone, then the chancellor of the State University of New York (SUNY) and a founding member of the Pew Higher Education Roundtable, told colleagues that the best way, perhaps the only way, to have colleges and universities cost less would be to starve them for revenue. His implication was that when facing the prospect of a major budgetary shortfall, colleges and universities would prove capable of cutting those things that mattered least and/or had the fewest advocates outside the academy itself. Johnstone's bromide was then being tested in New York, and, sure enough, SUNY's institutions reduced enough of their costs to rebalance their budgets, though not, as it turned out, to alter their business models or recast their educational programs.

Most faculty in public higher education, along with some of their administrative colleagues, still want to argue that what has worked in the past will work again now—that state economies, once healthy, will again yield sufficient tax revenues to allow publicly funded institutions to say, "What has been will be again."

Most commentators, however, believe that will not be the case. After thirty-plus years of increased operating costs substantially in excess of inflation, public higher education is now, and will be for the foreseeable future, on a revenue diet more stringent than Bruce Johnstone ever imagined. In the spring of 2012, the Demos organization published John Quinterno's *The Great Cost Shift*, which starkly laid out just how extensive the states' disinvestment in public higher education had already become:

- A review of financial data from 1990 onward suggests that a structural change in state support for higher education is under way.
- While state spending on higher education increased by $10.5 billion in absolute terms from 1990 to 2010, in relative terms, state funding for higher education declined. Real funding per public full-time equivalent student dropped by 26.1 percent from 1990–1991 to 2009–2010.
- Over the past 20 years there has been a breakdown in the historical funding pattern of recessionary cuts and expansionary rebounds. The length of time for higher education funding to recover following recessions has lengthened for every downturn since 1979 with early evidence suggesting that the recovery from the Great Recession will be no different. (Quinterno 2012, 3)

It is private liberal arts colleges, and not public institutions, that have worried the most about whether their business model is broken or their current educational programs sustainable. At the same time *The Great Cost Shift* was being published, Swarthmore and Lafayette colleges, with funding supplied by *US News & World Report*, among others, convened a three-day conference attended by more than 50 presidents and 150 senior administrators from the nation's top-ranked liberal arts colleges. Convened to explore "The Future of the Liberal Arts College in America and Its Leadership Role in Education Around the World," the Swarthmore-Lafayette conference was, as *Inside Higher Ed* observed, but one of several such liberal arts college gatherings scheduled over the next few months, each asking, "would liberal arts colleges . . . have to make significant changes in the next few years if they are to remain relevant (or present) in the current educational market?" (Kiley 2012a)

The speakers at the Swarthmore-Lafayette conference, major liberal arts college leaders and faculty all, found themselves inherently torn between what they believed to be in the best interest of American higher education and what they were observing in their daily lives as academic leaders. Or, as *Inside Higher Ed*'s Kevin Kiley observed, "A common refrain from the conference was that it's not the liberal arts colleges that are broken, but rather the conversation that they have been caught up in." The convening presidents, Rebecca Chopp of Swarthmore and Daniel Weiss of Lafayette, put the matter directly: Chopp said more softly, "We need a narrative that provides a rationale to our many publics and guides our decision making and life together"; Weiss spoke more sharply, "We must continue to stay the course, not make concessions to a population that does not understand what we do, and make the case that what we do is valuable" (Kiley 2012b).

Vassar's president, Catharine Bond Hill, supplied a tougher set of comments. A veteran of the Williams College economics department, which over the last three decades has supplied no fewer than five presidents to elite liberal arts colleges, Hill began by describing the complex dance of costs, sticker price, and net price at institutions like Vassar. Echoing Immerwahr's *Iron Triangle*, she said the task at hand was to maintain affordability while preserving quality. More could be done, for example, to facilitate student borrowing, including more income-contingent loans. But exercising the price option would only buy so much time. Eventually, she suggested, liberal arts colleges will have to take a hard look at their costs and ask, what can we stop doing? And "Why haven't we innovated? We have, but in ways that have pushed costs up." Ahead was a reconsideration of the ways institutions like Vassar allocated faculty time, perhaps including a rebalancing of teaching, research, and governance duties. "There's room for shifting faculty time to high-value inputs with students," ever so gently touching private higher education's third rail. And then she went further. "I think we could all sign on to no more climbing walls and saunas. . . . But what about average class sizes and teaching loads, and the number of languages being taught? It's much more difficult to agree on those things" (Hoover 2012).

It was left to *Inside Higher Ed*'s Kiley to suggest where the balance lay, for most of the leaders attending the Swarthmore-Lafayette conference:

> Despite significant looming challenges related to affordability, access, public skepticism about value, changing student demographics, and the influence of technology on students and education—which all the attendees readily acknowledged—most of the presidents of the liberal arts colleges here this week aren't planning on substantively changing how their institutions operate or their economic models. (Kiley 2012b)

Both in public and private, it remains fair to say, too many institutional leaders are still whistling in the dark. But there is also a growing subtext that says economically driven change is now possible, indeed probable, perhaps even inevitable. The important question that remains is whether the nation's principal colleges and universities will shape that change or fall victim to it.

Leaderless in Seattle, Lost in Indianapolis

The second of the circumstances now forcing changes in how colleges and universities educate their students and organize themselves is a growing recognition that higher education in general, and more elite higher education in particular, is in danger of becoming isolated—less relevant, more selfish in its defense of its own interests, more dismissive of those who keep asking why costs have risen so outlandishly.

For much of the last decade, the absence of strong national leaders speaking for and to the nation's colleges and universities has helped explain how and why American higher education became so moribund and why the schools have too often been unresponsive to the changes that swirled about them. Now a pair of aggressive, self-aggrandizing, and wondrously wealthy foundations, which have taken as their task the reshaping of the nation's colleges and universities, is filling that void. To their supporters, principally policy makers and wonks from outside the academy, the Bill and Melinda Gates and Lumina foundations, in Doug Lederman's words, see themselves as having "driven more significant (and beneficial) change in five years than American higher education has seen in decades. To their critics, the two behemoths and a band of collaborating groups and think tanks (call them the 'completion mafia') have hijacked the national agenda for higher education and drowned out alternative perspectives" (Lederman 2012).

The occasion of Lederman's commentary was a paper delivered to the annual meeting of the American Educational Research Association that sought to document just how much traditional higher education philanthropy had changed and how it had become a handmaiden to a campaign to make the nation's colleges and universities less focused on scholarship and more willing to make participation and affordability the principal, if not the sole, measures of their accountability. Braving the wrath of the two remaining philanthropic supporters of research on higher education, the authors of the paper, Cassie Hall and Scott L. Thomas, argued that Gates and Lumina: "have taken up a set of methods—strategic grant-making, public policy advocacy, the funding of intermediaries, and collaboration with government— that illustrate their direct and unapologetic desire to influence policy and practice in numerous higher education arenas" (quoted in Lederman 2012).

The assessment was gingerly put, and, as a consequence, still wide of the mark. Not that long ago a handful of major foundations and their smaller partners—Ford, Pew, Carnegie, Mellon, Kellogg along with Teagle, Danforth, and Atlantic Philanthropic Services (APS)— provided much of the venture capital that underwrote research and experimentation across higher education. To be sure, much of the grant- making was scattershot, often reflecting the personal interests of the foundations' officers and trustees. But even more of their grants provided the seed funds for the innovations that from 1950 onward made American higher education an enterprise envied by everybody. In those days, if you had a good idea you could take it to a foundation— and occasionally to one of the research programs funded by the federal government—and just maybe get the funding you required to conduct and disseminate your research.

At some point during the 1990s, the world of philanthropy began to change. Some of the players ended their support for higher education research (Pew, Kellogg, and APS, for example) or closed down altogether (Danforth). Grants became harder to acquire as the remaining players became more skeptical that improving higher education would lead to the kind of social benefits to which the foundations had turned their attention. Then emerged the two new players, the organizations Lederman labels "megafoundations," Gates and Lumina. Here, drawing on the occasion of the Hall and Thomas critique, Lederman's story continued:

> But the unmistakable shift that the two foundations have led in higher education grant-making, Hall and Thomas argue, has been away from giving to institutions and toward closely collaborating with state and federal policy makers and a series of "intermediaries" (nonprofit groups created with the foundations' funds, think tanks, consultants, etc.) who are interested in carrying out the philanthropies' agenda. The change has been driven, the Hall and Thomas paper argued, by "an increasing level of distrust that higher education institutions can successfully enact reforms that will result in meaningful changes to our postsecondary system." (Lederman 2012)

Since 2007 both Lumina and Gates have sponsored a string of reports that document the problem by using language full of thunder and lightning (a distant cousin to smoke and mirrors) but woefully short of any notion as to how to actually fix the problems so elegantly and persistently highlighted. In a sense, it is Charles Miller and his hopes for the Spellings Commission all over again. This singular message is clear and to the point: to avoid further shame, it is time for higher education to fix itself, choosing leaders and managers who know how to corral a reluctant faculty and move forward with an agenda that ensures that all Americans will benefit equally from the nation's investments in its colleges and universities.

The problem is that this change strategy has largely marginalized the professoriate at the institutions the foundations are seeking to reshape. Faculty become part of the problem, but not part of the solution. This approach turns higher education's traditional pecking order on its head, making community colleges and public comprehensive universities the major arenas, in general, in which the battle for more completions and lower prices must be fought.

This marginalization of the faculty, particularly those at the elite liberal arts colleges and major research universities is, I think, no accident. Most of the staff at the foundations likely to support higher education in general (and/or those having joined with Lumina and Gates to push the completion and affordability agenda) are highly educated, often possessing a doctorate or other advanced degree. Remarkably few, however, have ever been a full-time faculty member at a college or university. They are, for the most part, eloquent writers and commentators, but not often scholars or teachers. They can tell us what we need to accomplish, but cannot tell us how, having never themselves walked the path they now want us to travel.

The careers of the two foundation officers most responsible for the Lumina and Gates initiatives—Hillary Pennington at Gates and Jamie Merisotis at Lumina—exemplify how separate the worlds of academic and foundation leadership have become. Pennington, a 1983 graduate of the Yale School of Management, started her career as a senior fellow at the Center for American Progress and then became the founder and CEO of Jobs for the Future, an organization she led for twenty-two years. After Jobs for the Future, she joined Gates as head of the foundation's Postsecondary Education Initiative, departing in 2011. Merisotis was the founding president of the Institute for Higher Education Policy, a Washington, D.C., think tank launched with the support of the Kellogg Foundation in 1993. He joined Lumina as president and CEO in 2008. Prior to the founding of the Institute for Higher Education Policy, Merisotis, a Bates College graduate, served as executive director of the National Commission on Responsibilities for Financing Postsecondary Education, a bipartisan commission appointed by the U.S. president and congressional leaders. He was largely responsible for the commission's 1993 report *Making Colleges Affordable Again.*

Merisotis has also been the most forthcoming of the new foundation executives in explaining what they are trying to accomplish. He told Lederman on the eve of the public presentation of the Hall and Thomas paper: "I think it's very important to recognize that Lumina sees that unique capacity that it has as having dimensions that take us well beyond the traditional grant-making role." From Lederman's perspective it was a pretty slender reed to stand upon, and he noted that Merisotis, "while conceding that Lumina's 'advocacy' approach may differ from how other higher education foundations have behaved in the past, he compared its work to the Ford Foundation's advocacy for civil rights in the 1960s, when it 'tried to build public will, inform and influence public policy, and worked with a diverse set of actors in the field'" (Lederman 2012). Given that Lumina's efforts have yet to change even the trajectory of completions or flatten the trend of increased college costs, the more apt comparison just might be Lloyd Bentsen's reply to Dan Quayle in their 1988 vice presidential debate, when the latter tried to wrap himself in the mantle of John F. Kennedy, "Senator, you're no Jack Kennedy."

Merisotis, no doubt, would respond (and with some justification) that Lumina has fundamentally changed the debate over what is wrong with American higher education. Though he would not likely add the following, it would be equally true: Lumina has, in the process, helped reduce the public standing of the nation's research universities and their elite liberal arts college partners. Does it matter? To be honest, I am not sure. Unless Lumina's grant-making produces more results in the future than it has in the past, the foundation's marginalizing of tenure-track faculty and our role in reshaping our institutions will hardly be remembered. If faculty in general, and those at the top of their field in particular, come, however, to understand and take action by accepting responsibility for controlling college costs and understanding how and why too few students complete their college educations, then Merisotis and the others can take credit for an unintended consequence that just happens to achieve the larger goals they set out to accomplish. That possibility—that enough major college and university faculty will perceive the dangers inherent in having been sidelined by the foundations' completion and affordability agendas—just might prompt a more purposeful response on the part of the professoriate in much the same way as life in a financial desert has, thus making change, if not more palatable, at least more likely.

Houston, We Have an Alternative

In much the same way, the emergence of a market-savvy for-profit higher education sector is making change possible—and that is the third of my triad of changing conditions that may allow higher education to escape its Ecclesiastes moment. Since the turn of the twenty-first century, for-profit higher education has been the target of a host of regulators and influential legislators decrying the growth of the sector. For-profit institutions, they argue, are too often little more than degree mills, almost wholly focused on vocational training at the expense of liberal learning. The most successful of these institutions succeed by making promises about job placements and salaries they cannot keep. The for-profit sector, these critics point out, is uniquely dependent on the largesse of the federal government's student aid programs.

Other commentators, however, celebrate the success of for-profit colleges and universities as harbingers of things to come, and they offer them as prime examples of what Clayton Christensen has called a "disruptive innovation." From this perspective, the for-profit sector is cast as an emerging force capable of upending higher education's established order. For-profit higher education is credited with having reached out to markets long ignored by traditional higher education (adult education, for example) and investing in alternative teaching modalities (online education, for example) that offer the promise of lower costs as well as higher completion rates. How else, these commentators ask, can one explain how an enterprise that was once viewed as second rate and of dubious quality has come to account for nearly 12 percent of all higher education enrollments in the United States?

Perhaps what most intrigues these commentators is the possibility that for-profit institutions can offer an alternate model for a higher education enterprise: more cost conscious, more welcoming of working and disadvantaged students, and more interested in developing new ways to teach and train. My colleague William Massy has summed up this side of the argument as well as anyone. He begins by labeling the largest and most successful for-profits as "industrialized universities." What is important about them is that they go about their business in wholly different, what Massy calls, "industrialized" ways. There is, for example, an emphasis on top-down design "using teams of their own experts and consultants from across the higher education sector. Then they develop optimal delivery and assessment strategies that are replicated again and again using relatively low-cost (though still professional) labor. Online and hybrid teaching approaches often are utilized, but the industrialization model does not depend on any particular teaching methodology." Standardization leads to low incremental costs and offers the additional advantage of being "a powerful enabler of continuous improvement" (Massy 2011, 1).

The importance of Massy's commentary lies in the notion that for-profit universities as "industrialized" entities produce a different product in an importantly different way. Because design is top down, it involves substantial front-investment and a cadre of course designers. The educational products are standardized; they are assessed relentlessly and delivered by teams of internal experts and consultants.

Wholly missing is the idea of traditional faculty who own their own courses and who both teach and contribute to the knowledge base that underlies their teaching. In terms of the organization of their production functions, Massy's industrialized universities are nearly orthogonal to the academy as we have come to know it. Indeed, in ways that all too few within the academy recognize, the industrialized model Massy describes is becoming a full-blown alternative that could, over time, become the dominant model for postsecondary education, save that which is offered by major research universities and elite liberal arts colleges.

The most obvious difference between what has been and what could be, as I have already noted, is the change in the role of the faculty, but that change actually flows from a more basic shift involving the very purposes of higher education. Industrialized universities pursue educational purposes more aligned with training than with liberal or traditional learning. They place a premium on students having and purposefully pursuing short-term goals—often the certification or licensure that earns the successful student a quick and remunerative entry into the labor market. Most such training is, in fact, tactical as well as vocational. In the best of these for-profit entities, students are provided clear as well as organized pathways to the degrees or the other outcomes they seek.

In many ways this organizational structure is ready-made for the completion and affordability agenda being championed by Lumina and Gates, but, as for-profits, few of Massy's industrialized universities are eligible for philanthropic grants. Instead, Lumina and Gates have focused their attention on community colleges and less selective public comprehensive universities because they too are likely to focus more on training than on liberal learning and are more likely to develop curricula that employ the kind of top-down design principles now extensively used by the most successful for-profit institutions. All that stands in the way of having community colleges, in particular, come to resemble Massy's industrialized universities are the labor unions that represent community college faculty, yet even that obstacle is surmountable if the community college can provide sufficient as well as sustainable levels of compensation. Faculty at public comprehensive institutions are more likely to object to the introduction of a more industrialized mode of organization; then again, those institutions, along with very small private liberal arts colleges, are now and for the foreseeable future facing the greatest financial challenges.

Though only an extrapolated hypothesis, these trends suggest a possible future in which a dual-track system of postsecondary education emerges in the United States—ironically one not unlike the dual-track university/polytechnic system that held sway in the United Kingdom through 1992. As it does now, one track would comprise the 60-plus major research universities belonging to the Association of American Universities (AAU), another 125 or so research intensive institutions (for the most part private universities), and an additional 50 or so elite private liberal arts colleges. The training track would comprise all other institutions, both for-profit and not-for-profit, offering accredited degrees.

In the training or polytechnic-like track, curricula would become increasingly standardized as well as vocational. In this tier that educated upward of 85 percent of all undergraduates and absorbed upward of 90 percent of federal student aid funds the gainful employment rules would most likely apply. The track's instructional staff would likely have a diminishing proportion of PhDs educated at research universities, would see and define their roles as almost exclusively instructional, and over time would likely surrender their governance roles in return for long-term financial security.

Life among the nation's scholarly and traditional institutions would initially be unchanged. Tenure would be awarded to those with a demonstrated capacity for research. Deans and department chairs would be selected by and from the faculty, as would provosts, though perhaps to a lesser extent, and presidents would increasingly come from outside the ranks of the faculty. Individual faculty members would continue to act as independent agents responsible for choosing how and what they taught in courses for which they alone were responsible.

But change probably would come in unwelcome ways. There would be fewer graduate students to train. Legislators in states with major public flagship universities would begin asking why institutions focusing on training and completions were able to provide outcome measures while faculty at research-intensive institutions continued to insist that the advantages they provided their students were immeasurable, at least in the short run. Top-tier institutions would increasingly become bastions of the well-to-do. As such they would face renewed assaults, charging them with becoming "gated communities" no longer deserving the special attention and privileges they had historically enjoyed (for example, see Kroll 2009). Ultimately, I suspect, either the accreditors or the federal government, flushed with the success of remaking the polytechnic-like track of the industry more responsive as well as less costly, would seek to curtail those privileges through either outright regulation or changes in the tax code. The ultimate result would be a diminishing of the capacity of the American professoriate to champion change, exemplify the importance of the life of the mind, or serve as models of a just and fair society.

Each element of my triad of dislodging events—a growing scarcity of financial resources, a diminished faculty voice eclipsed by a new cadre of policy wonks and their wealthy foundation patrons, and the emergence of a dual-track system of postsecondary education—represent changes already under way. The question is not whether a dual-track system will emerge but rather what will be the relative size of each track. If the drift of the last decade continues—if faculty at both elite and comprehensive institutions continue to sit on the sidelines—my best guess is that an 80–20 split will prevail, with the entire for-profit and community college sectors, along with most pubic comprehensive institutions, aligning with the training/polytechnic track. These institutions would come to exemplify Massy's idea of an industrial university.

In this scenario, faculty at traditional and scholarly focused institutions would likely remain passive, pursuing their own interests and careers separately while largely accepting a further diminished public role. Alternately, these faculty might grow more petulant, lamenting ever more loudly that academic purposes and the life of the mind are too easily being dismissed and ending with a Churchillian shout, "Up with this I will not put."

The third possibility is that my triad of dislodging events will combine to form a proverbial perfect storm. Change would be more difficult to predict as well as to thwart. Unlike in previous epochs, the past would not be the guarantor of the future. My guess is that a dual-track system of postsecondary education would likely still emerge, but one in which the two tiers would be more closely balanced as well as linked, one with the other, through a variety of partnerships and joint ventures. There would likely be greater borrowing of successes both up and down the food chain—fueled, in large part, by recognition that increasing completion rates would be everyone's business.

It is, then, just possible that emerging from this perfect storm are neither battered institutions nor a diminished role for faculty, but rather an enterprise in which faculty, both singularly and collectively, succeed in having scholarship and learning retain their central importance as values to which all of higher education is committed. For this future to win the faculty must be newly willing to reconceptualize their responsibilities—to their institutions, to one another, to their students, and to the communities from which their students come—as Lori Carrell and her colleagues did at Oshkosh.

There is some evidence that similar stirrings and reform efforts are beginning among some departments within the nation's most prestigious and research-oriented universities. The Stanford Department of English, for example, recently found itself confronting the problem of a diminishing number of Stanford undergraduates interested in majoring in English. What followed was a three-year process of self-discovery that led to a redefinition of the scope and purpose of the major along with a major recasting of how individual faculty members worked with one another to deliver the curriculum. In the *ADE Bulletin* the department's chair, Jennifer Summit, described what she and her colleagues did, using language that makes clear the context in which a faculty-driven reform effort must take place:

> My department became convinced of the need to revise its curriculum after surveying our majors and recent graduates, followed by a series of focus groups. These told us that students were very happy with the individual classes they took, most of which we offer as small, intense seminars whose sharp focus is honed by the time constraints of the quarter system. At the same time, our majors and graduates felt that the major as an aggregate lacked coherence. Again and again, students asked us plaintively for a big picture that would supply connections between and across their classes: they confirmed what many of us have long perceived and lamented, that they lack a basic grid of historical knowledge that could give broader perspective and unity to their individual classes. Repeatedly, they told us that they felt the absence of an arc in which their classes could fit together; and in the focus groups, they passionately expressed their collective wish for a historical core or survey class that could provide the background and connections that they lacked. (Summit 2010, 47)

What followed was not just a recasting of the subjects to be taught, but also a reconceptualization of how that curriculum would be taught, including a renewed sense of collective responsibility.

> We created a three-quarter sequence aimed at delivering broad, synthetic perspectives and organized around literary-historical throughlines and paradigm shifts over the broad sweep of thirty weeks, with the collaborative participation of many faculty members from many fields. In so doing, we strongly agree with the Teagle report's call for seeing the major as "a collaborative educational project." Where the report's authors offer team teaching as a way of enlivening pedagogy, we see it as a necessary disciplinary bridge across the historical isolation of the fields. The collaborative and team production of this new sequence is essential to its character and differentiates it from the old survey or core, in which the major periods were defined as sequential yet autonomous. (Summit 2010, 51)

My hope, though I confess it to be just that, a hope, is that in increasing numbers faculty at institutions committed to the traditions of scholarship will use their standing and smarts to define and then implement the kind of changes Carrell and Summit have pursued.

The Things We Must Do—Together

In the twenty-some years since Bill Massy and I worked out the logic for the *Policy Perspectives* essay, "The Lattice and the Ratchet," most of my published research and commentary have been shaped by the conviction that higher education is the faculty's business. In the kind of perfect storm I have imagined, it is what we do and what we take responsibility for that will matter most. On our teaching and explorations will depend the academy's continuing commitment to the scholarship of learning and discovery. Achieving that future as opposed to one of diminished faculty roles will require forceful but, more important, collective action on our part. As individuals we will have to abandon that sense of ourselves as independent actors and agents. The financial crisis of the new century has taught us that talking about "my money" or "my students" or even "my research" brings few benefits and no friends. We need to be frank about the need to share the money. We will have to understand that we neither own nor possess our students, though we have an important responsibility to ensure their successful learning. Hence my checklist for change begins with a more detailed understanding of just how much we faculty must change, sooner rather than later.

✓ *Relearn the Importance of Collective Action*

I would start by having faculty relearn the importance of collective action—to talk less about shared governance, which too often has become a rhetorical sword to wield against an aggrandizing administration, and to talk instead about sharing responsibility for the work to be done together. Already much of the research we do, we do with others—colleagues in our own departments and institutions as well as colleagues literally across the globe. Collaborative research, it turns out, is more productive, more efficient, and, most of the time, more intriguing as well as more fulfilling.

Collaborative teaching confers the same benefits, provided that there are both shared purposes and shared designs. Collaborative teaching requires first and foremost an articulated consensus as to what a student is expected to learn and the modalities by which that learning is expected to take place. Team teaching is one form of col-laboration that works, but individual courses taught to a cohort of students whose schedules are either identical or nearly identical bring the same benefits. The kind of paired courses that Whittier has developed also establishes similar benefits, when two faculty mem-bers agree to teach different aspects of the same subject, often cross-ing disciplinary lines, to a common group of students. In each case, the first benefit of collaboration is the necessity of the faculty to talk with each other about their teaching—how each defines the problem or subject that is at the center of the course, what each wants to accomplish, and how each would assess the progress of the students they are teaching together.

There is a similar need for more collaborative work that turns a department into what might best be described as a learning cooperative—shared tasks, shared responsibilities, shared purposes and goals. Doing so probably means more meetings and places a premium on identifying those colleagues who, as chair, will prove to be effective facilitators. Ultimately a successful learning cooperative yields the capacity to invest substantial energy in common projects both within the depart-ment and across the institution.

✓ Put an End to Rhetorical Excesses

To increase collaboration among faculty, and between faculty and administrative units, will require a de-escalation of the rhetoric now too regularly employed to diminish and embarrass perceived opponents. The battle in New Hampshire described earlier in this volume is a prime example of the use of overheated language whose purpose all too often is limiting compromise and making collab-oration difficult. Faculty who enjoy these battles will want to argue that strongly held opinions, particularly when the rights and autonomy of the faculty are at stake, require strong language that forcefully draws lines in the sand that no right-thinking member of the faculty will want to cross.

Instead, those faculty who have better things to do mostly with-draw, leaving their more combative colleagues to duke it out either with each other or, as is more often the case, with the administration or the trustees or some misanthropic governor or state legislator. In this environment sustained, idea-centered discussions become a rarity—too much shouting, too many arguments that become personal, and as a consequence, too little listening as opposed to broadcasting.

I am aware that I am perilously close to arguing that ending the marginalization of faculty requires that we behave better. For that minority of the faculty, who have defined themselves as "take-no-prisoners" combatants, I am arguing for exactly that—civil behavior. My real concern, however, is with the great majority of us who have simply abandoned the fray and thereby allow the combatants to erect nearly impermeable barriers to the kind of collaboration that, on the one hand, yields a renewed sense of shared responsibility and, on the other, makes certain that we as faculty play a leading role in determining how our institutions respond to the changes swirling about us.

✓ Empower a Different Kind of Faculty Leader

The next battle we will have to fight is to make certain that our leading scholars are those we choose to lead our faculty organizations. Forty-five years ago, when I started as an assistant professor at the University of Pennsylvania, the lions of the Senate dominated academic discussions across campus. They were both experienced leaders and major scholars. Over time, the Senate at Penn, like Senates on most campuses, atrophied. Those who served were well meaning, but they were seldom if ever an institution's academic stars. In a world in which faculty have become independent contractors in all but name, no one is much interested in mastering the discipline of herding cats. Service on an institution's budget and priorities committee (or its equivalent) still attracts top-name academics, but they act more like trustees exercising a watching brief over their institution than like active players in the development of policies and strategies. That, nearly everyone now argues, is the task of the administration.

It is interesting to note that in the reforming of the curriculum at the University of Wisconsin Oshkosh, the Senate and its committees were the final arbiters of the process. The heavy lifting, however, was done by a cadre of senior and influential faculty that the provost recruited to serve on one or more of the special taskforces charged with bringing a coherent set of proposals for the Senate's vote. Today, that is a good strategy for ensuring that reform is a faculty enterprise. For the long term, however, those same faculty who led the reform effort as members of one or more of the ad hoc taskforces will need to take up leadership positions within the Senate itself so that body increasingly becomes an initiator of the kind of complex reforms Oshkosh has now put in place.

It is actually relatively easy to know how important the Senate (or its equivalent) and its leaders are on any campus. There are two obvious telltale signs: are the faculty's elected leaders still actively doing research, and are those who run the Senate most often permanent associate professors whose scholarly careers plateaued shortly after they earned tenure? A further sign of a moribund elected faculty organization is a slate of officers who have been in charge for a long stretch of time—in some cases, decades. These men and women have, in fact, become professional senators, as much interested in protecting their positions and privileges as preserving the autonomy of the faculty.

The solution, to repeat the observation made earlier, lies not in changing the rules or procedures of the Senate, but in establishing an academic context in which a different set of scholars lead the Senate and its executive committee. From an administrative perspective, it is a chicken and egg problem. Most presidents, provosts, and deans would welcome the faculty taking a more active leadership role, provided that the men and women the faculty choose to exercise that responsibility are senior, serious, and interested in exploring alternative means for achieving the institution's mission.

Campuses with collective bargaining face a more complex challenge exemplified by the union-sparked controversy at the University of New Hampshire. There, as a bargaining tactic, the union temporarily brought discussion of the modest changes in how UNH went about its business to a standstill. In concert with the UNH Faculty Senate, the union claimed it was protecting the faculty from unwanted changes in the calendar and perhaps from a more major realignment of instructional responsibilities and obligations. Almost uniformly, faculty unions have made protection of the status quo the standard by which to judge their success, along with their ability to win salary increases for their members—the tasks one expects a good, well-connected, well-organized union to undertake.

The protective role these unions play is well understood by the faculty despite their willingness to lament the rhetorical excesses of the union's leadership. As before, the union's trump card remains the fact that its leadership is democratically elected. At UNH, for example, about every third electoral cycle, there emerges from within the faculty an opposition slate that runs on the theme that the union's leadership is holding the university back or that it has been in power too long or that its bargaining tactics are holding the university up to public ridicule. When the ballots are counted, however, the opposition learns, once again, that it has garnered no more than a third of the votes. As long as faculty at unionized institutions like UNH perceive the union as protecting them from unwanted change, they will leave the union leadership in place. Having retained their power and perquisites, the union's leaders will quickly remind their administrative adversaries that they intend to keep the Faustian bargain they have struck with their faculty colleagues.

✓ Recast the Faculty Staffing Table

No doubt the most serious structural change that faculty face is the need to redefine the tasks, responsibilities, and privileges assigned to faculty of differing ranks and qualifications. At one time, the faculty's approach to this challenge was remarkably straightforward: faculty of nearly every stripe and discipline declared that they sought more tenured or tenure-eligible faculty just like they were—fully salaried, fully employed, fully engaged in the production of scholarship and the provision of instruction. Today, almost no institution has the resources to sustain a full-time faculty solely comprised of tenured or tenure-eligible professors. Since the mid 1990s one institution after another has drifted—some would say lurched—toward an academic workforce that often has as many contingent workers as it has tenured and tenure-eligible faculty. The contingent side of the staffing table includes a host of titles—adjunct, clinical or practice professor, postdoctoral fellow, research professor, instructional staff—as well as an equally wide variety of compensation schemes. In general, the contingent workforce that serves undergraduate education is paid less, teaches more, and labors without a longer-term contract and often without benefits.

This situation begs to be rationalized in a manner that is more efficient for the institution and more stable, as well as equitable, for the members of the contingent workforce. Both the University of Minnesota Rochester and the University of Wisconsin Oshkosh have put in place dual-track faculty staffing tables that provide both efficiency and stability. At Oshkosh, a full-time, fully qualified instructional staff category is currently responsible for just over half of all undergraduate instruction at the university. This category provides a broad umbrella of titles and responsibilities, but the core of the group are full-time instructional staff members who teach five courses each semester, participate in university governance, and have compensation packages noticeably lower than those of the tenured and tenure-eligible faculty. Instructional staff members do not have tenure, but many have been fully employed for a decade or more.

The University of Minnesota Rochester has much the same dual-track scheme with an important twist. The tenured and tenure-eligible faculty are appointed to the design faculty, signaling that they have prime responsibility for designing the overall shape of the curriculum as well as individual courses. Roughly half of the research and scholarship on which their eligibility for tenure and promotion rests is expected to focus on the learning processes and strategies that underlie instruction in their discipline. Within UMR, the design faculty are their institution's scholars—in the best and fullest meaning of the label—and as such are responsible for making UMR a place of inquiry and discourse.

When exercising their instructional responsibilities, design faculty at UMR complete much of their work in teams rather than as individuals. They frequently consult with one another as well as with members of the instructional staff who will join them in delivering the curriculum and courses they have designed. About half of the instructional staff with whom they work have earned doctorates. Instructional faculty teach more courses, but, unlike adjuncts elsewhere, they have full benefits and multiyear contracts.

For most institutions a similarly constructed dual-track faculty staffing table will bring a host of benefits—most important, a fully qualified instructional staff component that understands its principal function to be the teaching of undergraduate courses and the provision of undergraduate advising. The financial advantage of a dual-track staffing table derives not from the fact that instructional staff members do not enjoy benefits or are paid less for equivalent work, but rather from the fact that instructional staff are expected to teach more courses and spend more time with their undergraduate students. My guess is that over the years institutions will have to learn how best to strike a numerical balance between tenured and tenure-eligible faculty, on the one hand, and instructional faculty on the other.

Initially, the small liberal arts colleges will most vociferously object to a dual staffing table. They will want to argue that their special advantage is that across the curriculum their courses are taught by scholars who are either tenured or tenure eligible. Most liberal arts colleges are learning, however, that they can no longer afford a faculty composed exclusively of tenured and tenure-eligible faculty. So they, too, have begun hiring adjuncts, paying them less, and too often treating them as academic travelers. The better plan is to include within their faculty substantial numbers of fully qualified faculty whose principal, if not sole, responsibility is the provision of under-graduate instruction and advising.

A dual-track faculty system holds out the additional promise of ending the practice of assuming that a staffing table is akin to an immutable periodic table of faculty elements arranged by disciplinary specialty. No institution, no matter how big or wealthy, can any longer afford one of each, though the impulse on the part of faculty is to demand that if a colonial historian retires or leaves the institution, she needs to be replaced with a scholar whose interests are remarkably similar if not actually identical. Given that in a dual-track faculty sys-tem, there will likely be fewer tenure-eligible slots than there are now (because some of the funds necessary to fully salary and benefit the instructional faculty will necessarily come from the conversion of tenure slots into instructional faculty slots), institutions and their fac-ulty will have to become more adept at clustering their tenure slots both within large departments and, in smaller institutions, across departments.

✓ Make the Academic Department the Unit of Instructional Production

There is one final structural alteration on my list of changes faculty need to adopt to better lead what will likely prove a tumultuous change process. In pursuit of ensuring equity among all faculty in terms of what is expected of them, most colleges and univer-sities made the number of courses taught by each member of the faculty—that is, the course or teaching load—a single standard of pro-duction. This labor standard all but guarantees that faculty discharge their teaching responsibilities as independent agents.

The absurdity of this situation is probably best reflected in the machinations faculty must go through if they want to jointly teach a course. The standard rule is that each faculty member receives a half-course credit even though each attends every class session. The course load arithmetic, particularly at an institution with a collective bargain-ing agreement that provides detailed rules for defining each faculty member's teaching load, further fractures the faculty's sense of collec-tive responsibility by converting service assignments into course equivalents. Each job or service responsibility is separate, with its own course equivalent, separate stipend, or both.

The alternative is to make the department (or equivalent) rather than each individual faculty member the base production unit. Assign to the department a collective amount of instruction (courses plus other instructional activities) that must be provided, and then let the department decide how best to distribute those instructional activities among its members. Joint teaching then becomes immediately feasible. Individual faculty could teach more during one semester and less the next. The department could decide when to give release time for course design and development. Service activities would not be converted into course equivalents. At the same time, the department would have to learn how best to work together, thus beginning the process of becoming an instructional cooperative instead of an industrialized production unit, principally composed of interchangeable members.

These five changes, then, make up the faculty's checklist:

✓ Relearn the Importance of Collective Action
✓ Put an End to Rhetorical Excesses
✓ Empower a Different Kind of Faculty Leader
✓ Recast the Faculty Staffing Table
✓ Make the Academic Department the Unit of Instructional Production

None of these changes is sufficient in itself for an institution either to better control its operating costs or to increase the proportion of its students who graduate more or less on schedule. In 1980, I might have argued that these five changes would have been sufficient to ensure the continued vitality of American higher education. Today, however, they are necessary without being sufficient in and of themselves. These five changes will, however, ensure that faculty continue to play the dominant role in defining and designing the academic programs whose principal focus remains scholarly activity—whether it be the scholarship of teaching or the scholarship that contributes to content knowledge.

11 A Competent Curriculum

Much of the clamor surrounding the high cost of a college education has focused on the numbers rather than the processes that produce the numbers. The result, more often than not, is more proclamation than analysis. Colleges and universities are portrayed as being inefficient to the point of being sloppy or undisciplined or simply indifferent to the impact their higher prices have on middle- and low-income students. Everyone blames someone else. Faculty do not teach enough, are too self-centered, or are simply out of touch with a changing America. Administrators are too fond of their perks and too quick to add more staff to their departments. Government regulation now consumes a large part of every research grant, while a substantial portion of every tuition bill goes to cover the cost of filling out more forms, on the one hand, and, on the other, providing mandated services that no one wants badly enough to pay for out of their own pocket. Some even blame students and their parents for insisting on the latest amenities—saunas and climbing walls, for example—and further increases in merit-based student aid.

Even when the intent is not particularly polemical, most analysts assume that higher education's principal cost drivers are its classic employment categories: faculty, administration, student services, and advancement. Higher education's apologists reinforce these assumptions every time they point out that higher education is a labor-intensive enterprise filled with not just smart but also inherently expensive people.

A Better Way to Look at Costs

There is, however, an alternative to this focus on the number and salaries of the people colleges and universities employ. What drives higher education's operating costs upward are the nature and organization of its basic functions: the provision of teaching, research, and public service. The organization of these functions determines their costs, including the number of personnel required to produce a quality product. From this perspective, the set of activities that make up each function matters most. Although it is true that a given function will cost less if the salaries of those who perform that function are reduced or if the number of service providers is similarly trimmed, it is equally likely that such arbitrary reductions will yield a product of diminished quality.

For the instructional side of the ledger, the organizational arrangements that matter most are those imbedded in the curriculum. It is, to evoke Willie Sutton, where the money is. Curricula create expense in three direct ways. A college's curriculum defines what is to be taught and by whom, the order in which subjects are to be taken, and the requirements for a degree. A substantial portion of the increase in operating expenses at most colleges and universities can be explained, for example, in terms of the faculty collectively teaching (and often requiring) more subjects but individually teaching fewer courses than before. It is, to repeat an earlier observation, the propensity problem—the irresistible urge to add new subjects reflecting the ever-expanding nature of the knowledge base, while almost never deciding *not* to teach something else. Majors expand, and advisors encourage students to take double majors to increase their chances of landing the jobs they want; as a result, graduating transcripts become increasingly likely to record 140 credits or more rather than the standard 120 units students would earn if they took five three-unit courses per semester for four years. In many institutions the propensity problem also increases the probability of more under-enrolled classes. Often the pool of students pursuing a specific major or specialization has, through the continuing addition of new and advanced courses the faculty want to teach, been divided and then divided again until at any given moment only a handful of students are available to take a given course at a given time.

The style and mode of instruction also determine the underlying cost associated with a particular course. Here the cost analysts are seriously handicapped because almost no data are collected detailing the specific costs associated with each activity within a given curriculum.

In the 1990s, however, an interesting innovation at Rensselaer Polytechnic Institute (RPI) suggests how a different kind of cost accounting can better highlight how and why a college or university spends its money.

RPI had recruited Jack Wilson, who, in addition to being a professor of physics at the University of Maryland and an IBM consulting scholar, had served as the executive officer of the American Association of Physics Teachers (AAPT). Wilson came to RPI as the dean for undergraduate and continuing education, with the specific charge to help put in place "studio physics"—an alternative way of teaching introductory physics that did away with the biweekly lectures and discussion sessions that had traditionally anchored the curriculum. In their place, studio physics substituted two four-hour studio sessions per week during which pairs of students working on a souped-up personal computer conducted the experiments and worked through the problem sets that are the bread and butter of an introductory physics course.

Faculty are present in the studio, but principally and often solely as resource experts. At any time, students having difficulty understanding a particular concept, experiment, or problem can ask one of the circulating faculty for help. Frequently faculty, as they roam the studio, can also pick out the student pairs who are about to need proactive help. The souped-up PC has one other feature. Because significant portions of the RPI physics faculty had doubted that the computerized sessions in the studio would prove sufficient to pass introductory physics standard exams, the PC also provides a video lecture giving the basics of the problem or experiment on which the student is working. All of these video lectures are delivered by the member of the department judged best to deliver that particular lecture (RPI 2012).

This last innovation—making available a more traditional form of instruction against which to compare that being offered through the PCs in a studio format—yielded the cost analysis I am interested in here. Even before they launched studio physics, Wilson and his colleagues knew that more than 80 percent of the class frequently skipped the biweekly lectures delivered by the senior faculty. The biweekly discussion sections, also presided over by a regular member of the physics faculty, were frequently skipped by 50 percent of the class or more. Only the lab sections, the least expensive delivery system, had nearly perfect attendance, though the students often complained they had difficulty understanding their graduate student instructors. As Wilson was fond of pointing out, the students turned the course's cost pyramid on its head.

In two important ways the introduction of studio physics buttressed Wilson's claim. The least used element of the PC's support environment were the video lectures, which were accessed by less than 5 percent of the students over the course of the semester. Wilson was also guessing that watching or attending the senior faculty lectures would not matter. Here, the proof would be how well the studio students did on the standard exams administered to all students enrolled in introductory physics.

Initially the physics faculty had agreed to a three-year trial of studio physics in which one-third of the 500-plus first-year students enrolled in introductory physics would have a studio experience while the other two-thirds would be taught in the traditional way. As it turned out, the faculty needed but a single year's data to judge the experiment a success. The third of the students enrolled in the studio physics section on average did as well as (and frequently up to 10 points better than) the students enrolled in sections utilizing the traditional format. Just as important, the studio students spent more time "in studio" than did their classmates in the traditionally taught sections, and studio students came away from the experience more satisfied with not just what they had learned but also how they had learned.

The successful introduction of studio physics at RPI teaches a variety of lessons. First, it is advantageous to disaggregate the traditional instructional format into a set of more or less discrete activities. Second, faculty can in fact change their minds. Studio physics as developed at and for RPI was the superior learning product—a fact underlined by both the studio students' performance on the standard exams and the same students' evaluations of their learning experiences. Because the faculty had to confront evidence they accepted as valid—the performance on the standard tests—the curriculum could be changed without the faculty perceiving the change as an assault on either themselves or their values.

Third, the RPI experiment reinforces the necessity of an activity-based accounting of the costs generated by a particular strategy for teaching a particular course. There was, to begin, the initial investment in the souped-up PCs, their programming, and their installation in dedicated rooms that became the studios of studio physics. Course directors—skilled in the manipulation of the software as well as clever in their use of the PCs to demonstrate the basic concepts studio physics was expected to teach—had to be recruited and compensated. Though it was the proverbial third rail neither the RPI physicists nor their administrative colleagues wanted to touch, the kind of activity cost-analysis briefly described above makes one want to ask, "Just how many physicists are really needed to teach introductory physics to 500-plus first-year engineering and science students?" The answer, never taken advantage of by RPI, is "fewer than before—perhaps even a lot fewer if one doesn't count the graduate students who are necessary to the grading of the problem sets that the students turn in each week."

Posed in this way, the even more difficult unanswered question—the one that dogs nearly every attempt to change a collegiate curriculum—becomes more difficult: to what extent is the real purpose of a college curriculum today to distribute enrollments in such a way as to preserve faculty slots? Recall that, at the University of Wisconsin Oshkosh, the general education requirements had become a de facto peace treaty whose only apparent rationale was to guarantee departments with diminished student appeal sufficient enrollments to preserve the faculty lines they already had. It is not a wholly cynical observation to note that faculty shy away from both redesigning their curricula and better controlling the number of credits their majors acquire en route to graduation because they have little appetite for risking changes that will reduce their claim on tenured or tenure-eligible appointments.

If one accepts the RPI experience as a potential template for curricular change, then, among other elements, curriculum revision requires the ability to disaggregate instructional activities so that their costs can be determined separately and their contribution to the student's ultimate mastery of the material can be evaluated independently.

Taking Charge

If, as I have already argued, the first prerequisite for a successful campaign to recast the undergraduate curriculum is a strong, take-charge faculty voice, then the second necessary condition is faculty that are willing and able to take charge of the process by which their institution intends to recast its basic curricula. That certainly is the lesson embedded in the successful campaign to recast the Oshkosh general education curricula; in every sense it is a curricular change whose design was first promoted by senior faculty leaders, whose adoption was agreed to by the faculty at large, and whose implementation was wholly in the hands of the faculty. The third necessary condition is a faculty voice that seeks the kind of changes necessary to yield an undergraduate curriculum that is more efficient in a triple sense: students learn more, more students attain their degrees, and there is a genuine possibility that instructional costs can be controlled if not reduced without diminishing either student learning or student attainment.

Meeting this goal requires a broad menu of changes we faculty need to consider. Not all may prove necessary, but change is unlikely to result if none of my proposed alterations is adopted in one form or another.

✓ Commit to a Designed Curriculum

By definition, the undergraduate curriculum at a baccalaureate college or university provides the pathways undergraduates must travel en route to earning a baccalaureate or associate's degree. At a minimum, an undergraduate curriculum spells out how many courses or units a student must complete, the distribution of those courses among the offerings of individual departments and programs, and the minimal level of success, usually reflected in an aggregate grade-point average (GPA) the student must achieve prior to graduation. In most institutions the undergraduate curriculum is no more proscriptive. What you see is what you get: a list of minimal requirements that seldom if ever tests whether a student has successfully achieved the educational goals the faculty have endorsed.

It is a curricular frame that is the result of accretion. Most curricula have, as the faculty is fond of pointing out, evolved. Changes have been made slowly and largely piecemeal, often reflecting pressures that emerge and then recede with almost no one taking full account of what time and happenstance have wrought. Not surprisingly, then, no one owns the curriculum; instead, it becomes what each individual member of the faculty has inherited upon taking up his or her position at the college or university. Faculty, largely as individuals, shape their own courses, drawing on their own values and the instructional modalities with which they are most comfortable as well as the most recognizable traditions of their disciplines.

Thus, a faculty-centered curriculum preserves faculty choice. Similarly, a student-centered curriculum enshrines student choice if the list of requirements is short and students are expected to be academic shoppers constantly exploring differing perspectives. My proposal, however, does neither and in fact curtails both. Colleges and universities now require designed curricula in which the individual courses and learning experiences together sum to more than they do individually. Good design, moreover, starts with a clear statement of purpose—not so much what we expect students to know, but rather what we expect them to be able to do.

For too long, as faculty we have shied away from making such statements. In part we have done so because we suspect a codified definition of purpose will ultimately limit our ability to teach what we know in ways that make the most sense to us as individuals. We do know that once such a statement is in place we stand to be judged by whether our students can accomplish what we have said they ought to be able to accomplish. By not defining the competency we seek, we also make it nearly impossible to calibrate failures.

Without a statement of purpose—that is, without a practical elaboration of the competencies we expect our students to master—good design is simply not possible. For introductory physics at RPI, the credible statement of purpose begins with an elaboration of the principles and concepts the students must employ to pass the course's schedule of exams.

At the University of Wisconsin Oshkosh, the statement of purpose begins not with the individual University Studies courses that students will take to satisfy the revised general education requirement, but with an overarching commitment to yield students who are familiar with and can engage in purposeful discourse focusing on the following questions:

- How do people understand and create a sustainable world?
- How do people understand and engage in community life?
- How do people understand and bridge cultural differences?

Depending on which Quest course an individual faculty member is designing, the statement of purpose establishes an initial set of parameters for what the student will encounter: "As the first class in a student's college career, Quest I with its embedded FYE [First Year Experience] will expose students to the campus' three *Signature Questions* and will itself address one of those questions in greater depth. Approximately 25 percent (or more) of the Quest I content will focus upon and/or integrate that *Signature Question*" (USP 2012, 19).

To ensure that the Quest courses built around a signature question implement the new curriculum, Oshkosh took the further step of linking the implementation of the new curriculum to an altered governance mechanism newly labeled the University Studies Program Council

(USPC). The USPC will review all new proposals from departments for Quest courses to make sure that they in fact fulfill the Quest design requirements and then periodically review the Quest courses being taught to ensure that they continue to fulfill the stated purposes of a Quest course.

I understand that in making a commitment to design the first requirement of a competent curriculum I am, at best, swimming in muddy waters. Individual faculty will have no problem arguing that the courses they currently teach are well designed. What will give many, probably a majority, of currently serving faculty pause is my arguing that a truly designed curriculum—one that begins with an elaborated statement of purposes and proceeds to the elaboration of the specific means that will achieve those purposes—requires the equally purposeful linking of those "individually owned" courses through the deployment of what might best be called a curricular template. Almost everything that I have included in my checklist for achieving a competent curriculum proceeds from the assumption that such a template is not only feasible but necessary.

✓ Substitute Competencies for Seat Time

There is, of course, one element that is already common to nearly every undergraduate curriculum leading to a baccalaureate degree: graduation requires that a student must earn a minimum of 120 credits, which is the equivalent of eight semesters, five courses per semester, and three credits per course. Over the last several years this 120-unit requirement, plus the stipulation that a semester must be at least fifteen weeks in length and that each of the five courses in which the student is enrolled provides at least three hours of instruction per week, has become *the standard* that the U.S. Department of Education wants the accrediting bodies to use to determine whether students at a particular institution meet the requirement for full-time enrollment embedded in the legislation authorizing the disbursement of federal student aid funds.

This standard presumes—to steal from Gertrude Stein's observation—that a course is a course is a course: most likely self-contained, often specifically belonging to an individual faculty member, and almost always ready to be packaged as a key entry into the menus of courses that define the major, on the one hand, and, on the other, the general education and degree requirements. Course credits then become what students collect en route to graduation. Course credits, in other words, serve as the fungible units that constitute most collegiate degrees and hence, for most students, define their undergraduate education.

The basic problem with this template is its reinforcement of fracturing faculty effort. At the same time, defining a collegiate curriculum as a collection of interchangeable courses enshrines seat time as the principal measure of educational attainment; what matters is not what you know, but how much time you spend learning it. The U.S. Department of Education now regularly argues that it requires an enforceable standard that prevents "cheap degrees" from flooding the market. Making students spend enough real time in classrooms becomes the means to that end.

I have a friend who, having recently become an accreditor, winces every time I pursue this argument as a prelude for calling for a three-year baccalaureate degree that requires 90 as opposed to the standard 120 credits. She asks me, "Would you want a gallon of milk to be redefined as three quarts as opposed to the standard four?" I have begun responding by asking, "Aren't you more interested in the container's measurements than in the quality of the contents—that is, in the quality of the milk itself?"

The only way to resolve this argument I suggest is to agree on a metric that speaks directly to how much "milk" the student needs and then defines the milk I am interested in as the skill and competencies mastered rather than time spent in the classroom (or in front of a computer, if the education is being provided online). At this point she smiles knowingly and asks, "And just where is that metric to come from? Who gets to play Solomon? Who gets the power?" And I reply, "The faculty have the power if they choose to use it."

Thus the argument is joined. The only way to avoid enshrining seat time as the test of a valid undergraduate education is to bite the bullet and define what we expect undergraduates to be able to do when they graduate. Doing so means defining in very practical—and yes, measureable—terms the skills and competencies we want them to acquire as well as the values and learning attitudes we expect them to be able to demonstrate. In the lingo of curricular reform, I am proposing the development of competency-based curricula that explicitly substitute demonstrable competencies for recorded seat time and a passing grade.

The range of competencies I have in mind extends well beyond what an individual course is expected to teach. For example, medical schools now regularly define their challenge as providing their students with the capacity to complete the tasks that represent efficient medical practice. The medical boards taken during a medical student's third and fourth years are the first steps toward licensure as a physician as well as the tool most hospitals use when evaluating candidates for a residency. The United States Medical Licensing Examination (USMLE), the formal title of the set of examinations that medical students take, is designed to "assess a physician's ability to apply knowledge, concepts, and principles, and to demonstrate fundamental patient-centered skills, that are important in health and disease and that constitute the basis of safe and effective patient care" (USMLE 2012).

A second example of a competency-based curriculum comprising both specific and summative competencies is reflected in the requirements the Boy Scouts of America have spelled out for those seeking to become an Eagle Scout—earn a total of twenty-one merit badges, twelve of which must come from a prescribed list stressing commitment to community and family, personal fitness, and exploratory skills. Of interest here is the ability of the scouting organization to specify in considerable detail what the scout must demonstrate and how those judging the scout's performance are to know whether the demonstration is adequate. The full details of this curriculum are available on the Boy Scouts of America website (BSA 2012).

Those who want to argue that a detailed specification of outcomes is an exercise in dumbing down a curriculum ought to peruse the BSA website while noting just how summative the spelling out of a set of requirements can be. Among those worth looking at in particular, always remembering the specifications are addressed to youngsters under the age of eighteen, are merit badges for Chess, Geocaching, Oceanography, Robotics, and Whitewater. You will discover an emphasis on demonstrating, explaining, doing, and, interestingly, teaching someone else what has been mastered in pursuit of the particular merit badge.

Of more immediate interest, perhaps, are the curricula that sustainability movements are beginning to put in place, particularly on smaller college campuses. Students interested in mastering the values and propositions that a commitment to sustainability requires quickly learn that no one course and certainly no one discipline is sufficient. Nor is it possible to assemble the necessary skills and competencies in isolation; rather, the ability to combine as well as to apply what has been learned is the skill that matters most. Some sustainability curricula have also embraced the same "demonstrate, explain, do, and teach" requirements that are often the basis of the Boy Scouts curriculum.

Nearly all the curricular innovations on the remainder of my Checklist for Change become more attractive, as well as more likely to yield increases in student learning and attainment, if they are put in place in an environment in which, not seat time, but well-enumerated learning outcomes and competencies have become the basis for awarding academic credit.

✓ Explore Learning Pathways and Cohorts

A well-designed curriculum is a map telling the student the particular skills and competencies that must be mastered and in what order. Like any good map that helps the wanderer navigate an unfamiliar forest, a curricular map's basic component ought to be a series of "learning pathways" that guide the student from one experience to another in such a way that the student becomes familiar with the terrain without getting lost. A learning pathway can be as simple as a series of linked courses. Most undergraduate pre-med curricula, for example, are learning pathways, with easily recognized "exit ramps" (organic chemistry, for example) that help students to decide where to head when they discover medicine is not for them. Curricula in schools of engineering and nursing, along with those in the military academies, are for the most part similarly organized, as are the curricula of most conservatories. In these cases, the learning pathway stretches for three or even four years. Other learning pathways can be much shorter, depending on the purposes being served. The new University Studies Program at Oshkosh is a two-year learning pathway guiding new students toward a fuller understanding of the three basic themes or quests that comprise Oshkosh's general education curriculum. In each of these examples, student (and by extension faculty) choice is constrained, but not eliminated. Sometimes students have a choice of different sections or even courses that focus on a specific skill or competency; Oshkosh uses this strategy to make sure that all of its initial Quest courses have no more than twenty-five students. Sometimes a particular pathway will specify three or four of the courses to be taken next, an option that leaves students to complete their schedules by choosing among a roster of "free electives." In a curriculum defined as a series of learning pathways, students make the ultimate choices about which pathway to take and when to change direction by moving to an alternate pathway.

In the humanities and social sciences such pathways are practically nonexistent, except in very small institutions in which the limited number of faculty dictates that student choice must be curtailed. In the 1980s, these curricula drew the particular ire of the authors of *Integrity in the College Curriculum*. In the ensuing quarter-century, not much has changed for the better. Specialties have been added along with a marked increase in the number of boutique courses that teach but one aspect of those specialties. In a variety of these disciplines peace is maintained among the faculty, particularly when the discipline itself is rent by theoretical and methodological discord, by not inquiring too deeply and often not at all into what and how each teaches his or her own courses. Discussions of learning outcomes are largely dismissed in favor of celebrations of the kind of depth and breadth the smorgasbord curriculum provides. As a result, the students, again under the banner of the importance of student choice, are assigned responsibility for making sense of their varied learning experiences by figuring out what goes with what. Students often respond with a minimizing strategy for accumulating the necessary credits for graduation. In making their specific choices, students are often guided by the hour and the day of the course (never before 10:00 in the morning and preferably not on Friday), how much written work and how many examinations, and the grading history of the professor teaching the course—a series of characteristics that provide the core of most surveys whose purpose is to "rate my professor."

Changing this pattern will not be easy. Students will object, faculty will resist, and the inertia of leaving things as they are will want to prevail. The only way to enlist the faculty in the development of an alternative set of learning pathways that will constrain their choices and those of their students is to commit to a discussion of curricular purpose. Such a discussion cannot begin with a commitment to coverage, as Jennifer Summit and her Stanford colleagues learned. In fact, no discipline can still hope to teach undergraduates all the content they might need to know. Two alternatives are possible. The first and the easiest to adopt is a purposeful sampling of specialties, much like the smorgasbord menu now in place. The second is to build a learning pathway that instills the inquiry skills that form the basis of a particular discipline. Some of those skills are means to an end—statistics, writing, bibliographic search. Other skills pertain more to the ability to explore topics of particular interest or importance to a given discipline. Still other skills are really rules of behavior. Archeologists, for example, are guided by the dictum, "leave something for succeeding generations to find," which translates into "sample a dig site, rather than fully exposing it."

Faculty who safely navigate these initial discussions and emerge from them with an enumeration of purposes, skills, competencies, and attitudes must next turn to the more difficult task of defining learning pathways. Except in very small departments, there is no reason to define a single learning pathway leading to a major or a minor; what becomes crucial is that each pathway must specify courses to be taken in order, with some choices among courses at specific junctions along the learning pathway.

The first cousin of a learning pathway is a learning cohort—a group of students who take some, though most or all would be better, of their courses together. A learning cohort could be either a group of first-year students working their way along a general education learning pathway together or a group of history majors exploring their disciplinary pathway together. Cohorts not only make for collaborative learning in which students teach one another but also provide support mechanisms whose stickiness reduces attrition and promotes attainment—a lesson being learned by both community colleges using a cohort model to retain at-risk students requiring remedial education and graduate school programs finding it easier and more efficient to teach graduate students in groups. At the same time, the cohort model is substantially more efficient. Each course has a guaranteed enrollment equal to the size of the cohort itself. Faculty effort can be distributed more equally over the several years the cohort is in place.

Some will argue—as did the faculty unions in Pennsylvania and California in rejecting Joni Finney's and my argument that a reengineered curriculum employing cohorts would both reduce costs and increase attainment—that what works for advanced graduate students is not appropriate for traditional-aged college students who, because they are unsure of what they want, need a period of experimentation before settling on a major and an appropriate set of minors. I have always been a bit dumbfounded by this response because it essentially argues that inexperienced first-time undergraduates are better able to make (or at least survive a process in which they are asked to make) complex choices than experienced graduate students. I also like to point out that the cohort model works as well for at-risk students in remedial programs. For me, as should now be clear, the more essential element is adequate design rather than more elements from which to choose.

✓ Offer Credit by Examination or Demonstration

The simplest of my curricular changes to explain is the need to offer college credit by examination or demonstration. In its most basic form, credit by examination says to the student, if you can pass the final examination in course A and submit acceptable papers matching those submitted by students fully enrolled in the course, then you need not take the course to receive full credit. Courses that teach basic skills—calculus, foreign languages, English composition, even general chemistry and introductory physics—and have final exams used across all sections of the course would be the easiest to make available to students who believe they have independently mastered the material being taught in the course.

Credit by examination or demonstration works much less well when the course is didactic in nature. When the purpose of such a course, however, is to teach inquiry skills and scholarly rules of behavior, then a standard examination becomes much more possible. Hillary Pennington, before she left the Gates Foundation, was exploring the possibility of establishing a standard curriculum for the twenty-five basic courses that could be found in most general education curricula. I am less interested in a standard curriculum (that is, one size fits all) for those courses as in the real possibility that there could be a battery of twenty-five standard examinations that students could take if they believed they had mastered what one of these basic courses was expected to teach. Such a battery of examinations would begin to look like the Boy Scouts catalog of merit badges, each of which has the virtue of a very specific enumeration of the skills and attitudes a successful candidate is expected to be able to demonstrate. A standard catalog of externally generated and verified general education examinations has the further attraction of yielding a set of learning metrics by which institutions could gauge the effectiveness of both their learning pathways and the individual courses representing their general education curriculum.

✓ Develop a Three-Year (90-Credit) Baccalaureate Degree

Though talked about more often now than when I first raised the issue in *Making Reform Work*, the idea of the three-year baccalaureate degree is no closer to reality. A few, for the most part smaller, private colleges have begun putting in place accelerated bachelor's programs in which students earn the standard 120 credits over three calendar years during which the students work through the calendar year. My original argument was for a 90-credit three-year degree, an idea that makes traditionalists fume and chief financial officers tremble.

Originally I saw in the idea of a three-year baccalaureate degree an intriguing stalking-horse. If nothing else, the task of designing a true three-year degree would demonstrate anew that traditional undergraduate curricula are only about time-on-task. To the frequently asked question, "Do you think three years gives undergraduates enough time to learn what they need to know?" I have responded by asking, "What exactly do you think they need to know?" The answer, more often than not, is a quick change of subject.

The more I lobbied for a three-year degree for argument's sake, however, the more I came to see in the idea an interesting answer to many issues now confronting higher education. For families and students, a three-year degree would reduce the cost of a baccalaureate degree by 25 percent. Converting to a three-year, 90-credit baccalaureate degree would force college faculty to separate the wheat from the chafe in that they would have to decide what was and, just as importantly, what was not central to an undergraduate education. The conversion process would be a dislodging event of sufficient magnitude to hasten the consideration of other kinds of changes—changes to definitions of work, teaching load, and perhaps even tenure. Redesigning degree requirements could lead to the kind of curricular simplification that initially boosts retention and ultimately attainment. With more and more students seeking master's and other post-baccalaureate degrees, spending just three years on the first phase of their collegiate education makes sense because many will be spending more rather than less time attending a college or university.

✓ Invest in Learning Management

One key theme critics have been flogging recently is that American higher education remains trapped in a Luddite universe in which technological innovation is often talked about and then disparaged rather than being taken seriously and then adopted. This argument would have a better chance of gaining traction if its adherents better understood that most of the new computer-dependent providers—for-profit distance learning enterprises in particular—employ electronic pedagogies that pay little or no attention to how students actually learn.

The irony is that real lessons are to be learned beyond discovering that just using computers either online or in the classroom is not enough. I have already sketched how the University of Minnesota Rochester is putting in place a curriculum that requires faculty to add continuously to an electronic database of tagged and evaluated learning objects. Currently the reigning expert in this field is Candace Thille of Carnegie Mellon University, who heads the Open Learning Initiative (OLI), a major project being funded by the Gates and Lumina foundations. Thille's mantra is that effective, technologically assisted learning requires both design and management. The OLI project draws first on what the neurological and cognitive sciences are telling us about how learning takes place and the kinds of exercises and presentations of material that have the best chance of yielding a learned and retained outcome. The key OLI innovation is the embedding of what Thille and her colleagues call *intelligent tutors* within the computerized learning environments they are designing. Intelligent tutors, like the human tutors they seek to emulate, work alongside the student, constantly at the ready as the student works through the material being presented. As Thille describes this role, the intelligent tutor makes "comments when the student errs, answering questions about what to do next, and maintaining a low profile when the student is performing well." This approach, she notes, "differs from traditional computer-aided instruction in that traditional instruction gives didactic feedback to students on their final answers, whereas the OLI tutors provide context specific assistance during the problem-solving process." It is important to note that Thille's intelligent tutors make good the promise of having the instructor—in this case a sophisticated electronically mediated learning environment—become a guide on the side as opposed to a sage on the stage (Thille 2012, 5).

Just as important, OLI's intelligent tutors manage the learning process through the collection of real-time data tracking the student's successes, failures, and reactions. This activity makes possible the kind of data mining in the commercial world that has become the hallmark of smart computer systems that serve clients and shoppers. With the student's permission, the intelligent tutor collects and stores the student's responses, including the questions the student asks and his or her answers on exams and quizzes, and then makes those data available to the computer program itself and to the team of experts who monitor how well the students and their computerized learning environment are doing. Or, as Thille put it, the team of experts analyzed "the data stream to see what was working and not working to produce improvements in the next iteration of the course." In time "the data were put to another use—to support research about how people learn" (Thille 2012, 5).

Another example of a computerized learning environment that employs a complex learning management system is that developed by the American Public University System (APUS), a regionally accredited, for-profit distance education provider. While all the APUS courses are delivered online, they are nonetheless courses, either eight or sixteen weeks in length, with weekly schedules of projects, homework, quizzes, and examinations. Each course has a maximum of twenty-five students enrolled simultaneously who interact with each other as much or as often as with their instructor. Students in the basic public speaking course, for example, regularly upload YouTube videos of themselves delivering their weekly speeches that all members of the class are expected to watch and offer comments.

The APUS learning management system tracks all this activity. Under pressure from its accreditors and the U.S. Department of Education to document that its students log the minimum required hours to continue to qualify for federal student aid grants, the APUS learning management system takes attendance, is used by the instructor to comment on as well as grade student work, allows students to communicate with each other, and supports students engaged in group projects. All emails and other communications are preserved just in case there is a subsequent appeal of either the student's grade or his or her claim that sufficient work has been submitted to satisfy the course's basic requirements. Not just the student's performance is being tracked and evaluated; the instructor's activity is equally on view, becoming over the course of each year the basic data that make possible a quarterly audit of each instructor's performance.

Skeptics will note that the APUS learning management system has something of a "big brother" quality in that it is all-seeing, all-remembering. The learning management system, however, makes possible a complex set of learning analytics that allows APUS management to continuously improve the university's courses, knowing that when new things are tried, there will be data available to help judge whether the experiment is worth pursuing.

APUS has two additional noteworthy characteristics. First, it has not had a tuition increase in eleven years. Instead, managed growth—both in terms of the number of students enrolled and the range of degree programs and individual courses offered—has provided the margin the for-profit company requires to satisfy its stockholders and the internal capital needed to develop new offerings. The ability of the learning management system to readily test learning strategies undergirds much of the confidence APUS displays when it mounts a new degree program or course sequence.

Second, these additional characteristics offer a wholly different way to calibrate faculty effort. The 400-plus (out of a total of 1,600) full-time faculty members are each required to have approximately 400 enrollments in the course of a calendar year. The number of students taught, mentored, and graded becomes the currency of effort rather than the number of courses or course sections taught. Four hundred enrollments translate into roughly 5.3 courses every four months; APUS does not have traditional semesters because new courses start every month. When queried about what appears to be a very heavy teaching load, APUS senior staff are quick to point out that instructors often teach the same course three or four times a year, thus limiting the time required to do new preparations. More important, APUS instructors teach in a curriculum that is composed of standardized course sections that have the advantage of a centrally defined and tested template as well as the full range of capacities embedded in the APUS learning management system.

My guess is that traditional higher education has more to learn from the APUS learning management system than from its actual use of the technology to deliver instruction online. Combining the APUS learning management approach, with its emphasis on learning analytics, and the OLI's computerized intelligent tutors and accompanying learning analytics holds the promise of a revised curriculum that is more student centric, more flexible, and, in the long run, less costly to deliver.

✓ Establish a Credible Testing Regime

Richard Arum and Josipa Roksa, sociologists at New York University and the University of Virginia respectively, are the most recent examples of scholars within the academy whose research focuses on what higher education has failed to accomplish. Their book, whose title *Academically Adrift: Limited Learning on College Campuses* pretty much sums up their argument, has become an academic sensation, providing fodder for those who argue that higher education resists standardized testing of learning outcomes only because of an ingrained suspicion that readily available metrics will prove that there is, in fact, no there there to a college degree.

Academically Adrift used results from the administration of the Collegiate Learning Assessment (CLA) to 2,300 college freshmen and sophomores at two dozen four-year colleges and universities. The CLA is an essay test specifically designed to assess critical thinking, analytic reasoning, and written communication. The CLA, however, assesses changes in student learning, not at the individual level, but rather at the institutional level by having the test administered to relatively small, randomly selected samples of students.

The CLA had already gathered a fair amount of attention prior to the publication of *Academically Adrift* and drew accolades from a whole range of disparate critics ranging from Charles Miller, chair of the Spellings Commission, to Richard Ekman and his Council of Independent Colleges (CIC). The CIC had sponsored a thirty-three-institution consortium of CIC members who were using the CLA as an instrument for measuring institutional contributions to gains in student learning. For Ekman the importance of the CLA resided in its ability to prove "that cognitive growth in small private colleges would be more than in other types of institutions" (Basken 2008).

Academically Adrift unfortunately taught a different lesson, as summed up by Clayton Christensen and Louis Soares as they sought to demonstrate how a disruptive innovation could bring quality and affordability to postsecondary education. *Academically Adrift* demonstrated, they proclaimed, that

- 45 percent of the students whom they were following "demonstrated no significant gains in critical thinking, analytical reasoning, and written communications during the first two years of college"
- 32 percent did not, in a typical semester, take "any courses with more than 40 pages of reading per week"
- 50 percent "did not take a single course in which they wrote more than 20 pages over the course of the semester" (Soares 2011)

Writing in the *New York Times*, Arum and Roksa made clear the link between their analysis and the commentary championed by most of higher education's critics: the fact that students didn't learn meant that colleges and universities were not adding value. "We found that large numbers of the students were making their way through college with minimal exposure to rigorous coursework, only a modest investment of effort and little or no meaningful improvement in skills like writing and reasoning" (Arum and Roksa 2011). Ultimately the high-stakes claim that the CLA could do what higher education had so long claimed was not possible drew considerable attention to Arum and Roksa's methodology. Scholars with a technical interest in assessment were already worried about the high correlation between SAT scores and CLA results. There were open doubts about whether individual-level data could be mustered in such a way as to yield valid measures of an institution's collective contribution to the learning of all of its students. Some of us fussed that it was not possible to view as valid the results of an assessment in which those being assessed did not have a direct stake in the result—and that was precisely what the CLA did because those who took the CLA on behalf of their institutions were repeatedly assured that the results would not affect their subsequent education or careers.

In February 2011, Alexander Astin, the dean of educational researchers focusing on assessment, weighed in with an angry essay in the *Chronicle of Higher Education*. The message embedded in Astin's critique of Arum and Roksa's work is that the conclusions they drew, particularly that 45 percent of the students they followed drew no measurable learning benefits from their higher education, were not based on sound statistical analyses. By the end of his tour of Arum and Roksa's methods, it is clear that *Academically Adrift* is as mistaken as it is misleading. His conclusion is short and to the point:

> These considerations suggest that the claim that 45 percent of America's college undergraduates fail to improve their reasoning and writing skills during their first two years of college cannot be taken seriously. With a different kind of analysis, it may indeed be appropriate to conclude that many undergraduates are not benefiting as much as they should from their college experience. But the 45-percent claim is simply not justified by the data and analyses set forth in this particular report. (Astin 2011)

Astin's critique focused on questions of methodology; four months later, Braden J. Hosch of Central Connecticut State University provided the kind of evidence that should have diminished much of the fascination with both the CLA and *Academically Adrift*. Central Connecticut was one of four Connecticut institutions administering the CLA to a sample of its students as part of the Voluntary System of Accountability (VSA) project of the Association of Public and Land-Grant

Universities (APLU) and the American Association of State Colleges and Universities (AASCU). When reviewing three years of CLA results for his institution, Hosch noticed a remarkably strong correlation between the time the student took to complete the CLA and the student's score. Hosch's observation importantly implies that the CLA may very well be measuring not learning, but motivation. In fact, institutions that have administered the CLA have almost uniformly acknowledged that getting a representative sample of students to take the CLA has proved a major problem. The answer, the *Chronicle* reported, was to turn to "low-level bribery. Seniors who volunteer to take the test now have their $40 cap-and-gown fees waived" (Glenn 2010). Hosch's suspicions were validated: students who took their bribe and breezed through the test got lower scores than those students who, having been challenged by the CLA, took the test seriously and as a result earned higher scores.

Calling attention to the CLA's wobbly methodology has made hardly a dent in the critics' embrace of *Academically Adrift*. The *New York Times* columnist David Brooks is but the latest convert. Labeling the volume a "landmark study," Brooks proclaimed: "There's an atmosphere of grand fragility hanging over America's colleges. The grandeur comes from the surging application rates, the international renown, the fancy new dining and athletic facilities. The fragility comes from the fact that colleges are charging more money, but it's not clear how much actual benefit they are providing" (Brooks 2012). Higher education cannot win this argument simply because there is no evidence to the contrary. Those of us inside the academy have so consistently argued that what we provide is beyond simplistic assessment that we no longer have much standing in the argument about whether a higher education does anything more than hold out the promise of more remunerative employment.

It is also an argument we need to abandon because the curricular changes I am urging require the kind of assessments for which nearly all of higher education's critics have been calling. We need to know what works and what doesn't—what is a waste of time, what requires more time, and when enough is enough. A more refined CLA is not what the academy needs. We don't need a single test that is expected to be equally relevant to all institutions; we don't need a test of dubious statistical value; and we don't need a test that principally rewards motivation, and whose results too often reflect a student's score on the SAT.

Rather, we need a portfolio of examinations that map the broad range of skills, competencies, and attitudes whose acquisition ought to be the central purpose of an undergraduate education. Such a portfolio must clearly and persistently reflect a faculty voice and our commitment to scholarly inquiry. Finally, we need a portfolio of examinations that we as faculty embrace, not reluctantly, but whole-heartedly because an effective assessment system is so much in our interest.

Some examinations will necessarily test content knowledge much like the subject matter tests that are already key elements of the Graduate Record Examination (GRE) developed and administered by the Educational Testing Service. The more difficult examinations and the ones yet to be developed are those that test summative and cumulative learning. These exams need to be much more like the USMLE that schools of medicine use to assess their students and evaluate their performance as teaching institutions. Such exams must be developed externally and used by a wide variety of institutions, though not necessarily by all institutions. The system I have in mind resembles the Boy Scouts system of merit badges in that what is being assessed is the student's mastery of a broadly defined and carefully enumerated set of purposes, skills, and attitudes.

12 A Federal Commitment to Fix, Fund, and Facilitate

Had I been drafting *Checklist for Change* thirty years ago, there would have been no need for a twelfth chapter focusing on the federal government's responsibilities in a process meant to recast American higher education. Thirty years ago, the federal government was largely seen as a disinterested source of critical funding that helped to ensure both U.S. continued supremacy in scientific research and education and family/student financing of undergraduate educations. Outside a handful of administrators at major research universities, who were suspicious of attempts to rationalize how their universities calculated the indirect costs they charged the government on their federal research grants, no one worried about what the "feds were up to."

Today nearly everyone worries simply because the federal government has become a principal obstacle to many, perhaps even most, of the items on my Checklist. What began as a grand experiment in providing financial assistance to underwrite student aspirations, research ambitions, and the labor requirements of an increasingly complex economy has become a tale of unexpected consequences, bureaucratic snafus, and an increasingly strident game of "gotcha," in which both major political parties have taken turns in pillorying higher education for a seemingly endless list of deficiencies. In recent years Republicans have focused on costs, accountability, and a professoriate that, from the perspective of the party's base, neither works hard enough nor is right-thinking often enough. Democrats now worry most about access, the peccadilloes of a burgeoning for-profit sector, and higher education's inability to explain, let alone control, operating costs.

While this more or less constant harping makes life for college and university presidents troubling, the big problem—and the one that has inconveniently made the federal government so important to the change narrative—is that Washington, without intent or design, has de facto become higher education's principal third-party payer, providing more than $130 billion a year in direct grants and subsidized and guaranteed loans to students and their families. Where once the federal government was satisfied to just supply the money, while asking few questions and making even fewer demands of colleges and universities, today Congress, the White House, and the Department of Education have each weighed in with their own notions of how to make higher education more accountable, more welcoming to disadvantaged learners, and more able to satisfy employer demands for smart workers. In most cases the message to colleges and universities is direct: "if you take the money, then you must do things my way." Increasingly "my way" has meant more regulation and more compliance, all of which has tended to freeze current practices to the point of thwarting the changes most reformers have thought necessary.

Given the bitter partisan battles that reining in the federal deficit have already sparked, the fate of purposeful changes in federal policy remains an open question. What is clear—to me at least—is that absent significant changes in how the federal government interacts with higher education, there is little prospect for much progress. Nonetheless, my catalog of the changes and initiatives that are necessary for change to take place follows. The result ought to be a new national agenda for higher education that presupposes a commitment to an appropriately American intergovernmental cooperation.

Things to Be Fixed

Federal student aid poses the fundamental problem—not the amount of student aid, but the way it is distributed, tracked, monitored, and, in the case of student loans, paid back. At best, the federal government's programs of assistance to students and families inhabit a hodgepodge of poorly connected programs yielding unintended consequences without increasing the probability that more disadvantaged learners will earn a baccalaureate degree. Much of the money is wasted in the sense that it is spent on students who, given the current rules of the game, are not likely to graduate. The students who need help the most—for example, those requiring substantial remediation—are told they cannot use federal funds to pay for the necessary remediation. Institutions, while benefiting from their ability to charge higher tuitions, find themselves responsible for loan default rates, though they have a remarkably small role in determining who can borrow how much under what terms of repayment. The single largest failure of the program is the federal student aid's voucher system that rewards first-time enrollments rather than degree completions. Fixing these problems has become an imperative.

✓ Provide Incentive Funding to Institutions for Graduating Disadvantaged Learners

Much of the current discussion of how to improve federal student aid programs centers on rewarding institutions that graduate disadvantaged learners in substantial numbers. The most direct way to accomplish this end is to create a federal trust fund that can award substantial grants to baccalaureate institutions that consistently improve the percentage of their disadvantaged students earning a baccalaureate degree within six years or less. The benefiting institutions would be required to invest the funds in activities whose principal purpose was to improve undergraduate education—in other words, the grants, which ought to be substantial, could not be used to cover other operations.

To further guard against institutions in general—and the for-profit sector in particular—becoming diploma mills living off the federal bounty for successful completions, an external verification process must document that the graduating students have the requisite skills and competencies at the core of a successful undergraduate education. The testing regime described in chapter 11 could supply that verification as long as all graduates in a particular program were tested.

A second approach would be to award grants from the completions trust fund to community colleges based on the number of their students who transfer to a four-year institution and earn a baccalaureate degree. For these awards testing would not be necessary, but the system would require better tracking of students who start in one institution and subsequently transfer to one or more other institutions.

A third approach that would proactively fund completions is to have the trust fund award competitive grants to baccalaureate institutions with promising programs to increase the graduation rates of disadvantaged learners. Some form of post-program verification would be necessary here as well.

✓ Make Students Enrolled in Remedial Education Programs Eligible for Pell Grants

As with so many federal student aid programs, the intentions were right, but the policy was not. The idea was to prevent the federal government from paying for the secondary educations students ought to have received before proceeding to a postsecondary institution. The basics—reading, mathematics, and writing—were to remain the responsibility of the local school districts; students with substantial educational deficits were not expected to be passed on to postsecondary institutions with their high school diplomas in hand. But in increasing numbers starting in the 1970s, high schools did just that; they sent to college disadvantaged students who, with embarrassing regularity, failed the standard placement tests most institutions use to determine college readiness. These students needed good, old-fashioned remedial education to fix what the high schools had left broken. By the rules and regulations governing federal student Pell Grant eligibility, remedial courses not qualifying for college credit do not count in the calculation of full-time status. And only full-time students are eligible for full Pell Grant awards. To get around this catch-22, most institutions place these students in "developmental courses" that do award college credit but often are not sufficiently remedial.

There are several ways around this dilemma. The most straightforward plan allows students enrolled full-time in collegiate-level remedial education programs to be eligible for federal student aid. I would extend this proviso such that students enrolled full-time in a remedial education program would be granted an additional year of federal student aid eligibility. If the newly restated goal of student federal aid is to increase the rate at which disadvantaged learners complete a college degree, then it makes little or no sense to penalize the very students their colleges and universities have identified as needing up to an extra year of full-time enrollment to remediate a basic educational deficit.

Were the three-year baccalaureate to become a national standard, I would make a further shift in eligibility for federal student aid programs: guarantee all students who qualify as requiring financial assistance up to four years of eligibility. Students requiring remedial education would use their first year of eligibility to become truly college ready. Students who graduated from college in three years could use their fourth year of eligibility to begin their post-baccalaureate educations.

✓ Make Institutions Active Players in the Student Loan System

In the new federal system of student financial aid Congress created in the 1970s, colleges and universities were excluded from direct participation. Instead, federal monies would go to students who would vote with their feet by choosing which institutions to attend. That institution needed to be accredited, needed to certify a student's enrollment, and frequently was expected to act as a dispensing agent; but the fundamental relationship was between the student and the federal government.

This relationship also sounded better in theory than it has proved to be in practice. As loans in general, and federally guaranteed and subsidized loans in particular, have become an ever larger part of the standard financial aid packages undergraduates receive to help pay for their educations, the question of who is responsible when students default on their loans has become something of a political football. In the federal government's view loan defaults are fundamentally an institutional problem. High and persistent default rates by the institution's current and past students can render future students enrolled at that institution ineligible for federal student loans as well as other forms of federal student aid. Indeed, making institutions accountable for their former students' federal loans has become an integral part of the government's scrutiny of a for-profit higher education industry whose students are more than twice as likely to default on their loans as students attending either public or private not-for-profit baccalaureate institutions.

The problem is that no institution—for-profit, private not-for-profit, or public—has much say in which of its students are eligible for a federal student loan, whether those students are likely to prove creditworthy, and, most troubling of all, how much debt those students should be allowed to take on. At a minimum, the total cost of attending an institution (i.e., tuition, room and board, fees, and living expenses) ought to set an upper limit on federally subsidized student loans for which individual students are eligible. It would be better, but no doubt politically tricky, to develop a set of maximums that would both curtail the institutions' reliance on tuition increases and limit the students' appetite for more expensive institutions, increased spending money, or both.

This, the simplest of the changes, would have two immediate effects. Bundling the cost of attendance and undergraduate student loans with each other would make more obvious, perhaps even transparent, the link between the pricing and the financing of a college education. The more important impact would be a modest, but still significant, reduction in the amount of educational borrowing, particularly on the part of students with the greatest need. Such a limitation might also help reduce the possibility of treating the proceeds from a student loan as supplemental income, though the need for such a supplement would not be altered.

A more substantial change would be to integrate the institution and its own programs of student financial aid with the federal programs. Pell Grants are already integrated because almost all institutions treat those monies as "first dollars in." The other forms of aid—institutional grants, state grants, federally subsidized and federally guaranteed student loans along with parental loans, and, where applicable, tax credits—remain separate and separable. Ultimately, some institutions would see an advantage of being a provider or a guarantor of loans to their students—an agent if you will, using its own creditworthiness and ability to bundle loans as a means of securing the most favorable terms possible for the debt their students and their families take on to pay for a college education. Many, perhaps most, institutions would be leery of playing a more direct role in the packaging of student debt, though in time a wide variety of providers—and not just the for-profit sector—would, I think, come to see in this change an opportunity to better order their own finances while helping students and their families see the total cost of the educations they are pursuing.

✓ Establish a Federal Regulatory Environment Distinct from Accreditation to Oversee Federal Student Aid

There is little likelihood that any of the changes I have recommended above, or those that follow, will succeed as long as the federal government continues the awkward practice of punishing accrediting agencies that refuse to serve as compliance police. There is simply too much money—$130 billion and counting—in federal student aid each year to leave its monitoring to what is, in fact, a jumble of quasi-public agencies that have shown little aptitude for or interest in serving in that role.

The basic questions the federal government needs to ask have little to do with the questions accreditors have traditionally asked in order to ensure that the institutions over which they have suzerainty meet minimum quality standards. Instead of focusing on the details of the curriculum, the availability of educational resources (for example, the number of books in the library), the qualifications of the teaching faculty, or whether the institution is committed to shared governance—all conditions of fundamental importance to the accreditation process— the federal government must regularly as well as forcefully ask: Does the institution practice "truth in pricing" and "truth in lending," and does its advertising make false claims guaranteeing remunerative employment? Does the institution comply with federal health and safety regulations? Finally, is the institution accredited (that is, in the view of its peers is it offering a credible education)? Both stipulating and enforcing definitions of full-time enrollment and gainful employment, and whatever other criteria the federal government puts in place regulating the awarding of federal student aid, ought to be the business of an independent federal regulatory agency. And, not so incidentally, the federal government must fund this agency, instead of today's reliance on accreditors absorbing the cost of monitoring compliance.

✓ Change the Timing and Flow of Federal Student Aid Dollars

Last on my list of things the federal government needs to fix is the timing and flow of federal student aid dollars. Because the current program of Pell Grants is first and foremost a voucher system, it has proved a powerful incentive for institutions to recruit and enroll new disadvantaged learners. The institutions get their money up front in the form of tuition payments that are disconnected from the student's retention through graduation.

The reality, as every university and most college chief financial officers will tell you, is that first-year students are eminently less expensive to teach than advanced students. They enroll in large courses, and they do not take advanced science courses that require complex laboratories and that frequently attract just a handful of students. First-year students do not participate in the supervised field experiences required for licensing. And, particularly if they are disadvantaged learners, they take the minimum, as opposed to the maximum, number of courses that duel-majoring advanced students are more likely to take in their third and fourth years. As a result, most baccalaureate institutions and certainly those with large first-year enrollments make a hefty margin on their first-year curricula. The more first-year students—particularly when matched with a more modest number of advanced students—the heftier the margin. When the federal government supplies a substantial Pell Grant with which the student pays his or her tuition, the better the deal. Throw in a ready supply of federal student loans and the deal becomes even sweeter, particularly when combined with state funding mechanisms that similarly reward students for initial enrollment. It is no wonder that so many institutions in general, and for-profit institutions in particular, responded with such alacrity to the federal challenge to increase access by increasing the number of first-year and first-time students.

As the federal government shifts its policy to place greater weight on completions, it will need to make a fundamental adjustment in both the timing and flow of federal student aid dollars to the institutions whose behavior it seeks to influence. The most direct way to accomplish this shift is to make a Pell Grant progressively more valuable to the institution enrolling Pell recipients—in short, pay a bonus, such as a direct payment to the institution of $1,000 for every Pell recipient with sophomore standing, a $2,000 payment for Pell recipients with junior status, and a $3,000 payment for Pell recipients with senior status.

Given the current focus on reducing the federal deficit, there is little likelihood that Congress would authorize a near doubling of the current Pell program. A second possibility for rewarding institutions that retain their Pell recipients is to redirect a portion of the current Pell funding to cover the cost of the kind of bounty or bonus program I have just outlined. Such a shift would likely result in institutions reaching out less aggressively to first-time disadvantaged learners, thus forcing an explicit acknowledgment that ultimately a trade-off exists between access and attainment when there is a fixed limit to available funding.

A more radical suggestion is to have the federal government increasingly responsible for covering the cost of advanced undergraduate enrollments and the institutions themselves responsible for all, or almost all, financial aid distributed to first-year students. This suggestion does not materially differ from my first idea, but it would require institutions to make substantially larger investments of financial aid in their first-year students if they wanted to benefit from the substantially larger grants available to institutions for enrolling disadvantaged learners as they neared graduation.

No doubt my most radical suggestion is to end federal student aid altogether and replace it with a reimbursement program much like the reimbursement system that pays hospitals for the care they provide. Colleges and universities would submit invoices detailing the actual cost of instruction at a unit level and what proportion of those costs could be reasonably assigned to the instruction received by students qualifying for federal assistance. If such a program would ever prove politically attractive enough to be enacted, some key problems would have to be tackled. First, colleges and universities must develop an activity-based cost accounting system of sufficient robustness to allow for the detailed segregation of costs by specific instructional activity. Theoretically such a system is feasible; it would, however, require not only the acquiescence of an instructional staff to submit the data necessary to make the system both achievable and auditable but also the development of a computerized cost-tracking system much like the one the federal government is helping to put in place in the medical arena.

The second problem that would have to be addressed is the variability of instructional costs reflected in Howard Bowen's classic theorem that universities will raise all the money they can and spend all the money they raise. Across higher education, costs reflect not what things cost to produce, but rather how much revenue the institution is able to raise and then spend on the things important to it. To make workable the activity-based cost accounting being envisioned here, the federal government would have to establish minimum acceptable costs criteria not unlike the diagnosis-related groups (DRGs) that, with admittedly mixed results, were put in place to help standardize reimbursement rates across the health care industry. Putting in place such a system would become, in itself, a powerful tool for first understanding and then limiting the cost increases that have plagued higher education since the 1980s.

To control the federal outlays needed to fund a federal student aid program that reimbursed institutions for allowable costs, the reimbursement rates would have to reflect minimum necessary costs, on the one hand, and, on the other, the proportion of students at the institutions meeting the federal program's eligibility requirements. As in my earlier example, the reimbursement rates for advanced courses could also reflect bounties or bonuses for moving disadvantaged learners from first-time, first-year enrollees to students with advanced standing about to graduate. The defining of these incentives and their actual specification would, no doubt, prove politically difficult, but nonetheless necessary.

In offering each of these suggestions my point is not necessarily to settle on one, but rather to suggest that a range of possible actions deserves consideration, along with all other serious suggestions for changing the timing and flow of federal dollars in support of undergraduate education.

✓ Fund Two New Federal Agencies for Accountability and Compliance

In the past, most discussions of federal student financial aid have centered on the need to increase the program's funding, principally by increasing the standard Pell Grant award. The discussions that took place during the Spellings Commission meetings, for example, focused on how to increase appropriations for Pell Grants such that each year the average Pell Grant would be equal to 70 percent of the average in-state tuition of a public college or university. The commission's only comment on the general design and effectiveness of federal student aid programs was a plea for consolidation and simplification. While the latter has largely been ignored by both Congress and the Department of Education, spending on Pell Grants has increased substantially, with the maximum Pell award rising to $5,550 per semester.

I argued within the commission, and I have similarly argued in this volume, that the issue is not the level of funding but the nature of the program's incentives and its rewarding of first-time enrollments as a means of promoting greater access. It should come as no surprise, then, that my Checklist does not include more money for grants; rather, I advocate for new money to put in place two support mechanisms that federal student aid programs and undergraduate education have required for more than a decade.

✓ Fund a National Testing Regime Documenting Undergraduate Learning

To repeat an earlier observation, it no longer matters that most faculty continue to oppose the systematic testing of students to determine what their undergraduate educations have equipped them to accomplish. It doesn't even matter that faculty, whatever their personal views on testing, will be the principal beneficiaries of a testing regime that allows a dispassionate evaluation of what does and doesn't work. The truth is simple: testing is now a political necessity that as faculty we need to accept and facilitate if we are to maintain control over what and how we teach.

The means of accomplishing the testing assumes importance now, and the method remains to be determined. From my perspective the characteristics of a successful testing regime would include the following:

- The recognition that the student, not the institution, is being tested, although the aggregate scores of students from the same institution could be seen to reflect that institution's capacities.
- Students and institutions can choose among a variety of tests.
- The tests must, in fact, be tests and not satisfaction surveys; to be tested through examination and demonstration is what the student knows, what the student is capable of doing, and how well prepared a student is to learn what he or she does not know.

What will not suffice are tests like the CLA, which is no test at all because it is taken by just a sample of students and the students themselves have no direct stake in the test's outcome. Nor is the NSSE sufficient. What I have in mind are tests more like the subject matter tests that are part of the GRE, though subject matter expertise is just one aspect of what must be tested.

I have already suggested that the USMLE could provide a model of what such a national testing regime might look like. In each case that examination asks, "What do you know?" and "Do you know how to apply what you know to the delivery of patient care?" Unlike the USMLE—a set of interrelated exams derived from a single field of study—the undergraduate level requires a full portfolio of exams, each focusing on different courses of study and different educational goals. But like the USMLE, in each case the specific test must focus on two aspects: each test should combine subject matter knowledge and its application; an external agency, reflecting truly national standards, must develop, administer, and score each test.

Developing the necessary portfolio of tests will not be easy, but it is doable. By my estimate, approximately forty separate tests will be required. For students seeking admission to a graduate or professional program, scores on the relevant tests will likely become part of their admissions file. Included in the portfolio of tests will be those necessary for professional licensure in most, if not always all, of the fifty states (a role the USMLE now plays for the licensing of new physicians). In time, employer communities would come to see the advantage of requiring new job applicants to have taken one or more specific tests, perhaps including a general test of communication skills, both written and verbal.

Once a national undergraduate testing regime is in place, graduating students will view the taking of the specific tests that their degrees, future plans, and attending institutions require as a natural culmination of their undergraduate education—much like the role the SAT and ACT play for graduating high school seniors. The tests included in the national testing regime I am proposing would, however, test content knowledge, related processes for applying that knowledge, and inquiry skills to be employed when additional knowledge and skills are required.

In the past, the demand for certification, often at the state or local level, was sufficient to spur the development, testing, and dissemination of tests employing national standards. The demand on the part of colleges and universities for better, more neutral information on their applicants, for example, spurred the development of both the SAT and ACT as a means of demonstrating an applicant's college readiness. The SAT and ACT are largely funded through user fees and by the membership fees charged to institutions by the sponsoring organization. The USMLE is similarly funded by user fees, now in excess of $1,200 for students who take the clinical as well as the applied-knowledge exams.

In some fields, particularly those offering highly remunerative employment, the market may possibly fund the development of a successful test. Currently, the Bloomberg Institute is test-marketing the Bloomberg Assessment Test (BAT) targeted for "aspiring financial professionals" who want "to demonstrate their value to top employers." The BAT is an online, monitored test that has multiple modules among which the student can choose. Students taking the BAT do so at a Bloomberg LP office or at a university that has signed up to host a test session (Bloomberg Institute 2012).

For most fields, however, market demand, at least initially, will not be sufficient to launch a successful testing regime. The only entity with sufficiently deep pockets is, in fact, the federal government, which is also the only entity with a fundamental need for having in place a national system of educational certification that can be used to measure the scope and quality of American baccalaureate degrees. Over the next five years the federal government is expected to spend in excess of $600 billion to fund students pursuing both associate's and baccalaureate degrees; therefore, it's not unreasonable to expect the federal government to fund the development of the requisite program that certifies the undergraduate educations received by recipients of federal student aid—Pell Grants, guaranteed and subsidized student and parental loans, and the host of smaller federal programs that provide direct student financial aid.

The federal government is also uniquely positioned to establish the agency that will be needed to first develop and subsequently administer the proposed portfolio of certification examinations. Traditionally, when required to perform such a task, the federal government has called upon and funded the efforts of one or more working committees established by the National Academy of Sciences, but in this case, the federal government would need to be certain it was asking for the development of a valid testing regime and not an evaluation of the feasibility or fairness of putting in place a system of national certification.

✓ Establish a New Federal Agency Responsible for Monitoring Institutional Compliance with the Rules and Regulations Governing the Disbursement of Federal Student Aid

Given the contretemps of the last five years, the federal government's assumption of direct responsibility for ensuring institutional compliance in the disbursement of federal student aid is well overdue. Since 2007 we have learned that turning the accreditors into compliance police is bad policy and worse practice. The six regional accrediting agencies, lacking both the requisite financial resources and the "gotcha" instinct sought by the federal government, are simply not equipped for the role of compliance monitors.

Required instead is a mini-federal agency, preferably one independent of the Department of Education but combining elements of the revamped federal consumer protection agency and the regulatory perspectives of the Securities and Exchange Commission. This new agency would have responsibilities: monitoring student loan default rates; ensuring compliance by proprietary institutions with the federal 90–10 rule governing the proportion of an institution's revenues that must come from other than federal resources; determining whether specific degree and certificate programs lead to gainful employment; deciding what constitutes full-time study for purposes of distributing federal student financial aid; and, in the case of institutions awarding the associate's and baccalaureate degree, ensuring that the awarding institution is accredited. This new federal agency will avail itself of the results of a national certification system for undergraduate education, if such a system were in place, to evaluate which institutions, in addition to being fully accredited, would be eligible as dispersing agents for federal programs of student financial aid.

To the extent the accrediting agencies used the results of the national certification examinations to accredit individual institutions, the two requirements could be combined.

Making It Happen

My Checklist is nearly complete—nineteen initiatives for changing American higher education.

TO ENSURE A STRONGER FACULTY VOICE:

- ✓ Relearn the Importance of Collective Action
- ✓ Put an End to Rhetorical Excesses
- ✓ Empower a Different Kind of Faculty Leader
- ✓ Recast the Faculty Staffing Table
- ✓ Make the Academic Department the Unit of Instructional Production

TO DEVELOP MORE COMPETENT CURRICULA:

- ✓ Commit to a Designed Curriculum
- ✓ Substitute Competencies for Seat Time
- ✓ Explore Learning Pathways and Cohorts
- ✓ Offer Credit by Examination or Demonstration
- ✓ Develop a Three-Year (90-Credit) Baccalaureate Degree
- ✓ Invest in Learning Management
- ✓ Establish a Credible Testing Regime

TO GUARANTEE THAT FEDERAL POLICIES SUPPORT A NATIONAL PROCESS OF PURPOSEFUL CHANGE:

- ✓ Provide Incentive Funding to Institutions for Graduating Disadvantaged Learners
- ✓ Make Students Enrolled in Remedial Education Programs Eligible for Pell Grants
- ✓ Make Institutions Active Players in the Student Loan System
- ✓ Establish a Federal Regulatory Environment Distinct from Accreditation to Oversee Federal Student Aid
- ✓ Change the Timing and Flow of Federal Student Aid Dollars
- ✓ Fund a National Testing Regime Documenting Undergraduate Learning
- ✓ Establish a New Federal Agency Responsible for Monitoring Institutional Compliance with the Rules and Regulations Governing the Disbursement of Federal Student Aid

I am uncomfortably aware that agendas, like the one I have now detailed in these pages, are often dismissed as being quixotic or impractical or simply too foolish to be taken seriously. I have confounded the problem by producing a Checklist rather than a menu of possibilities, each of which deserves separate consideration. In my Checklist the initiatives are not just linked, but interdependent. For example, the curricular shifts I have called for are not likely, absent a national testing regime for which the federal government must take first responsibility, along with a reinvigorated faculty voice that supports the effort. Even the simplest changes—offering college credit by examination or demonstration—would require changes in how the federal government calculates full-time enrollment for purposes of eligibility for federal student aid assistance, the acquiescence of the accrediting bodies, and again, the support of a faculty less committed to seat-time requirements that protect faculty teaching slots.

The changes I have envisioned all require a strong faculty voice, a curriculum that promotes competency as well as creativity, and a federal government that understands that change is not possible unless Washington is prepared to fix what it has broken, fund a testing regime, take primary responsibility for monitoring compliance, and be the first mover in what must ultimately become a multifaceted, multiyear campaign to improve the nation's higher education system.

What won't work is yet another jeremiad on that system's shortcomings. There is no need to search for villains or miscreants, for there are none. Much more often than not, those policies and practices that ardent reformers proclaim to be broken began life as good ideas that time and unintended consequence have rendered problematic. Nor will it help to point out more quietly that the nation's colleges and universities are failing, that U.S. college attainment rates now trail those of many of our nation's principal economic competitors, or that as a nation we are losing our edge in the race for scientific supremacy. The simple truth is that most colleges and universities are not failing, though not enough of them could be said to be fully thriving. College attainment rates for purposes of international comparison are like quicksand, having all the appearance of a solid foundation until one actually gives weight to the comparisons being drawn. Even the current angst over STEM (science, technology, engineering, and mathematics) too often conflates cause and effect and misunderstands the consequences of other nations now doing what the United States has done so well for so long.

If a campaign for ending the stalled progress that has characterized American higher education since the 1980s is to have any chance of succeeding, it will have to acknowledge the singular importance of a college degree in the twenty-first century, as well as the historical strengths and standing of the colleges and universities that award those degrees. It will have to be a campaign for improvement recognizing that, as a nation, doing things better is what we do best. And it will take time—no quick fixes, no national commissions expected to spend a year defining what's broken and then proposing their own set of fixes.

One question remains: "What has to happen to make it happen?" In the concluding chapter of *Making Reform Work*, I asked a similar question and suggested that the United States might look to Europe and its Bologna process for instruction if not inspiration. Alas, most commentators on *Making Reform Work* assumed that my fascination with the Bologna process was a function of my advocacy of a three-year degree, which the European Union was putting in place. No, my interest was, in fact, with the process itself—in how a tangle of different jurisdictions and differing definitions of self-interest could build a broadly framed consensus on how to improve a long-established and historically self-important set of institutions governed by their faculty and largely funded through public appropriation.

As I wrote then, the challenge Europe's political leaders tackled was a higher education environment too fragmented and too dependent on local customs to allow the continent's universities to become major players in the emerging worldwide market for higher education. The process—and again, it is the process that is worth consideration as applying in an American context—they put in place was one of extended consultation and cooperation that would ultimately propel their separate systems of higher education along a path of greater integration and cooperation. Everybody had a role, and everybody was consulted, although the ministers of education, acting with the political authority of their prime ministers, kept the process on track. Meeting by meeting, year by year, communiqué by communiqué, the continent's principal higher education constituencies defined and then oversaw the implementation of protocols and agreements that have gone a long way toward creating commonality and interchangeability among and between Europe's competing institutions of higher education. What began slowly, almost haltingly, perhaps even accidentally, is now rightfully celebrated as a remarkable achievement in multinational cooperation and reform.

What can American higher education and its would-be reformers learn from their European counterparts? At least three characteristics of the European process are worth consideration in Washington:

- The change process was conceived of as a multiyear, decade-long undertaking. No need to hurry; no need to try to fix everything in a single year of frantic activity.
- It was a process explicitly linking six sets of key actors: ministers of education (and by extension, their prime ministers), university leaders, student leaders, leaders of international organizations, European Union bureaucrats, and policy wonks. The latter analysts helped define the issues and shaped the agenda. The European Union bureaucracy helped staff the meetings and ensured that schedules were kept and deliverables delivered. University leaders, elected by their faculty, served as much needed brakes by insisting that the policy wonks' proposals have institutional traction. Student leaders, when not overly strident about the fee issue, kept the process honest. The ministers of education became the final authority by providing the necessary political muscle to implement reforms.
- Finally, the process proved both disciplined and focused. A limited number of goals were set, with clear benchmarks leading to verifiable implementations.

Could such a process work in an American political environment? Just possibly, is my tentative answer, which yields the twentieth and final entry on my Checklist for Change. Here I have assigned first responsibility to the federal government.

✓ Facilitate a National Process of Continuing Improvement in the Nation's System of Higher Education

As I have observed before, imagining an American political process with the capacity to promote change over time is akin to a parlor game where the rules are not very clear and the outcome not necessarily important. I write just after a quadrennial presidential election knowing that this volume will appear after a new secretary of education has been confirmed and a fractious Congress has again taken up the task of righting the federal government's finances, no doubt at the expense of some, if not all, of the national programs that for two decades and more have helped underwrite spending on higher education. The process I have in mind will probably last through at least one additional presidential election and, given the current partisan divide, will necessarily have to draw on leaders from both political parties, preferably from their centrist rather than their ideological wings.

Even though my proposed campaign will be national, it must also be rooted initially in a handful of states with strong governors, who will play the same role in this effort as the ministers of education have played in the Bologna process; that is, these governors will be responsible to keep the process within their individual states on time and on track, meaning in most cases the timely passage of enabling legislation at the state level.

The proper national convener is the president of the United States; his office and his command of the necessary discretionary resources as well as the people will keep the process on time and on track at the national level. He will need to designate a principal facilitator for the process, probably someone from the other party. A re-elected President Obama, for example, might well choose Tennessee's Senator Lamar Alexander—a former secretary of education, governor of Tennessee, and president of the University of Tennessee. A President Romney, however, might have chosen former Secretary of State and former Senator Hillary Clinton, who as First Lady and a coauthor of the Clinton administration's plan to revamp the nation's health care system, would have understood well just how difficult the task at hand will be.

The first decision will be which states to recruit initially. Again there needs to be a partisan balance as well as states with large complex systems of higher education including research universities, liberal arts colleges, community colleges, and comprehensive public and for-profit institutions. They must be states with strong institutions in both sectors of the dual-track system that is becoming the distinguishing feature of American postsecondary education. Among the current mix of governors and educational landscapes, I would think about California, New York, and Colorado, all currently with Democratic governors, and from the Republican side, New Jersey, Michigan, and Virginia. The second decision will be appointing an effective steering committee for the process, to be chaired by the facilitator appointed by the president. Such a working group—and here the emphasis is rightly on *working*—might include the chiefs of staff of the six governors, a senior staff member from each party on the relevant committees in the U.S. Congress, up to six institutional presidents (or former presidents) from across the spectrum of postsecondary education providers, and finally, up to six or more policy wonks, who are seen as neither party warriors nor take-no-prisoners advocates of specific policy initiatives.

Just three more specifications are necessary. First, all who sign on need to understand that what is being undertaken is a multiyear process—probably not the same ten years initially devoted to the Bologna process but closer to ten than to one. Second, the process must continuously blend detailed analysis, purposeful conversation, and sustained implementation into a seamless stream of activities. Constituents should expect no summative report, no detailed list of legislative enactments to be submitted to either Congress or the relevant state legislature for immediate enactment. Some of what needs to be tried will frankly be experimental, and its success must be evaluated over time. Some temporary legislation will be needed as well—for example, changing the rules for federal financial aid that apply only in the states that have signed on to the president's change process. Once enough states are ready, Congress may want to consider the first appropriations to support a testing regime or legislation that shifts responsibility for monitoring students' financial aid in the participating states to a temporary federal agency. Again, the watchwords are, "We are engaged in a work in progress that will necessarily change over time." In time, more states will need to join. After a majority of states have signed on to the process, concerted as well as summative congressional action will become increasingly necessary. At regular intervals, the president may want to weigh in, perhaps hosting a Camp David conference for participating states, their governors, their chiefs of staff, key congressional leaders and their staff, and finally that handful of policy wonks who will be expected to help shape the actual policies and practices the process puts into place.

One last stipulation: all twenty initiatives—including the initiative that gives the federal government prime responsibility for organizing a facilitated change process—ought to be on the table. In time, specific initiatives could be altered, even discarded, but initially all twenty would be given serious consideration. In time, as well, new ideas and initiatives could be added, but I would hope the fundamental balance of the Checklist I have outlined would be preserved. As a result, by 2024 we could all say that most characteristic of the nation's colleges and universities is the collective strength of their faculty, their curricula that help institutions control costs while ensuring a growing flow of graduates who know what they are doing whether at work or at play, and a federal government that is central to a change process that eschews playing "gotcha" and chooses instead to be a responsible monitor and a creative facilitator.

References

AAC (Association of American Colleges). 1985. *Integrity in the College Curriculum: A Report to the Academic Community.* Washington, DC: Association of American Colleges.

Academic Senate of the California State University. 2010. "Opposition to Participation in the Zemsky-Finney Re-engineering the Undergraduate Curriculum Proposal." AS-2962-10/FA, May 6–7. http://www.calstate.edu/AcadSen/Records/Resolutions/2009-2010/documents/2962.pdf.

American Radio Works. 2011. "Podcast Friday: Learning Group." American Public Media, August 18. http://arwpodcast.tumblr.com/post/9096831523/group-learning.

Arum, Richard, and Josipa Roksa. 2011. "Your So-Called Education." *New York Times,* May 14. http://www.nytimes.com/2011/05/15/opinion/15arum.html?scp=2&sq.

Astin, Alexander W. 2011. "In 'Academically Adrift,' Data Don't Back Up Sweeping Claim." *Chronicle of Higher Education,* February 14. http://chronicle.com/article/Academically-Adrift-a/126371/.

Barkey, Dale. 2008. "Letter [to Full-time Faculty] from Dale Barkey [Chapter President, AAUP-UNH], February 4, 2008." American Association of University Professors-University of New Hampshire Chapter. http://aaup-unh.org/?m=200802.

Basken, Paul. 2008. "Test Touted as 2 Studies Question Its Value." *Chronicle of Higher Education,* June 6. http://chronicle.com/article/Test-Touted-as-2-Studies/23503/.

Baum, Sandy, Jennifer Ma, and Kathleen Payea. 2010. *Education Pays 2010: The Benefits of Higher Education for Individuals and Society.* New York: The College Board Advocacy and Policy Center. http://trends.collegeboard.org/downloads/Education_Pays_2010.pdf.

Baum, Sandy, and Michael S. McPherson. 2011. "Sorting to Extremes: An Economic Analysis." A presentation prepared for the Center for Enrollment

Research, Policy, and Practice, University of Southern California, Los Angeles, CA, January. http://www.usc.edu/programs/cerpp/docs/USC_SortingtoExtremes_January2011mm.pdf.

Berrett, Dan. 2011. "When Bitter Bargaining Bleeds Over." *Insider Higher Ed*, April 28. http://www.insidehighered.com/news/2011/04/28/faculty_at_university_of_new_hampshire_vote_no_confidence_in_president#ixzz1z6bec54Y.

Bloomberg Institute. 2012. Bloomberg Assessment Test. Accessed July 2, 2012. https://www.bloomberginstitute.com/bat/start/.

BLS (Bureau of Labor Statistics). 1970. *National Survey of Professional, Administrative, Technical and Clerical Pay, June 1970* (Bulletin 1693). Washington, DC: U.S. Department of Labor.

———. 2010. *National Compensation Survey: Occupational Earnings in the U.S. 2010*, Table 3: Full-time Civilian Workers, Mean and Median Hourly, Weekly, and Annual Earnings and Mean Weekly and Annual Hours. Washington, DC: U.S. Department of Labor. http://www.bls.gov/ncs/ncswage2010.htm.

Blumenstyk, Goldie. 2006. "Chairman Blasts Accreditation." *Chronicle of Higher Education*, November 3. http://chronicle.com/article/Commission-Chairman-Blasts/33664/.

———. 2010. "Beyond the Credit Hour: Old Standards Don't Fit New Models." *Chronicle of Higher Education*, January 3. http://chronicle.com/article/News-Analysis-Thinking-Beyond/63349/.

Bollag, Burton. 2006. "Spellings Wants to Use Accreditation as a Cudgel." *Chronicle of Higher Education*, November 24. http://chronicle.com/article/Spellings-Wants-to-Use/9275.

Breneman, David W. 1994. *Liberal Arts Colleges: Thriving, Surviving, or Endangered?* Washington, DC: Brookings Institution.

Brooks, David. 2012. "Testing the Teachers." *New York Times*, April 19. http://www.nytimes.com/2012/04/20/opinion/brooks-testing-the-teachers.html.

BSA (Boy Scouts of America). 2012. Accessed July 2, 2012. http://www.scouting.org/sitecore/content/Home/BoyScouts/AdvancementandAwards/Merit Badges.aspx.

CETL (Center for Excellence in Teaching and Learning), University of Wisconsin Oshkosh. 2012. Accessed July 2, 2012. http://www.uwosh.edu/cetl.

Christensen, Clayton M., Michael B. Horn, Louis Caldera, and Louis Soares. 2011. *Disrupting College: How Disruptive Innovation Can Bring Quality and Affordability to Postsecondary Education.* Center for American Progress, Washington, DC, and the Innosight Institute, Mountainview, CA, February. http://www.americanprogress.org/issues/2011/02/pdf/disrupting_college.pdf.

Chronicle of Higher Education. 2011. "College Groups Ask Education Dept. to Rescind Credit-Hour Rule." The Ticker, *Chronicle of Higher Education*, February 22. http://chronicle.com/blogs/ticker/college-groups-ask-education-dept-to-rescind-credit-hour-rule/30740.

CLI (Center for Learning Innovation), University of Minnesota Rochester. 2009. "Section 7.12 Departmental Statement (March 26, 2009)." http://www.r.umn.edu/prod/groups/umr/@pub/@umr/documents/content/umr_content_236562.pdf.

Cochran, John B. (Factfinder). 2009. "In the Matter of Fact Finding between the University of New Hampshire Chapter of the American Association of University Professors and University System of New Hampshire Board of Trustees, University of New Hampshire" (March 31). http://aaup-unh .org/wp-content/uploads/2011/04/UNH-and-AAUP-Factfinding-Report.pdf.

Eaton, Judith. 2008. "The Future of Accreditation?" *Inside Higher Ed*, March 24. http://www.insidehighered.com/views/2008/03/24/eaton.

Epstein, Jennifer. 2009. "Defining 'Gainful Employment.'" *Inside Higher Ed*, December 10. http://www.insidehighered.com/news/2009/12/10/employ.

————. 2010a. "Linking Debt and Income." *Inside Higher Ed*, January 18. http://www.insidehighered.com/news/2010/01/18/rules.

————. 2010b. "Shellacking the For-Profits." *Inside Higher Ed*, August 5. http://www.insidehighered.com/news/2010/08/05/hearing.

————. 2010c. "Splitting the Difference on Gainful Employment." *Inside Higher Ed*, July 23. http://www.insidehighered.com/news/2010/07/23/ gainful.

————. 2010d. "What Harkin Wants." *Inside Higher Ed*, August 10. http://www.insidehighered.com/news/2010/08/10/forprofit.

Field, Kelly. 2011. "Gates Foundation Weighs In on Credit-Hour Rule." *Chronicle of Higher Education*, June 16. http://chronicle.com/article/Gates-Foundation-Weighs-In-on/127933.

FSA (Federal Student Aid). 2009. "Proprietary School 90/10 Revenue Percentages from Financial Statements with Fiscal Year Ending Dates between 7/1/2008 and 6/30/2009." Report, 2007–2008 Award Year. FSA Data Center. Washington, DC: U.S. Department of Education. http://federal studentaid.ed.gov/datacenter/proprietary.html.

Gerald, Danette, and Kati Haycock. 2006. *Engines of Inequality: Diminishing Equity in the Nation's Premier Public Universities*. Washington, DC: The Education Trust. http://www.edtrust.org/dc/publication/engines-of-inequality-diminishing equity in the nation's premier public universities.

Gladieux, Lawrence E. 1995. "Federal Student Aid Policy: A History and an Assessment." Financing Postsecondary Education: The Federal Role. Proceedings of the National Conference on the Best Ways for the Federal Government to Help Students and Families Finance Postsecondary Education. Charleston, SC, October 8–9. http://www2.ed.gov/offices/OPE/ PPI/FinPostSecEd/gladieux.html.

Glenn, David. 2010. "Scholar Raises Doubts about the Value of a Test of Student Learning." *Chronicle of Higher Education*, June 2. http://chronicle.com/ article/Scholar-Raises-Doubts-About/65741/.

Goldman, Charles A., and William F. Massy. 2001. *The PhD Factory: Training and Employment of Science and Engineering Doctorates in the U.S.* Boston: Anker Publishing Company, Inc.

Haydock, Michael D. 1999. "The GI Bill." Originally published in *American History*, April 19. http://www.historynet.com/the-gi-bill-cover-page-october-99-american-history-feature.htm.

Hebel, Sara. 2005. "The Hard Birth of a Research University." *Chronicle of Higher Education*, April 1. http://chronicle.com/article/The-Hard-Birth-of-a-Research/65376/.

Hechinger, Fred M. 1971. "Federal Aid: Nixon Plan Is Small Comfort to Colleges." *New York Times*, February 28. http://select.nytimes.com/gst/ abstract.html?res=F60F1EF63A5B137A93CAAB1789D85F458785F9.

_____. 1972. "Some Badly Needed Money for Colleges." *New York Times*, June 11. http://select.nytimes.com/gst/abstract.html?res=F70D11FD3E5E1 27A93C3A8178DD85F468785F9.

Hicks, Steve. 2010. Letter to John Cavanaugh, Chancellor, Pennsylvania State System of Higher Education [from Steve Hicks, President, Association of State College and University Faculties], March 23. [Note: typographical error in opening date of letter.] http://www.cs.csustan.edu/~john/Post/CFA/ Reengineering/hicks-responds-to-reengineering.pdf.

Hoover, Eric. 2012. "A Liberal-Arts Leader Weighs Costs and Quality." Headcount, *Chronicle of Higher Education*, April 10. http://chronicle.com/ blogs/headcount/a-liberal-arts-leader-weighs-costs-and-quality/29924.

Huddleston, Mark W. 2011. "New Hampshire State Finance Committee, FY12–13 USNH Operating Budget Hearing, April 18, 2011, Testimony by Mark W. Huddleston, President, University of New Hampshire." http:// www.unh.edu/president/concord-testimony.

Immerwahr, John, Jean Johnson, and Paul Gasbarra. 2008. *The Iron Triangle: College Presidents Talk about Costs, Access, and Quality.* October. Palo Alto, CA: National Center for Public Policy and Higher Education and Public Agenda. http://www.publicagenda.org/files/pdf/iron_triangle.pdf.

Inside Higher Ed. 2009. "Taking Stock of Education Dept. Appointment." *Inside Higher Ed*, April 22. http://www.insidehighered.com/quicktakes/2009/04/ 22/taking-stock-of-education-dept-appointment.

Johnson, Nate. 2009. "What Does a College Degree Cost? Comparing Approaches to Measuring 'Cost per Degree.'" Delta Cost Project White Paper Series, May. Washington, DC: Delta Project on Postsecondary Education Costs, Productivity, and Accountability. http://www.deltacostproject.org/ resources/pdf/johnson3–09_WP.pdf.

Kelderman, Eric. 2011. "Education Department Asks Accreditor to Better Explain a Curriculum Review." *Chronicle of Higher Education*, September 19. http://chronicle.com/article/Education-Department-Asks/129080/.

Kiley, Kevin. 2010. "U. of California at Merced Turns 5 Amid Growing Pains." *Chronicle of Higher Education*, November 14. http://chronicle.com/article/ U-of-California-at-Merced/125366/.

_____. 2012a. "Everybody's Worried Now." *Inside Higher Ed*, April 11. www.insidehighered.com/news/2012/04/11/lafayette-conference-shows-concern-about-liberal-arts-colleges-economic-future.

_____. 2012b. "Changing Their Tone." *Inside Higher Ed*, April 12. www.insidehighered.com/news/2012/04/11/lafayette-conference-shows-concern-about-liberal-arts-colleges-economic-future.

Kroll, Andy. 2009. "Shut Out: How the Cost of Higher Education Is Dividing Our Country." TomDispatch.com, April 2. http://www.tomdispatch.com/ post/175054/andy_kroll_the_crisis_of_college_affordability.

Landscape. 1999. "Telling Time: Comparing Faculty Instructional Practices at Three Types of Institutions." *Change* 31(2), March/April: 55.

Lederman, Doug. 2006a. "Dropping a Bomb on Accreditation." *Inside Higher Ed*, March 31. http://www.insidehighered.com/news/2006/03/31/accredit.

_____. 2006b. "Regulatory Activism?" *Inside Higher Ed*, August 21. http://www.insidehighered.com/news/2006/08/21/regs).

_____. 2007a. "Key GOP Senator Warns Spellings." *Inside Higher Ed*, May 29. http://www.insidehighered.com/news/2007/05/29/alexander.

_____. 2007b. "Someone Didn't Get the Memo." *Inside Higher Ed*, December 19. http://www.insidehighered.com/news/2007/12/19/naciqi.

_____. 2011a. "CLA as 'Catalyst for Change.'" *Inside Higher Ed*, November 14. http://www.insidehighered.com/news/2011/11/14/cla-experiment-focused-private-colleges-attention-assessment.

_____. 2011b. "The True Significance of 'Gainful Employment.'" *Inside Higher Ed*, June 13. http://www.insidehighered.com/news/2011/06/13/explaining_the_true_significance_of_gainful_employment_rules.

_____. 2012. "Foundations' Newfound Advocacy." *Inside Higher Ed*, April 13. http://www.insidehighered.com/news/2012/04/13/study-assesses-how-megafoundations-have-changed-role-higher-ed-philanthropy.

Lewin, Tamar. 2011. "For-Profit College Group Sued as U.S. Lays Out Wide Fraud." *New York Times*, August 8. http://www.nytimes.com/2011/08/09/education/09forprofit.html.

Massy, William F. 2011. *Modeling Instructional Productivity in Traditional Universities.* Discussion Draft, August.

Moltz, David. 2011. "Educators See Federal Overreach." *Inside Higher Education*, March 14. http://www.insidehighered.com/news/2011/03/14/members_of_congress_and_college_officials_debate_higher_education_regulations.

NCEE (National Commission on Excellence in Education). 1983. *A Nation at Risk: the Imperative for Educational Reform.* A Report to the Nation and the Secretary of Education, United States Department of Education, April. Washington, DC: U.S. Department of Education.

NCES (National Center for Education Statistics). 2009. National Postsecondary Student Aid Study (NPSAS). "Beginning Postsecondary Students Longitudinal Study (BPS): 2009 (enrolled for the first time 2003–2004 and followed for six years)." Washington, DC: U.S. Department of Education. http://nces.ed.gov/surveys/bps/.

_____. 2010. *Digest of Education Statistics 2010*, Chapter 3: Postsecondary Education. Washington, DC: U.S. Department of Education. http://nces.ed.gov/programs/digest/2010menu_tables.asp.

_____. 2011. Integrated Postsecondary Education Data System (IPEDS). Author's analysis of data, 1985–2010. Washington, DC: U.S. Department of Education. http://nces.ed.gov/ipeds/datacenter/.

Nelson, Libby A. 2011. "Concessions or Cave-In?" *Inside Higher Ed*, June 2. http://www.insidehighered.com/news/2011/06/02/new_gainful_employment_rules.

New York Times. 1970. "Text of Nixon Message to Congress Proposing Higher Education Opportunity Act." *New York Times*, March 20. http://select.nytimes.com/gst/abstract.html?res=FB0A1FFD385E157B93C2AB1788D85F448785F9.

_____. 1972. "Stratifying the Campuses." Editorial, *New York Times*, April 23. http://select.nytimes.com/gst/abstract.html?res=F60B15FB3455127B93C1AB178FD85F468785F9.

OLI (Open Learning Initiative), Carnegie Mellon University. 2012. Accessed July 2, 2012. http://oli.cmu.edu/get-to-know-oli/.

PHERP (Pew Higher Education Research Program). 1988. "Seeing Straight Through the Muddle." *Policy Perspectives* 1(1) September. Philadelphia: Institute for Research on Higher Education, University of Pennsylvania.

_____. 1990. "The Lattice and the Ratchet." *Policy Perspectives* 2(4) June. Philadelphia: Institute for Research on Higher Education, University of Pennsylvania.

Quinterno, John. 2012. *The Great Cost Shift: How Higher Education Costs Undermine the Future Middle Class.* March. New York: Demos.

http://www.demos.org/sites/default/files/publications/TheGreatCostShift_Demos.pdf.

RPI (Rensselaer Polytechnic Institute). 2012. The Mobile Studio Project in Physics. Accessed July 2, 2012. http://www.rpi.edu/dept/phys/MobileProject/Untitled-3.html.

Rhoades, Gary. 1998. *Managed Professionals: Unionized Faculty and Restructuring Academic Labor.* Albany: State University of New York Press.

Rosovsky, Henry. 1991. "Annual Report of the Dean of the Faculty of Arts and Sciences 1990–1991." Excerpted in the Pew Higher Education Research Program's *Policy Perspectives* 4(3) September 1992: Section B. Philadelphia: Institute for Research on Higher Education, University of Pennsylvania.

SACS (Southern Association of Colleges and Schools). 2009. "Substantive Change for Accredited Institutions of the Commission on Colleges-Policy Statement." Commission on Colleges, Decatur, GA, June. http://www.sacscoc.org/pdf/081705/Substantive%20change%20policy.pdf.

Schneider, Carol Geary. 2010. "The Three-Year Degree Is No Silver Bullet." Statements and Letters, June 3. Washington, DC: Association of American Colleges and Universities http://www.aacu.org/about/statements/2010/threeyears.cfm.

Soares, Louis. 2011. Presentation to the "Disrupting College Convening," Center for American Progress, Washington, DC, June 29.

Spellings, Margaret. 2008. "Congress Digs a Moat Around its Ivory Tower." *Politico*, February 6. http://www.politico.com/news/stories/0208/8361.html.

Stripling, Jack. 2009. "Buyer's Remorse." *Inside Higher Ed*, August 10. http://www.insidehighered.com/news/2009/08/10/merced.

Summit, Jennifer. 2010. "Literary History and the Curriculum: How, What, and Why." Association of Departments of English, *ADE Bulletin* 149: 46–52.

Thille, Candace. 2012. *Changing the Production Function in Higher Education.* Second in the Series Making Productivity Real: Essential Readings for Campus Leaders (February). Washington, DC: American Council on Education. http://www.acenet.edu/AM/Template.cfm?Section=Programs_and_Services&CONTENTID=44553&TEMPLATE=/CM/ContentDisplay.cfm.

U.S. Department of Education. 2006. *A Test of Leadership: Charting the Future of U.S. Higher Education.* A Report of the Commission Appointed by Secretary of Education Margaret Spellings. Washington, DC: U.S. Department of Education. http://www2.ed.gov/about/bdscomm/list/hiedfuture/index.html.

U.S. Senate. 2011. "Emerging Risk?: An Overview of Growth, Spending, Student Debt and Unanswered Questions in For-Profit Higher Education." Health, Education, Labor and Pensions Committee, Tom Harkin, Chairman, June 24. http://harkin.senate.gov/documents/pdf/4c23515814dca.pdf.

UC Merced (University of California Merced). 2012. "About UC Merced." Accessed July 2, 2012. http://www.ucmerced.edu/about-uc-merced.

UMR (University of Minnesota Rochester). 2012. "Growth of UMR." Accessed July 2, 2012. http://r.umn.edu/about-umr/growth/.

UNH (University of New Hampshire) Campus Journal. 2011."Faculty Senate Minutes Summary 4–25–11 and 5–09–11," June 8. http://unh.edu/news/campusjournal/2011/Jun/08min-509.cfm.

USMLE (United States Medical Licensing Examination. 2012. Sponsored by the Federation of State Medical Boards (FSMB) and the National Board of Medical Examiners (NBME). Accessed July 2, 2012. http://www.usmle.org/.

USP (University Studies Program), University of Wisconsin Oshkosh. 2012. "University Studies Program: General Education for the 21st Century." Last updated March 1, 2012. http://www.uwosh.edu/usp/pdfs/university-studies-program-booklet.

UT (University of Texas) System. 2012. "Charles Miller: Selected Accomplishments of Regent Miller (1999–2004)." Board of Regents, Former Regents of the University of Texas System. Accessed July 2, 2012. http://www.utsystem.edu/bor/former_regents/regents/Miller/accomplishments.htm.

Whittier College. 2012. "About . . . [Whittier College]." Accessed July 2, 2012. http://whittier.edu/About/.

Zemsky, Robert. 1989. *Structure and Coherence: Measuring the Undergraduate Curriculum.* Washington, DC: Association of American Colleges.

_____. 2009. *Making Reform Work: The Case for Transforming American Higher Education.* New Brunswick, NJ: Rutgers University Press.

Zemsky, Robert, and Joni Finney. 2010. "Changing the Subject: Costs, Graduation Rates, and the Importance of Rethinking the Undergraduate Curriculum." *National CrossTalk,* May. Palo Alto, CA: National Center for Public Policy and Higher Education. http://www.highereducation.org/crosstalk/ct0510/voices0510-zemfin.shtml.

Zemsky, Robert, and Gregory Wegner. 1987. "Diversity Competition and Costs: A Candid Look at Selective Admissions." Philadelphia: Institute for Research in Higher Education, University of Pennsylvania. http://www.usc.edu/programs/cerpp/docs/TobiLament.pdf.

Index

About the Author

In the *Chronicle of Higher Education*, Robert Zemsky described himself as someone "old and round enough to be mistaken for a pooh-bah." In his forty-year career he has proved to be a major commentator on the future of both American and global higher education. He has pioneered the use of market analyses for higher education, served as the University of Pennsylvania's chief planning officer, and was the founding director of Penn's Institute for Research on Higher Education. He has also served as the convener of the Pew Higher Education Roundtable, as chair of the Learning Alliance, and as a member of the U.S. Secretary of Education's Commission on the Future of Higher Education. His recent books include *Making Reform Work* (2009) and *Remaking the American University* (2005).